AUTHORITY AND THE TEACHER

ALSO AVAILABLE FROM BLOOMSBURY

Overschooled, but Undereducated, J. Abbott (with H. MacTaggart)
14–18: A New Vision for Secondary Education, K. Baker
Wasted, F. Furedi

AUTHORITY AND THE TEACHER

William H. Kitchen

B L O O M S B U R Y

LONDON • NEW DELHI • NEW YORK • SYDNEY

Bloomsbury Academic

An imprint of Bloomsbury Publishing Plc

50 Bedford Square	1385 Broadway
London	New York
WC1B 3DP	NY 10018
UK	USA

www.bloomsbury.com

First published 2014

British Library Cataloguing-in-Publication Data
A catalogue record for this book is available from the British Library.

ISBN: HB: 978-1-4725-2984-8
PB: 978-1-4725-2428-7
ePub: 978-1-4725-2980-0
ePDF: 978-1-4725-2367-9

Library of Congress Cataloging-in-Publication Data
Kitchen, William H.
Authority and the teacher / William H. Kitchen.
pages cm
ISBN 978-1-4725-2984-8 (hardback) – ISBN 978-1-4725-2428-7 (paperback)
1. Teacher-student relationships.   2. Education—Philosophy.   3. Authority.
I. Title.
LB1033.K533 2014
371.102′3—dc23
2014003695

Typeset by RefineCatch Ltd, Bungay, Suffolk
Printed and bound in India

To my late father

Who showed me the meaning of an unshakable and
at times illogical 'faith'

CONTENTS

FOREWORD

I do not want to create a society of robots who just know stuff.' In that it takes a kind of genius to sum up the whole educational zeitgeist in one short sentence, this delegate to this year's National Union of Teachers (NUT) annual conference deserves our congratulations.

He or she no doubt received rapturous applause from the couple of thousand teachers packed into the conference hall. Who, after all, needs to know 'stuff' when everything that has ever been known is instantaneously available on the Internet? Who, in their right mind, would want students, in all of their impressionable ignorance, to be initiated into forms of worthwhile knowledge by teachers who are older and wiser? Our children should be encouraged to discover things for themselves and come to their own unassisted conclusions, shouldn't they? We don't want unthinking little 'robots', do we?

I was fortunate enough to attend a grammar school in south London some fifty years ago. My teachers might, I suppose, have dragged anxiously on their cigarettes in their smoke-filled staffroom, pondering the nature of the educational enterprise. Somehow, I doubt it. We went to school to be taught things that mattered by men who were passionate about the subjects they taught. Some, inevitably, were not very good teachers. But the ideal was clear: this was a community in which the importance of knowledge and the fact that education depended upon the young submitting to the authority of experts and enthusiasts were taken for granted.

A lot has changed over the last fifty years in education. There are still schools that hold on to the ideas that knowledge matters and that the authority of the teacher must be absolute. But these are few and far between. The teacher who spoke at the NUT conference has become the norm. As I write, the proposals of the Secretary of State for Education for a new national curriculum rooted in worthwhile knowledge have provoked venomous opposition. A hundred academics working in university departments of education recently signed a letter to national newspapers dismissing Mr Gove and his wretched curriculum as a throwback to the educational dark ages when teachers, they allege, did nothing but cram facts into their pupils' heads to be regurgitated in examinations – and, in later life, in pub quizzes.

One of the greatest ironies of the current educational debate is that those who espouse most passionately the central importance of teaching the young how to think for themselves demonstrate a lamentable inability to reflect on the absurdity of their own arguments. The ability to think demands a basic knowledge of the thing about which one is thinking. I have opinions on, for example, the topic of global warming, but I do not have the scientific knowledge to think, in any meaningful sense of the word, about the strengths and weaknesses of opposing arguments.

Knowledge matters. The purpose of education is, as Richard Peters and Paul Hirst argued many years ago, to initiate the young into the different ways in which, over the centuries, men have organized their experience and understanding of the world. This initiation depends upon the ability of teachers to explain and inspire, and on the willingness of the young to engage in this enterprise with a proper humility. Most people who think at all about education, but who are not teachers or academics working within university departments of education, would probably raise an eyebrow at the idea that anybody could believe anything different. But most teachers in this second decade of the twenty-first century have been brainwashed into a Pavlovian rejection of what they believe to be an outdated and authoritarian view. They see their job as facilitators rather than teachers who have an authority in their subject and over their students. They aspire to a democratic relationship in which everyone in the classroom is a 'learner' engaged in the discovery of new knowledge and personal insights.

This is why this book is so important. William Kitchen draws on the work of Michael Polanyi, Michael Oakeshott and Ludwig Wittgenstein to construct a compelling philosophical defence of the educational ideals that have so nearly disappeared from our schools. It should be required reading in every teacher training institution – and, better still, should be a set text upon which every future Secretary of State for Education is tested before taking up office.

Professor Sir Chris Woodhead
Former Chief Inspector of Schools in England
Hendre Gwenllian, Penrhyndeudraeth
January 2014

PREFACE

t is difficult to outline the emotions that one endures while writing a book; it is equally difficult to outline the thought processes that go into making it happen. This book has been the product of three years of deliberation, culminating in no more than two months of writing. The ideas had been festering within me since I completed my teacher training as a mathematics teacher, listening attentively to my then lecturer and subsequent PhD supervisor Dr Hugh Morrison. He imprinted on me a version of education that seemed intuitive and natural, rooted in sound philosophy and careful consideration. The more I listened, the more I was convinced that the authoritative education of which he was so defensive was right and that the constructivist, progressive education of which he was so dismissive was fundamentally flawed. So it got me thinking – and, three years down the line, I have put these ideas into the book now in front of you.

The arguments for authoritative education are unattractive at first glance; it is tricky to overcome the word 'authoritative' and come out the other end with a positive description of authoritative approaches to anything, let alone education. The word stenches of dogma, strictness and coercion. It gives the impression that someone instructs and another simply passively absorbs. Such conceptions of education, once commonplace, are now considered to be intrinsically restrictive in an ever-changing world in which knowledge quickly becomes obsolete and 'skills' are the new cream of the crop. This book seeks to examine precisely why authority is viewed as an undesirable concept and why it is considered to be an educational plague, to be avoided at all costs. I have tried, then, to give an alternative view to the current educational trends steeped in constructivism (theoretically speaking) and progressivism (ideologically and pedagogically speaking), to outline that the propaganda-fuelled view of authority in education should not be cast aside, but rather embraced, in the hope of a truly liberating education, a far cry from the restrictive, dogmatic, coercive view of education that many try (and succeed) to circulate.

This argument is made from three main viewpoints. First, I have outlined why authority is needed in teaching and learning. Second, I have outlined why authority is needed in the transmission of knowledge. This may seem unusual, since current thinking in education would suggest that knowledge is inert, fixed and fast becoming obsolete. However, I make the argument that any education without knowledge transmission is not an education at all. Therefore I go on to demonstrate that the development of knowledge requires a submission to the authority of a master expert: the teacher. Finally, I outline the argument for authority in education in general, which in large part is a concatenation of the two previous arguments.

Once this rationale for authority in education is established, I introduce three noted and well-established philosophers to the debate. One of the philosophers – Michael Oakeshott – should not be a surprise, given his noted contributions to educational discourse over the years. The other two – Michael Polanyi and Ludwig Wittgenstein – are invoked to capture the entire essence of the argument: to offer, together with Oakeshott, a conclusive, coherent, philosophical account of the argument for authoritative education.

The book seeks to fill one lacuna in the current literature: to offer a philosophical argument into the educational debate surrounding authority. Previous arguments are largely anecdotal, and they serve their purpose as such. However, this book seeks to found teaching, learning, knowledge development and education in general within a philosophical framework – hoping to put an end to the constant educational reform that is carried out whimsically, as though experimenting with education as the solution to society's ailments were permissible.

I hope to champion the case against the constant drivel emanating from within education about 'what works', and the incessant changes that teachers, parents and, most importantly, students have to endure. My hope is that this book might serve to rid educational discourse of any more need for reform. If you are a teacher, it might serve to restore your eroded authority as a master in your subject. If you are a policymaker, I would advise you to pay close attention to what is within these pages. If you are a parent, the book should help you to envisage a brighter future for your child. And if you are a student, I hope that it will save you from being treated like an educational lab rat, on whom is tested the latest educational fad. Whichever the case, I hope you enjoy the book.

William H. Kitchen

Belfast

February 2014

ACKNOWLEDGEMENTS

I n the process of writing a book, any author will tell you that there are times when support is required – intellectual, emotional, professional, perhaps even psychological! I consider myself extremely fortunate to have received the support of many people, each of whom has played his or her role in making this book possible.

First, I thank my wife Victoria, who had to endure this project during the first year of our marriage. Her belief in me and her words of encouragement, as well as her understanding when the nights grew so very late during the 'heavy' stages of writing, made writing considerably easier. She knew what I hoped to achieve and stuck with me every step of the way.

Also, I thank my family, who were often forced to sit through many a draft reading. The look of bewilderment on their faces when I read to them – and then their expressions of sheer astonishment that I had somehow managed to pull this book together – made reading my book aloud significantly more entertaining. More importantly, for their enduring support of me in all of my academic endeavours, through to this early point in my career, I am forever indebted to them. I also dedicate this book to my late father, who had an unshakable trust and faith in me that sometimes transcended the bounds of sense. In the darkest moments, the residue of that faith often pulled me through.

I am grateful for the professional and intellectual support of Dr Hugh Morrison, who has become more than an intellectual mentor during the time for which I have known him. He is the living manifestation of an authoritative master, whose manner and guidance you seek to imitate when you are fortunate enough to act under his tutelage. Quite simply, he is the finest educator that one could hope to encounter and the greatest example of an intellectual guide, whose features and qualities are, I hope, captured in this book. In that I argue that a pupil can never truly break free from his master, given his intellectual capacity, I would never wish to break free from what he has taught me: he is simply never wrong.

I also thank Professor Sir Chris Woodhead both for writing the Foreword and for his encouragement along the way. He took an interest in my project when others had no time to spare and, for that level of humility, I am extremely appreciative.

Finally, I am grateful to Frances Arnold and Rosie Pattinson, whose editorial skills and expertise made the process of publishing this book swift, efficient and hassle-free.

Bloomsbury and the author wish to acknowledge with gratitude the following permissions for extracts reproduced within this book:

Moyal-Sharrock, D., 2007. *Understanding Wittgenstein's* On Certainty. Basingstoke: Palgrave Macmillan. Reproduced with permission of Palgrave Macmillan.

Oakeshott, M., 2001. *The Voice of Liberal Learning.* Indianapolis, IN: Liberty Fund. © 1989, Yale University Press. Thanks also to Professor Timothy Fuller for providing the electronic permissions for this text.

INTRODUCTION: AN EDUCATION FOR WHICH TO BE FEARFUL

Before this book can deliver what it sets out to achieve, some preliminaries must be established. There are various things of which I, as the author, need to make you, the reader, aware before I try to convince you that authoritative approaches to education are favourable. Indeed, there are a number of background arguments upon which this book will infringe by its very nature, some of which are perhaps not even the intentional target of the book. Primarily, however, consider this introductory chapter my attempt to convince you that what is bound together in these pages is worth reading – that is, the validity and coherence of the arguments found in the book you are now holding can be established and debated only once we agree that the debate is worth having. Having gripped your attention, I will then focus in subsequent chapters on gaining your agreement. But in the absence of such agreement, which is a feature of any healthy debate, we ought at least to agree that the debate is valuable.

I will begin by outlining what the core remit of the book is, as well as by clearly setting out its rationale. It is obvious from the title of the book alone that the aim is to examine the concept of authority in education, but there is value in unpacking this rationale a little further before we embark on the arguments that follow. Moreover, by sharing my reasoning for writing the book, I hope to transmit to you a reason for reading it; the best way in which to do this is to outline what, precisely, the book seeks to achieve.

Thereafter, it seems sensible to give insight into the background theoretical, philosophical and sociological context within which the book is likely to be placed. There are, of course, other arguments and counter-arguments for authority in education already present in the educational literature, and there is most certainly some value in examining what these arguments say and what this book seeks to contribute to the debate. In examining these, I will consider very briefly the work of Furedi, G. H. Bantock, R. S. Peters, Stenhouse and various other contributors in the argument *for* authoritative approaches to education. Each of these authors will contribute to a context-setting preamble of arguments that will make clear the views on education from various perspectives that span the disciplines.

It is also essential to make the reader clear of a potential counter-argument to what is being posited in this book. This will come in the guise of Carl R. Rogers' book *Freedom to Learn* (1983), which puts forward a standard case for non-authoritative approaches to education. Two things must be made clear at this stage: first, it is not my aim to step into the educational quagmire of messy theory and troublesome ideologies that are not required for this debate. In choosing, for example, Rogers' text as one anti-authoritative text within educational discourse, I acknowledge that there are many others. But an intensive review of the anti-authoritarian literature is not the remit of this book, nor should it be. Nevertheless, there is undoubted value in examining Rogers' take on anti-authoritarian approaches to education, to add extra weight to the rationale for pursuing the alternative authoritative approaches.

The second and final point of note for this introductory chapter is the context in which this book rests in relation to progressive ideology and constructivist educational theory. I am keen to dispel pre-emptively the notion that this book is, by its very nature as a text on authority, anti-progressivist. To be clear, there are various precepts of progressive ideology that will be given stern examination in this book – but this is a consequence, rather than the aim, of the arguments made here. The progressive–traditional debate is to be had elsewhere, and as much as I acknowledge that this book might well serve to undermine progressive ideology, it is important that it is clear from the outset that the book does not seek, as its core aim, to slay the progressive beast. There is, however, a fundamental attack within these arguments on the underpinnings of constructivist learning theory, the core postulates of which are categorically undermined within the bounds of the many arguments made.

Rationale, aims and objectives

As I outlined in the preface, the core motivation for me as the author of this book has been to address the topic of authority in education, with particular interest in why the adoption of authoritative approaches to education has become so unattractive in the modern time, particularly since the 1960s and 1970s. There is no doubt that the shift away from authority in education (and the submission to it) has coincided with the progressive education movement, which shot to prominence over the last century – thanks to Rousseau, Froebel, Pestalozzi and Dewey, in the main – and reached its height in the 1970s. To be clear, however, this overlapping of anti-authoritarianism and progressivism need not mean that these concepts can be considered educational equivalents. The challenge to progressivism, as I have already noted, goes well beyond the bounds of this text. In fact, there are elements of progressive ideology that this book – rather unusually, given its support of authority in education – adopts and supports. Indeed, this book argues extensively that education should be liberating: a process that culminates in the intellectual freedom of those who embrace it. The overarching purpose of this book, therefore, is to demonstrate, contrary to much of what is contested within educational discourse today, that authority need not be avoided in the pursuit of a liberating education. Moreover, the shift towards child-centred education – which is often sold as one of the core principles of progressive education – need not exclude the adoption of the type of educational authority that I propose in these pages. So let us be clear from the outset: being an ardent supporter of authoritative approaches to education need not see me subjected to criticisms of rigidity, dogmatism and coerciveness, as previous supporters of authority have been.

Indeed, the authority for which I argue here is a stepping-stone towards intellectual freedom and emancipation. It underpins knowledge and learning, and gives a view of education as a process that liberates through the guidance and leadership of authority. The paradox here is to realize that an initial submission to authority and a quest for freedom, rather than mutually exclusive or contradictive, are in fact mutually *compatible* notions. The initial submission to authority is part of the fabric of being a rational being, which eventually leads to freedom. In this way, authority underpins the freedom for which we all yearn. That is not to suggest that we ought to be credulous in any way; rather, it suggests that doubt, which is a feature of our freedom, is housed inside an authoritative framework.

In essence, if the game of doubting is predicated on the game of believing, in whom better might we place our faith than a master expert, with credentials and expertise? For this to be possible, the authority of the master expert must be absolute, since to induce doubt at the foundations will have troubling consequences (as will be shown later) for our eventual emancipation.

In this respect, a further rationale for this text was to set on a sounder philosophical footing the arguments that have previously been made about authority in education. The work of my predecessors will feature heavily in the first part of the book, and indeed the main arguments (in the second part) are a concatenation of philosophical ideas from three of the most powerful philosophers of the twentieth century. It became abundantly clear to me while reading the surrounding literature on authority in education that, despite the fact that there are examples (albeit only few) of significant contributions in support of authoritative education, there is a lack of philosophical underpinning to much of what has already been written. Moreover, in many texts to date, as I will demonstrate over the course of the first part of the book, there are embedded confusions about what authority *does* mean and *ought* to mean to education; in part, there are deep-seated misconceptions of educational authority as domineering, tyrannical and coercive – restrictive to the pupils, who have their creativity strangled by the grip of the authoritarian teacher. These misconceptions, it seems, are a feature of the confusion between power and authority. This book seeks to recalibrate the authority debate, to ensure that the terms of reference are clear, and to discuss the notion of authority in light of a consistent definition. If I were to submit to this confusion between power and authority, my writing would cease now. Let it be clear, henceforth, that I do not. The authority for which I seek to make the case within education is the authority that emanates from a master of his or her subject, whose knowledge, manner and insight command the authority of the practice from which he or she comes. I want to make the case for an authority that leads by example, not by the abuse of power or the coercive force imposed by punishment. This case for authority – the case that dismisses the potential ambiguity of authority as a destructive force – needs to be supported in the literature by sound philosophy and coherent reasoning. In the pages to follow, I hope that this is what you will find.

With the underpinning rationale for the book made clear, the method for delivering on this remit needs to be established. In aiming to prove that authority is of worth to education, I decided that the best way forward was to talk about the role that authority plays in teaching and learning, as well as in the development of knowledge. Consequently, the role that authority plays (or ought to play) in education is taken to be the concatenation of these two arguments.

The fact that this book examines the role that authority should play in teaching and learning is hardly a surprise. Indeed, any book about education will, at least in part, need to discuss the concepts of teaching and learning. However, this discussion will not take place on the backdrop of educational theory per se, as opposed to a general discussion about what teaching and learning are, and how authority is an essential component in each. This discussion is one of the core arguments in the book: that, at the foundations of learning, authority is indispensable. The role of the teacher in relation to his or her pupils, and the role that authority plays in such a relationship, is given particular interest. Polanyi, Oakeshott and Wittgenstein are each cited as making unique contributions to this argument, constructed within the second part of the book. This discussion will be entirely philosophical as a result of these contributors and references to learning theory are minimal. This means that the concepts of teaching and learning are set in a general context, and so the discussion of why authority is needed in each of these elements of education is not specific to one theory or another. The argument offered here for authority in teaching and learning is intended to *transcend* the boundaries of educational theory, and to blaze a trail through the messy plethora of theoretical perspectives on how children learn and how we ought to teach. It will be contested that the authority of the teacher in the teacher–pupil relationship should be absolute, but flexible. Philosophical backing will be offered for the view that, if learning is to be a truly liberating process, the process needs to begin with acknowledgement of the authority of one's intellectual superiors. This authority is not coercive or restrictive, but quite the opposite: it is insightful and liberating.

The discussion of the role of authority in knowledge development may come as a surprise given the anti-knowledge agenda in modern-day education. This book, however, seeks to overturn the view that knowledge has lost its verve, even in the 'fast-changing world' in which we live, and it seeks to do so in two ways: (a) by treating knowledge as the inheritance of intellectual riches, this book puts forward the case that knowledge should never lose its value; and (b) by outlining that knowledge is a dichotomy of information and judgement, I demonstrate that knowledge need not be fixed or inert, and that its transmission from one generation to the next need not be passive, but engaging. Indeed, if knowledge includes judgement as one of its components, what might it mean to acquire a judgement without engaging with the concept that one wishes to be able to 'judge'? Judgement requires action – it is dynamic – and so the discussion of knowledge put forward in these pages is one that gives rise to a dynamic, engaging, liberating education in which knowledge takes centre stage.

A common trend of this text will be to demonstrate that any education in which knowledge does not feature is not an education at all. But to make this argument stand up to the critic who contests that knowledge has become obsolete in education, we need a form of knowledge that embraces student engagement, without the need for an educational 'free for all', bereft of structure and boundaries. The role that authority plays in such a take on knowledge becomes pertinent when one asks: 'How do I acquire such knowledge?' The resounding answer will be that you must submit, in the first instance, to the authority of a learned master, whom you must trust to guide you through your education, who will offer you his or her informed insights, share with you his or her judgement, and allow you to assimilate his or her expert mannerism. It will be shown that embracing our knowledge inheritance is the liberating function of any education: a process that begins with the acknowledgement that the teacher is someone in whom we ought to place our faith, in the hope of avoiding ignorance.

Building on previous work on authority is something that is of particular importance, particularly given the apparent demise of pro-authority arguments within educational discourse in recent times. In Chapters 1 and 2, I will discuss, very briefly, some work from a sociological perspective on similar topics that I hope this book will underpin with sound philosophical foundations. Despite the fact that other authors have, in the past, made contributions to authority in an educational context (compare G. H. Bantock and R. S. Peters, as the main contributors), there remains a deficiency of philosophical reasoning about the topic within mainstream educational thinking. In personal correspondence while writing this book, Professor Sir Chris Woodhead, former Chief Inspector of Schools in England, told me that he found such a deficiency in the literature on authority in education quite troubling. Indeed, he contested that he could count on the 'fingers of one hand' how many worthwhile contributions have been made to support authoritative education. There is therefore a serious need for such discussion, even from among those who consider it necessary to resolve the deep-seated confusion of 'authority' and 'knowledge' within educational debates. To put this discussion on a philosophical level is essential and no less than the debate on educational authority deserves. The removal of authority and the undermining of knowledge within education have been permitted in many cases without opposition; this book seeks to 'right' that 'wrong'. The case for authority in education needs to be reopened and a fair hearing needs to be given to a version of authority that should appease the sceptic, without the need for weak or unfounded pedagogy and ideology.

One final note before some preliminary arguments are made: I have given this chapter a potentially troubling subtitle, 'An education for which to be fearful'. Be assured that this title is not scaremongering or hokum; rather, it is a forewarning that if what is posited in these pages is ignored, the potential for education going forward is a frightening prospect. If we continue to undermine the authority that is the lifeblood of successful education, we will eventually reach a stage at which our actions are beyond correction. If we continue to undermine the authority of the teacher in his or her classroom and to undermine his or her position as a master in his or her subject, we will arrive at an entire generation of children who lack humility and guidance, and who will be misinformed and lost. If we take 'child-centred' education too far, we need not be surprised if we find that we have reared a generation of self-centred children. If we continue to preach to the world that knowledge is no longer important in schools and that the 'feeling' of our learning is more important than the 'content' of what we learn, we will be telling our children to choose ignorance over enlightenment. The fact that I believe these things is immaterial; the arguments that I put forward as their justification over the course of this book, however, should not be ignored. If these arguments are ignored, I am fearful – and so might you be.

PART ONE

THE BACKGROUND

1 THE SOCIOLOGICAL BACKGROUND

A sociological perspective

It seems pertinent at this stage to acknowledge that, despite the fact that this book is entirely philosophical in nature, there is a requirement to discuss, very briefly, similar arguments made from a sociological perspective. I should be clear, however, in acknowledging also that this book deliberately avoids further discussions from a sociological perspective later in the text, since it seems that all that can be said from a sociological perspective has been said already. The remit of this book, therefore, is to add philosophical clout to previous arguments that have been made from different perspectives.

This chapter will examine a recent sociological argument made by Furedi (2009) in his groundbreaking book *Wasted: Why Education Isn't Educating*. In this book, Furedi offers insights into the sociological framework that the philosophical arguments in this book underpin. It is worthwhile to note now that Furedi's text is respected and representative as a pro-authority argument within educational and sociological discourse. The reader should therefore consider it to be the sociological companion to this book.

Let us now examine which parts of *Wasted* are pertinent to the discussion that will take place within the bounds of this book. By unpacking some of the core strands of Furedi's book, I hope to demonstrate that the debate for authority in education transcends the boundaries of discipline. Let the perspective put forward in this chapter serve, therefore, as a primer to what will follow in the core chapters of this book. When the reader examines the details of these preliminary arguments, I trust that he or she will recognize the need to substantiate the arguments with sound philosophical reasoning. In many ways, reading Furedi's take on authority prompted me into action in writing this book. I trust that the reader will recognize the pragmatism in what Furedi contests – but also realize the need for the arguments to be underpinned in such a way as to demonstrate beyond any doubt that authoritative education is not only intuitive (as Furedi demonstrates), but also grounded in firm and coherent conceptual reasoning.

There are several important arguments made in Furedi that are relevant for the scope of this book. *Wasted* begins by outlining what Furedi calls the 'paradox of education' (Furedi, 2009: 1). It is interesting that, in making this point, Furedi draws on philosophical evidence from Hannah Arendt. Indeed, the Arendt passage quoted by Furedi on the first page of *Wasted* makes clear the striking similarities between what he is arguing for sociologically and what I am arguing for philosophically. Moreover, the fact that Arendt's writings are invoked makes clear Furedi's own acknowledgement that there is a requirement for a philosophical argument to what he puts forward from a sociological perspective.

So what is this 'paradox of education'? According to Furedi, the more that we invest in education as a societal, political and social tool, the less demanding education becomes. Moreover, Furedi (2009: 1) argues that 'education has become a battlefield on which often-pointless conflicts are fought'. This is indeed a precept to much of what I have written in this book. In fact, it is the fundamental reason why educational policy and practice has been so radically shifted over the last century: education is seen as the solution to societal problems, and it is used as such to cure society of its ailments. Such a view of education, Furedi contests, gives rise to the paradox; indeed, if education is the solution and the solution does not work, then education will be blamed and subsequently changed. In this way, education has fallen prey to an 'anything goes' culture, both academically and in terms of discipline and expectations. Consequently, in an attempt to address societal issues through educational intervention, the anti-knowledge and anti-authority campaigns have gone into overdrive. Indeed, 'it is the reluctance of contemporary society to value and affirm the exercise of adult authority that undermines our capacity to develop the potential of the young people' (Furedi, 2009: 7). This is the core underpinning sociological notion of this book, as well as of Furedi's. The undermining of authority inevitably leads to the undermining of educational values. As I will argue in subsequent chapters, the demise of authority, in actual fact, leads to the demise of the fabric of teaching, of learning, of knowledge development and, consequently, of education also.

Furedi also offers five core preliminary arguments to outline areas of education that seem to have come under sustained attack in the anti-authority campaign. These five preliminaries once again serve as sociological precepts (and indeed sociological parallels) to much of what the reader will find in this book, written philosophically.

The first of these preliminaries outlines that the authority of adults is based on their status as the experienced section of society, whose task it is to transmit the 'legacy of human knowledge and cultural achievements' (Furedi, 2009: 7). This concept will be unpacked further later in this book, in relation to the writings of Michael Oakeshott, whose view of education was embedded in the belief that the adult (or, in his arguments, the teacher specifically) was responsible for the transmission, cultivation and development of the knowledge inheritance of human achievements. Furedi (2009: 7), however, outlines that the undermining of subject knowledge and the rejection of the 'authority of academic subjects' gives rise to an anti-knowledge and anti-authority approach to education. From a curriculum perspective, it seems as though knowledge is now undervalued in a world in which it is believed that what constitutes 'knowledge' has such a high turnaround that school curricula ought not to be knowledge-based. Furedi rejects such a view of things in *Wasted*, and I too reject it among the core arguments of this book.

Secondly, as Furedi outlines, there is another apparent 'paradox' in education (I would, in fact, simply call it a 'contradiction') – namely, the fact that we live in what is often celebrated as a 'knowledge society' or a 'knowledge economy', in which the value of knowledge is hyped, and yet we pursue educational agendas in which knowledge is consistently undermined (Furedi, 2009: 8). Despite the current obsession within education of so-called 'lifelong learning' models – now used in preference to so-called 'front-end models', which are about the here and now – there appears to be no place for knowledge in education that is expected to move beyond formal schooling. In fact, as Furedi contests, the concept of 'formal schooling' has been cast out as outdated and static. Lifelong learning models, in which inert knowledge is cast aside, are 'presented . . . as a demonstration of the seriousness with which education should be taken' (Furedi, 2009: 8). However, in pursuing lifelong learning models in which knowledge is of decreasing interest and value to the learner, 'implicitly, and sometimes explicitly, the authority of formal education is called into question' (Furedi, 2009: 8). There is no doubt that the undermining of the role of knowledge in education is synonymous with the undermining of authority, both of subject disciplines and of the teacher whose job it once was to develop such knowledge. Moreover, I agree with Furedi's sociological pre-analysis suggesting that the undervaluation of knowledge is contradictory to a so-called 'knowledge economy', the idea of which shot to prominence under Tony Blair's premiership, for instance. Where knowledge was once held as one of the cornerstones of education, such views of education are now regarded as inhibiting and restrictive to those who have it 'imposed' upon them. Along with such undermining of the role that knowledge plays within education goes the analogous undermining of authority within education. These concepts will be examined philosophically throughout this book, with particular interest in re-establishing that the anti-knowledge campaign is fraught with inherent and unavoidable blunders.

This realization of the attack on knowledge leads Furedi to his next preliminary sociological argument – namely, that the 'erosion of adult authority in general has a direct impact on the status of the teacher' (Furedi, 2009: 8). Once again, in a sociological context, there is no doubt that the authoritative role of the teacher as a master in his or her subject has come under a major degree of scrutiny. Indeed, if the knowledge-based curriculum comes under threat, the natural consequence is that the teacher who was once revered as a master of knowledge will also come under threat. Furedi contests that evidence of such an attack taking place can be found in the fact that teachers are being increasingly expected to regard themselves as 'learners' or 'facilitators' in their own classrooms. Such a notion, although romantic, is extremely irresponsible and serves only to erode the authority of the teacher in his or her own domain: the classroom. Some might contest that the classroom is not under the ownership of the teacher, but rather under the collective ownership of the pupils who inhabit it. However, a ship without a captain is destined for dangerous waters.

Let it be clear that the classroom is a place of learning, and that it is the *pupil* who learns and the *teacher* who teaches. These are the roles of the players in the classroom and no amount of tinkering with the rules of the game will ever change the scene. As I will argue later, in keeping with philosophers Polanyi, Oakeshott and Wittgenstein, the job of the teacher is to provide an expertly constrained framework within which the pupil will flourish. This framework is held together by the fabric of authority: both the authority of the subject that the teacher seeks to convey to his or her pupils; and the authority of the position of the teacher. Furedi's acknowledgement that the demise of adult authority in general – and the undermining and erosion of teacher authority, in particular – has led to the undermining of education requires further examination. Furedi himself does this sociologically in *Wasted*; I will examine this view philosophically later in this book. Unless we cease to undermine teacher authority, we will continue to undermine one of the pillars of education, which makes for successful teaching and learning, and knowledge development and transmission between the generations:

> The devaluation of the authority of the teacher is also reinforced through the loss of value accorded to subject-based knowledge. Many pedagogues regard the teaching of academic subjects in schools as irrelevant. Since the authority of teachers rests on their expertise in a subject, the current devaluation of academic subjects has a direct effect upon teachers' professional status. The cumulative outcome of these developments is the decline of the status of the teaching profession.
>
> (Furedi, 2009: 8–9)

The final preliminary arguments that Furedi makes are heavily focused on the sociology of this discussion. He contests that confusions surrounding adult authority in general have led to difficulties in socializing children and difficulties in disciplining children (Furedi, 2009: 9). The argument around socialization is of no consequence to what is put forward in this book and so will simply be noted at this stage; the concept of discipline is a potentially problematic discussion with reference to authority. Let it be clear now that, although Furedi puts forward a compelling case for the demise of authority and the demise of discipline being synonymous with one another throughout *Wasted*, it is not my focus in this book to develop these ideas in any real detail. Moreover, the confusion of authority and power as though they are one and the same concept is, in fact, critiqued in this book. Similar confusions are commonplace within educational discourse: about the concepts of discipline and punishment, for example. It must be understood that the authority for which this text argues so vehemently is *not* one that has confusions about authority and power. There is indeed a case to be made to suggest that the recent problems with school discipline are a consequence of the systematic undermining of the teacher's authority within his or her own classroom – but this debate is for another place and Furedi makes a sound contribution to it. I am more focused, however, on the roles that the authority of the teacher and his or her knowledge of his or her subject play in teaching and learning. The fact that our schools are now full of children and young people who are unruly and teachers who are either not capable or not permitted to discipline such children is an argument steeped in sociology to such an extent that I dare not contribute.

However, for the moment, these five core preliminary arguments, together with what Furedi calls 'the infantilization of education' (Furedi, 2009: 13), serve as the crux of the 'paradox of education'. These arguments culminate in the realization that 'paradoxically, the more that we expect of education, the less we expect of children; and the more hope society invests in education, the less we value it as something important in its own right' (Furedi, 2009: 16). From a sociological perspective, Furedi makes a compelling argument that this paradox is rife within educational discourse. This book therefore seeks to untangle the paradox and to place education back on safe ground. The anti-knowledge and anti-authority campaigns within education need to be halted before they do irreversible damage. Furedi argues that the intergenerational nature of education requires the authority of the teacher to be absolute, so that the development of knowledge can be successful. I will expand and develop this perspective on authority and knowledge. Furthermore, it is essential to stop the onslaught against the value of knowledge that is manifest in the modern day. By viewing knowledge as an inheritance of experiences and judgements, this book seeks to convey the notion that knowledge is *indispensable* in any understanding of education, and that the teacher is the one who enlightens his or her pupils and supports them in embracing their knowledge inheritance.

The core precepts of *any* education must therefore encompass, at least in part, knowledge development. Educated people must be knowledgeable people, equipped with a collection of historical intellectual wealth that has been transmitted to them through the actions of a distinguished master: the teacher. They must be equipped with a judgement that enables them to act, to create and to inspire others. The educated person, in his or her initial submission to the authority of the master, seeks to understand that master's way of acting and, in following him or her, becomes valuable to others: 'The principle achievement of education is an educated people and society' (Furedi, 2009: 20). An educated people and society is, indeed, the sociological focus of education; what, precisely, constitutes an educated people is what requires definition. This book seeks to convey the message that the educated person is one who has a wealth of knowledge, founded in his or her training and housed inside the authority of the master. The educated person is liberated by attaining his or her master's judgement and insights into ways of acting. The educated *people* is therefore a collection of educated persons – and their education is a process the genesis of which is founded in accepting the absolute authority of the teacher who seeks to train them.

Education for the future?

There is a current trend within education to obsess more over what education can *prepare* children for, rather than to focus on their development in the here and now. Make no mistake: in large part, this is a sensible notion. Education should, by its very nature, equip learners for future challenges. However, the manner in which this goal is strived for is less than sensible – perhaps not even honourable. In what Furedi (2009: 21) calls 'throwaway pedagogy', we now have an education system that is predicated on the belief that the best way in which to pursue an education for the future is to avoid knowledge development; the reason for this, it is often contested, is because knowledge quickly becomes obsolete, and so we ought to avoid its deliverance in the present moment, owing to its likely irrelevance in the not-too-distant future.

The general 'throwaway' and 'change' cultures that are in vogue within modern-day educational thinking have led to the demise of so-called traditional, academic education in a process that Furedi (2009: 23) calls the 'fetishization of change'. Institutions are valued less, in favour of 'personalized learning' and 'lifelong learning'. The constant changes in society have given rise to a demand that educational aims and educational focus must shift from an academic, knowledge-developing education towards a skills-based, lifelong-learning education. The so-called 'front-end' models of education that focus on the present moment are disregarded as static and stagnant, lacking vision and creativity, and are cast aside in favour of 'lifelong learning' models, which focus on how children and young people can face *future challenges and changes* in knowledge. It is therefore no longer acceptable to educate our children for the here and now, since the here and now changes so quickly that it will be gone before our knowledge of it is put to any use. Knowledge, therefore, is replaced by skills, with a focus on how these skills can help us to move forward with the times and to avoid remaining stuck in the past.

The focus of this movement within education is, according to Furedi, the result of a drive for change and a fear of remaining rooted in the past. This emanates from the carefully chosen rhetoric of governments and policymakers, who give the impression that 'change' is synonymous with 'improvement' (Furedi, 2009: 23): 'Typically, change is presented in a dynamic and mechanistic manner that exaggerates the novelty of the present moment. Educationalists frequently adopt the rhetoric of breaks and ruptures and maintain that nothing is as it was and that the present has been decoupled from the past.' However, such rationale for change and so-called 'forward thinking' within education is a far cry from the reality that, sociologically speaking, binds together the past and the future. To think of the present and the future as entirely divorced from the past – and from the collection of intellectual wealth on which we, in fact, *depend* for our future – borders on absurdity:

> [This] outlook is shaped by an imagination that is so overwhelmed by the displacement of the old by the new that it often overlooks important dimensions of historical experience that may continue to be relevant to our lives. The discussion of the relationship between education and change is frequently overwhelmed by the fad of the moment and with the relatively superficial symptoms of new developments.
>
> (Furedi, 2009: 23–4)

It follows, therefore, that to change the educational edifice so whimsically every time there is a societal, political, cultural or technological change serves only to undermine the stability that education ought to bring to society *in the face of change* – that is, regardless of the fast-moving world in which we now live, education should contain, at least in part, a calming knowledgeable influence. The wealth of human experience that would be missed – or worse, ignored – if we were to turn our collective backs on the knowledge of the past gives rise to troubling consequences of a knowledge-free or knowledge-deficient form of education. Indeed, while the world moves so quickly, one wonders if Euclid's geometry ever becomes redundant? As technology advances, are we to consider it beneath us to teach our children about the importance of reading the literary greats? Surely such knowledge *transcends* temporal restrictions, to the extent that it ought to be relevant and worthwhile in all times, to all men?

Moreover, the current tendency to deflate and downgrade knowledge to a statement of mere facts and figures serves little purpose other than to demonstrate a lamentable ignorance on the part of those who seek to dispense with a knowledge-led education. I often wonder what precisely a 'skills-based' approach to education might entail in the absence or deficiency of knowledge: if skills enable us 'to do', what might it mean to be able to *do* anything, in the absence or deficiency of knowing? Being able to *do* anything entails an ability to decide that it ought to be done in a certain moment: what might it mean to be able to act at the correct moment, in the absence of *knowing* that the moment is correct? In the absence of an underpinning knowledge, actions are entirely random. Skills require knowledge; they depend on it in order to give legitimacy to act. As I will contest later in the book, in keeping with Oakeshott's definition of knowledge, such ability to act is found in *judgement*: an indispensable facet of our knowledge reserves, which is developed only through close imitation of the teacher's way of acting, whose authority must be absolute.

The recent onslaught of 'change' in education has given rise to the notion that the past is to be put behind us where it belongs and largely ignored in the modern day. The use of empty rhetoric and idioms coming from educational policymakers and government officials has led to the undervaluation and undermining of a knowledge-based education. Furedi warns that this 'flight from the past' is particularly dangerous, in that to move forward in ignorance of what has come before is to be found guilty of intellectual arrogance:

> The dramatization of change renders the past wholly irrelevant. If we continually move from one 'new age' to another then the institutions and practices of the past have little relevance for today. Indeed, the ceaseless repetition of the proposition that the past is irrelevant serves to desensitize people from understanding the influence of a legacy of human development on their lives.
>
> (Furedi, 2009: 27)

The use of the words 'institution' and 'practice' are of particular importance in this case. Indeed, many who are ardent supporters of the anti-knowledge campaign would contest that institutions and practices ought to be changed, lest we remain fixed in the past. But this is precisely what Furedi is warning against in his defence of such notions. Furthermore, as I will demonstrate later – in a philosophical sense – institutions and practices are solid cornerstones of education, which ought to be well-grounded and firm. That is not to say that they should never change over time; rather, they should – by their very definition – be difficult to change. The modern-day onslaught on knowledge is synonymous with the undermining of institutions and practices that hold the wealth of historical knowledge together. The concept of 'change' and the idea that we have wave after wave of 'new ages' give rise to the belief that institutions and practices matter less, and that knowledge can be discarded frivolously. I will show that nothing could be further from the truth.

Furthermore, a 'new age' need not dispense with the 'old age'; in fact, sociologically speaking, a new age is more likely to flourish in recognition of the old age upon which it seeks to *build*, as opposed to replace. Change, therefore, is more responsibly replaced by *transition* between ages, and transition *never* discards the workings of the past. Institutions and practices are a part of the fabric of knowledge, and should form a part of a responsible transition between generations. Neither should knowledge once relevant to a 'previous generation' ever lose its value, regardless of advancements in technology or changes of ideology. In fact, quite the contrary: advancements in technology should give rise to new knowledge and new insights, in a new age, to build on top of the wealth of knowledge that already exists. It should not seek to replace the old with the new; rather, to cultivate the new within the old, to form a seamless transition between one generation and the next. Only in the most radical of cases in the total and absolute shift of ideology – perhaps in the aftermath of a trauma or disaster – should the slate ever be wiped clean and the old be cast aside as obsolete, no longer fit for purpose. In large part, however, the most sensible and responsible transition between 'ages' takes place in the context of an acknowledging the intellectual riches that have been left by the great and the good of yesteryear.

The underlying concern with the attack on institutions and practices is that it gives rise to subsequent attacks on authority and traditions. Once again, these terms of are particular importance for the bounds of this book, as the reader will note in the chapter dedicated to Polanyi's writings on authority (Chapter 5). Furedi (2009: 30) suggests that the deliberate disregard for the past is 'fuelled by the search for new forms of authority', outlining that 'authoritative institutions and traditions in western society have been contested for some time'. There is no doubt that this is the case in a more general sense than only that of authority within educational discourse. Nevertheless, education as an institution and as a tradition does not escape the contestation of authority. From a sociological perspective, Furedi (2009: 30) argues that this contestation of the authority of the institution and traditions of education is symptomatic of the fact that we have become 'cut off and estranged' from our past. Similarly, this 'estrangement' signifies 'a new world that has left the old one behind' (Furedi, 2009: 30). In this book, however, I seek to reinstate the institution and traditions of education, and to restore and protect the somewhat eroded authority of the teacher in doing so. The egalitarian, anti-knowledge, anti-authority campaigns within education must be brought to a halt, not with elitism in mind, but to protect the ideals that make education possible and responsible.

Within the remit of this book, I trust that the reader will see a form of education that has one simple sociological undertone: to protect the institution of education from becoming a 'free for all' and to place the authoritative teacher at the centre of this institution, leading the pupils under his or her tutelage towards their knowledge inheritance. I trust that the reader will also find within this model of authoritative education scope for transition between generations, so that the institution of education need not be stagnant or static. And, finally, I trust that the reader will conclude that a trust in one's teacher is not unfounded, regardless of the 'age' in which we live, and that we should not – and, indeed, do not – live in a world in which knowledge is redundant, worthless or obsolete:

The objectification of change is symptomatic of a mood of intellectual malaise where the notions of truth, knowledge and meaning have acquired a provisional and arbitrary character. Perversely, the transformation of change into a metaphysical force haunting humanity actually desensitizes society from distinguishing between novelty and qualitative change. That is why lessons learned through the experience of the past, and the knowledge developed through it, are so important for helping society face the future. When change is objectified, it turns into a spectacle that distracts society from valuing the important truths and insights that it has acquired throughout the best moments in history. Yet these truths that have emerged through attempts to find answers to many of the deepest and most durable questions facing the human species, and the more that the world changes, the more we need to draw on our cultural and intellectual inheritance from the past.

(Furedi, 2009: 41)

The fall of authority

Undoubtedly the most significant chapter of *Wasted* in relation to this book is its third chapter, in which Furedi outlines some 'confusions about adult authority' (Furedi, 2009: ch. 3). Evidently, there is an extensive discussion from within the adult community about the role (or demise) of authority in general. It was in reading this chapter of *Wasted* that many of my own core ideas began to develop in line with much of what I had already considered from my time in teacher training.

Furedi offers some sociological insight into why the demise of adult authority might have taken place over time. Not surprisingly, it is posited that the demise of adult authority has coincided with confusions about authority and where it 'fits' into the modern world. There is no doubt that the disregard for authority in recent times has coincided with confusion about what authority represents. This confusion has infested political authority, the authority of the State and the authority of the Church, for example, as well as the authority of the institution of education and the authority within school contexts. Furedi makes some general arguments about authority on a wider scale, to outline that the fall in authority in an educational context is, in fact, symptomatic of an anti-authority pandemic that has swept across other institutions also.

Generally speaking, there is an undervaluation of authority – in particular, the authority of the adult generation in relation to the younger generation. Authority is now considered to be an overrated, dogmatic notion owing to a societal perception (particularly within the younger generation) that adults are becoming increasingly 'out of touch' with a rapidly changing world. Also, authority is now viewed as an irrelevant and infringing force, which is no longer valued or respected by the younger generation. Moreover, the difficulty in establishing consensus within communities and societies – a concept that is required for authority to be legitimate – leads to the natural demise of adult authority in general. Values are less stringent than before and agreement on which 'values' ought to be transmitted to the younger generation is harder to establish (Furedi, 2009: 63): 'For some time, many western societies have found it difficult to forge a consensus through which they can affirm their past and the basic values they uphold. Traditional symbols and conventions have lost some of their power to enthuse and inspire, and in some cases have become irrevocably damaged.' In this view of things, the ideals and values of the adult generation seem to have lost 'their relevance to a "changed" world' (Furedi, 2009: 63), and as a consequence any values that are transmitted cannot be transmitted 'with conviction' to the younger generation.

This is one of the many reasons why I argue later in this book that authority is essential within education: without it, the transmission of anything between generations becomes difficult and ineffectual, to such a point that, one day, such transmission may cease altogether. The argument that the world is changing so quickly that the adult community is no longer fit to keep up simply does not stack up; in fact, quite the opposite is true. A child without guidance has the potential to act in a misguided manner; a child without judgement has the potential to act in a reckless manner; a child without knowledge is almost sure to act in an ignorant manner. The person who offers guidance, judgement and knowledge is the teacher; the one indispensable aspect of the teacher that makes the transmission of all of these qualities possible is his or her authority to act, his or her legitimacy to convey a set of ideals and values that have been set within the community that he or she represents.[1]

The anti-authority campaign attempts also to convey that a submission to authority goes hand in hand with a rejection of individual reasoning. Conversely, its proponents try to contest that if we can reason for ourselves, we ought to rebel against the word set down on us from on high. The rational beasts that we are demand that we reject authority and confirm things for ourselves. This is a post-modern shift away from traditional ideals that were established by an authority and transmitted to the masses through a chosen delegate (in the case of education, the teacher). It is also argued that, as a consequence, authority is seen as a stifling force on creativity and individuality, coercing those who submit to it to act in predetermined ways:

> [Q]uestioning the right of traditional authority to determine how people conduct their life has become one of the defining features of modern culture. Moreover, the very assertion of authority is increasingly perceived as an encroachment on individual freedom ever since traditional forms of authority have come under question, all

other forms have been challenged and sometimes castigated as arbitrary. Many people have come to regard authority as, by definition, the antithesis to freedom, and restricting its role is seen as the objective of movements fighting for the expansion of democratic rights.

(Furedi, 2009: 71)

This view of authority is particularly confused. Indeed, it is this muddled version of authority that this book seeks to overturn, to make it clear that authority need not be mutually exclusive of moments of creativity and inspiration, nor of the notion of freedom. Moreover, it is a particularly confused belief that creativity is a spontaneous faculty, which results only from moments of individualism. In fact, it seems entirely more sensible to suggest that creativity is generated from a foundation of habitual practice and disciplined behaviour – that is, that creativity and absolute freedom are not synonymous with one another. Furthermore, the entire essence of freedom is ingrained into responsible forms of authority. If a young child goes to place his or her hand on the fire, he or she is *free* to do so – but the responsible parent will act with authority to guide the child not to do so. The parent's authority is legitimized by the fact that he or she knows that the fire will burn the young child, whereas the child is ignorant of this fact. Perhaps we might suggest that, in the interest of preserving the young child's freedom, the parent ought to let him or her touch the fire? Alternatively, we can discard such a suggestion as nonsense and recommend the responsible thing: that the adult leads with authority, and that the child be guided and constrained by it.

By grasping the understanding that authority is founded in the legitimacy to guide and instruct others, we can move forward beyond the empty rhetoric that authoritative approaches to education ought to be avoided. The legitimacy is established in the ideals cultivated and perpetuated by a collective body – the community – and these core ideals are steeped in an acknowledgement of the traditions from which they come. As Furedi (2009: 66) contests:

Authority is not an attribute of individual behaviour: it is legitimized through shared ideals that provide a set of principles for the conduct of authoritative behaviour. Values, traditions and authority are closely connected to one another, and if one is undermined, so is the other. Yet the exercise of adult authority is indispensable for the running of an effective education system.

This legitimacy – which is very much a feature of authority that is often misconceived or ignored – is precisely what distinguishes authority from power. Where 'power' need not be legitimatized, authority is underpinned by a legitimacy to act. Therefore, where authority is often put forward as the 'antithesis' of freedom, it is, in fact, a more coercive force than authority that infringes on people's freedoms. Indeed, if *authority* is rebelled against, it is possible to enforce authority only by discipline. When *power* is ignored or rebelled against, the consequence is usually punishment or coercive force. Discipline need not be considered as a destructive force; it is not a tool with which to destroy the will of the individual in the same way as is punishment or coercive force. Discipline is the legitimate act of enforcing authority, with a view to positive outcomes. This book does not seek to equip the teacher or the institutions with more power, but rather to restore their eroded authority. In grasping the distinction between authority and power,[2] we grasp the notion that *authority* is a positive guiding force by definition, with safeguards inbuilt to protect from its abuse; *power* is open to being abused, and is more focused on dominance and the restriction of those who are dominated.

The role of the authoritative teacher, therefore, is 'to direct and guide children's growth' (Furedi, 2009: 69). Contrary to what is often posited of authority among the confusions that portray it as a restrictive and coercive force, there is a fundamental requirement that, 'in the relationship between the teacher and the child, the educator needs to initiate, direct and set the terms of the relationship' (Furedi, 2009: 69). In this way, education cannot be considered to be any different from any other arena in which authoritative relationships are essential to proper functioning. Over the course of this book, I aim to demonstrate that such authoritative relationships are at the core of educational interactions between teachers and pupils. This, however, requires justification. The current trend of discarding such authoritative interactions between the teacher and the pupil requires rethinking. For the moment, though, I will open this discussion (to be developed throughout the entire book) in agreement with Furedi (2009: 69–70), who contests that:

All authority relations are hierarchical, and the relation between a teacher and student is no exception. In education, a relationship of inequality founded on the primacy of adult authority is based on the recognition that only grown-ups can be genuinely responsible for the welfare of children and for the world. Education as a generational transaction presupposes the fact that the older generation has something important to impart that children need to learn.

This sociological notion of education as a 'generational transaction' is indeed one of the core concepts that this book seeks to underpin with philosophical evidence. In Chapters 5 and 6, for example, I will contest – in keeping with Polanyi and Oakeshott – that education is a cultivation of knowledge between a master and his or her pupils. Moreover, this 'transaction' that Furedi posits is an idea that I will develop philosophically, in grasping the idea that education is a process of initiation into a knowledge inheritance of intellectual wealth left behind by previous generations that we are to embrace.

The fear that is instilled into discussions about authority within education in the modern day is in need of being eased. As I will outline in Chapter 3 in providing some standard definitions of authority, there are often versions of authority put forward, particularly within educational discourse, which give rise to the notion that authority is a notion to be avoided and feared. Society, in general, has been encouraged to treat all forms of authority with 'suspicion' (Furedi, 2009: 71). However, the form of authority for which I argue in this book is one that should dispel any such fears or suspicions in relation to education. It is founded in a simple principle that has been captured – citing Bantock, another ardent supporter or authority in education, in the process – as follows:

> [T]he act of learning and the very pursuit of knowledge requires the acceptance of authority of the subject and of the teacher who represents it in the classroom. When children go to school, they rely on their teachers to guide them to comprehend new forms of knowledge. This reliance on the teacher involves *a leap of faith* which people only undertake if they accept the authority of the educator. 'Learning always involves a determination to grasp after what is as yet uncomprehended', observed Bantock.
>
> (Furedi, 2009: 70)

The idea that the fullest development of knowledge and the purest version of learning require a submission to authority seems, at least in part, to be intuitive. Indeed, when we view education in the terms that Furedi puts forward – as a generational transaction – we seem to ease closer to an understanding that there is a requirement for authority within any successful version of education, learning and knowledge development. I aim to show that foundational authority is required to make the notion of knowledge development coherent. Similarly, I aim to demonstrate that any version of learning must embrace the idea that there is an authoritative master who initiates the pupils under his or her charge and guides them authoritatively towards embracing their intellectual inheritance. And, finally, I aim to show that, in order to pursue a successful educational experience, one has to place one's faith in the authority of the teacher, who is the chosen representative of the community and the practice from which he or she comes. In such a version of education, we can learn to embrace the idea that the process of education serves as the responsible intergenerational transaction between the adult community and the younger generation, in which the adult community imparts knowledge and equips the younger generation with the insight required to make sensible and informed choices for the future. Moreover, in taking a careful look at how readily we ought to 'throw away' the intellectual riches and knowledge inheritance from the past, Furedi puts forward the case that we ought to *recycle* knowledge from one generation to the next, in such a way that knowledge will never lose its value or become redundant, regardless of how fast the world moves or changes.

Let us therefore be clear from the outset: authority is not a concept within education that ought to be avoided at all costs. This book supports the idea that education should liberate students and offer them opportunities to be the best that they can be. However, the view that such liberation comes only in the absence of authority is outright rejected. In fact, precisely the opposite is argued in this book – that is, that authority is the very concept that underpins a liberating education, leading to the eventual freedom of the pupils who are fortunate enough to experience it. This view of education, and the role that authority plays in making sure that it comes to fruition, adopts Furedi's conclusion that 'children are the rightful heirs to the achievements of human society' (Furedi, 2009: 212). These ideas will be developed in Chapter 6, where I will discuss the idea of inheritance within an educational context. It is important to grasp in this preamble of arguments that authority is required for a responsible intergenerational transaction between the adult community and the younger community. In education, it is the responsibility of the teacher (who represents the adult community in the classroom) to ensure that the pupils under his or her charge are made privy to the inheritance that is rightfully theirs. In the opposite direction, however, the responsibility of the pupil is to place his or her trust in the experienced master, whose responsibility it is to lead the way. An educated society results only from a collection of educated people; the people can be educated only if they yield to the superior insight, knowledge and judgement of their intellectual superiors; this superior insight, knowledge and judgement gives legitimacy to the authority of the teacher as an expert in his or her discipline. We ought not to undermine this authority, lest we undermine the very precepts upon which a successful education is built.

2 THE PHILOSOPHICAL AND THEORETICAL BACKGROUND

Given the nature of the debate surrounding authority in general, and its importance to education in particular, it will hardly come as a surprise to the reader that there are a number of arguments that previously have been made in favour of authoritative education. Indeed, there is a rather eclectic mix of authors who have made their own individual contributions to this debate, both for and against, some of which will be examined briefly over the next few sections. Furthermore, there are a few background arguments that need to be highlighted relating to the basic philosophical, ideological and theoretical areas into which the arguments of this book fit.

The existing arguments for authority in education: Background reading for this book

G. H. Bantock: The relationship between freedom and authority in education

Bantock is well known for his contributions to the discussion and debate surrounding authority and freedom in education. Indeed, his book entitled *Freedom and Authority in Education*, first published in 1952, was a pioneering piece of work, seen as the defence of authoritative education against the onslaught of progressivism in the middle of the twentieth century. The review offered by *New Statesman* of Bantock's book, set on its inside cover, reads: 'He is aghast, like many another, at the sloppiness of much of contemporary educational theorizing, and possessing a keen mind and a sharp pen he has a good deal of fun at the expense of well-intentioned but muddle-headed sentiments. If his strictures have the effect they deserve, they will have been well worth while.' This review, I hope, could capture the remit of this book equally as well as it did that of Bantock. In many ways, this book builds on ideas that Bantock initiated and brought to the debate – albeit from a different time, context and perspective – many years ago.

Take, for example, Bantock's overt critique of the progressive ideology that had become so overhyped at the time of his writing. His distaste for the obsession with change through educational means led Bantock to conclude that proponents of progressivism in his time had a muddled view of what traditions are and what they represent. Indeed, he contests that '[o]ur society, in the view of education that it encourages, is obsessed with the image of change which it believes itself to foster' (Bantock, 1970: 8). Progressivism, therefore, in trying to adopt this view of a changing world, is believed to be 'pragmatic rather than concerned with ultimate aims, materialistic rather than idealistic' (Bantock, 1970: 14). The consequence of this belief is that '[i]t displays a scepticism before the external world, and its reconstructions, such as they are, are synthetical and rationalistic rather than derived from received opinions and traditional modes' (Bantock, 1970: 14). Communities, traditions, practices and customs, as well as the authorities who act on behalf of these things, are cast aside in this view of education, giving way to the rational-thinking individual, whose atomistic supremacy overhauls the role of any authority figure. Nothing is to be taken as a foundation; everything must be questioned and justified. Such a view of education leads Bantock (1970: 14–15) to conclude that this is 'ultimately an education of pride and rejection rather than one of acceptance and humility. It involves the decay of the intellect, the decline of the will and the triumph of impulse.' It is an education in which 'everyone shuts himself up in his own breast, and affects from that point to judge the world', accepting no 'authority beyond themselves' (Bantock, 1970: 19).

This take on non-authoritative education leads Bantock (1970: 21–2) to ask: 'Should children be encouraged in the sort of egotistical self-inflation that the exercise of such control and the consequent diminished role of the teacher's authority might well beget?' This question is one of the core undertones of this book – that is, should we throw the classroom open to the romantic notion that children should be permitted to question all things that are told to them, regardless of the impact of such whimsy on the authority and the position of the teacher, and the consequential impact on the child's learning and his or her education in general? Perhaps such a view of education forgets what the role of the teacher is supposed to be. But Bantock (1970: 22) reminds us:

> The teacher is in a particular position; he is not appointed by children, and is appointed because he knows much more about his subject than the children do. Thus his authority, which in part, at least, derives from his subject (I am assuming his competence) cannot be called into question. If he says that the Battle of Hastings took place in 1066, it must be accepted; no dictate of the sternest tyrant could be more absolute. Thus, while learning is a matter of any importance in our schools, the teacher can never quite be reduced to the role of Big Friend or Cheer Leader, as seems to be the modern ambition.[1]

Another core element of Bantock's writings that is of importance and relevance to this work is his discussion and consideration of the relationship between educational freedom and educational authority. One of the main notions that this book seeks to overturn is that educational freedom comes only in circumstances under which educational authority is rejected. It is often posited, as Bantock outlines, that freedom and authority are mutually exclusive concepts, each the antithesis of the other. Nevertheless, such a view of things is fundamentally flawed; the truth is, in fact, on the contrary, in as much as intellectual and educational freedom seems to emanate from authoritative beginnings. As Bantock (1970: 25) observes, 'we are emotionally attuned to receive the notion of "freedom" – without thought about the ends this freedom is to subserve – whereas the notion of authority has to overcome a deep-seated emotional prejudice'. That is to say, we accept our freedoms without a second thought about our obligations to such freedoms; it is ingrained into our fabric as human beings that we have certain freedoms and liberties, and perish the thought that any of these freedoms be infringed upon. And yet we rarely ask where such freedoms come from, and how they can be attained and maintained.

Bantock concludes, as will I later, that authority and freedom are *not* in opposition to one another in relation to education. However, there are elements of authority that require defining, and safeguards must be built into any authoritative framework to detract from its abuse. However, when we acknowledge that authority is not, in fact, the dogmatic, restrictive force that some would have us believe, we can begin to appreciate the pivotal role that authority plays in our eventual educational liberation. As Bantock (1970: 25–6) contests: 'The authority which I am considering is the true source of "freedom" – that higher freedom which reasserts the dignity and worth of man. It is no mechanical, static thing … but a living, dynamic principle of a tradition of objective learning reinvoked and reabsorbed.'

To reinforce this point, it is also essential to make clear that authoritative education need not be in opposition to an education that is enjoyable. Rather, where non-authoritative education places at its centre the child's enjoyment, authoritative education sees enjoyment and interest as the by-products of good education, rather than its remit. Bantock recalls a conversation that he had with the headmaster of a school (bearing in mind that this was prior to his writing in 1952), in which the headmaster said to him: 'Of course, I don't very much mind what the children do here, provided they are happy.' I have encountered many similar instances in my own educational engagements with senior figures within schools. I recall one encounter with a vice-principal of a secondary school, who contested that the remit of any school was to give the children whatever freedom they required to explore their own world and to express it in whatever terms they saw fit. At my evident dismay, he responded in the same manner as did the headmaster to Bantock: by claiming that the children in his school 'had fun' and that this was 'what his school was all about'. For me, this is a frightening prospect. When I put forward the strange notion that schools are places in which learning should take place and in which teachers ought to teach, the vice-principal emphasized that it mattered more to him and his school that the students enjoyed their education, rather than that they were subjected to learning experiences 'forced onto them' by teachers. I, like Bantock in his encounter with the headmaster, had to 'wonder about the wisdom of such a statement' (Bantock, 1970: 64).

How on earth have we come to hold within educational thinking that enjoyment has superseded and triumphed over the development of a quest to learn? The counter-contestation might be that happiness leads to a greater propensity to learn. But such a view of learning seems to miss the fact that, at times, unsavoury work has to be done in order to arrive at the eventual 'happy ending'. As Bantock (1970: 64) observes, 'very often, one is met with the situations where present happiness must be sacrificed so that a greater happiness can be achieved'. I recall an instance in which, even in my advanced years as an undergraduate mathematician, a senior lecturer introducing the course to the body of undergraduate mathematicians warned us that if we hoped to be successful, we ought not to be frightened to 'get our hands dirty'. His advice, as a seasoned educator, was, of course, that we needed to be willing to slog through the difficult beginnings if we were to arrive eventually at our ultimate goal. We were not encouraged to go off on a rampage, seeking to make sense of the mathematical world on our own, for such advice would have been to dismiss his own role as our educator. In telling us that we were to get our 'hands dirty', he was also making clear that he did not want to shirk his educational responsibility to us, as the students under his charge. His authority was made clear and we were encouraged to follow his ways. The salient conclusion, for Bantock (1970: 64), is clear: '[I]t is often necessary to perform tasks that are at the moment distasteful so as to acquire skills which can lead to profound happiness in later life. One of the greater faults of "child-centered" education has been its tendency to make the child its own arbiter in its own destinies.' And in relation to the notion of educational freedom, this conclusion translates thus (Bantock, 1970: 67): 'All the higher freedoms of the human being imply the initial restriction and discipline essential to the process of becoming "free" to exercise the required will.' This initial restriction and discipline is found in the pupil's submission to his or her master, whose authority must be absolute, with the acknowledgement that 'to provide . . . freedom at too early an age can lead to even greater insecurity' (Bantock, 1970: 67).

Freedom, therefore, comes only after an initial submission to the authority of a master expert. This is the salient point of each of the chapters of this book, and requires philosophical and conceptual justification. Bantock's claim that '[n]o child is free to choose by the light of nature alone' (Bantock, 1970: 68) needs to be founded in sound philosophical reasoning. Moreover, I set about demonstrating why, precisely, 'no child is free to choose until he is already sufficiently disciplined to see the implications of his choice' (Bantock, 1970: 68), and why the role of the educator is 'to shield him from harmful impulses that may later militate against his freedom of choice' (Bantock, 1970: 68). In doing so, we can further the pupil's ability to 'discriminate' between reckless choices and informed ones. However, such ability to discriminate comes only once the pupil has adopted his or her master's expert mannerism, insights and judgement. To deprive the pupil of his or her ability to discriminate is 'not to free the child but to bind him' (Bantock, 1970: 69).

Let the importance of freedom in education be clear, as well as the role of a submission to authority in attaining such freedom (Bantock, 1970: 69): 'If then, the standard is to be freedom, that freedom itself implies the initial restraint and discipline inherent in the process of becoming free to exercise the required skill.' Moreover, this notion depends on 'an authority through which man achieves his freedom and dignity, and the acceptance of which is the pre-requisite to the attainment of such freedom' (Bantock, 1970: 182). Freedom and authority within education are therefore *not* opposing forces, nor are they mutually exclusive; rather, they are mutually interdependent. As I will argue later, particularly in Chapters 5 and 6, a truly liberating education depends greatly on a basis of authority from which such freedom and liberation can spring. In the absence of such authority, the very notion of liberation seems far-fetched and unfounded. A choice that is free from authoritative guidance has greater potential to be misinformed and misguided. And any version of freedom that emanates from misinformed and misguided judgements hardly constitutes a freedom that education should seek to circulate.

Lawrence Stenhouse: Knowledge as the great emancipator

The contribution of Stenhouse to the debate on authority in education is relevant to this work in light of what he posited of knowledge as a tool for the eventual 'emancipation' of the pupil who is exposed to it. A review of Stenhouse's work can be found in Hendricks (2002), who makes several points of relevance to this project. She claims, first, that 'the primary theme in Stenhouse's work was the idea of emancipation – both of students and teachers – through knowledge' (Hendricks, 2002: 118). This belief is also one of the core themes of this book. Indeed, as I will demonstrate later, calling on philosophical evidence from Oakeshott's writings on the topic, knowledge should be viewed as an inheritance of intellectual riches, passed on from one generation to the next. By viewing knowledge as a wealth that is to be inherited, one can embrace Stenhouse's view that knowledge is also the great emancipator. Indeed, for the teacher or educator, knowledge emancipates, liberates and frees him or her to instruct with authority and security. For the student who is exposed to knowledge, he or she can inherit that intellectual wealth and become liberated in the process. In reading Chapter 6 of this book in particular, I trust that the reader will come to appreciate the importance of knowledge as an emancipating tool, as Stenhouse contests.

Furthermore, as Hendricks (2002: 118) highlights, Stenhouse came to realize that knowledge was a tool that ought to be used to make sense of the world around him. In coming to grasp the idea that knowledge was required for a true and fulfilling liberation, Stenhouse was 'encouraged to use knowledge to make sense of his world so that he could become an authority in his own right' (Hendricks, 2002: 118). This is precisely what I will argue later, when I deal with Polanyi's and Oakeshott's contributions to the knowledge and authority debates, respectively, in educational contexts.

The most significant preliminary contribution to this book made by Stenhouse is the pride of place that he gave to knowledge in his vision of a successful education. One of the core arguments that this book seeks to put forward is the case that *any* education must have, as one of its core remits, the fullest development of knowledge. Stenhouse makes clear why knowledge is not only appealing within education, but also necessary to *any* successful educational process. Indeed, by viewing knowledge as the key to one's eventual emancipation, we can begin to see why the fullest development of knowledge within education might be so instrumental.

Moreover, precisely how knowledge is developed most successfully is also of concern. Hendricks (2002: 118) observes that Stenhouse 'challenged the traditional roles of authority in the educational system' and put forward the case for students to have 'more control over their learning'. These ideas will not be adopted in this book; rather, this book sets out to re-establish the belief that the authority of the teacher must be absolute. It is, however, interesting that, despite his contestations of 'traditional roles of authority' within education, Stenhouse (1983a: 214) himself observed that 'authority should rest with teachers'. Therefore, for the moment, we shall move forward in agreement with Stenhouse that knowledge is the 'great emancipator' – the tool required within education for our eventual liberation, both as students and as educators – despite the fact that there may be disagreements about the role of authority in the development of such knowledge.[2]

R. S. Peters

Richard Peters is widely regarded, along with Bantock, as making significant contributions to the debate for authoritative approaches to education and had a particular interest in fending off (as did Bantock) the prominent progressivist ideology of his time. This, I suppose, is the fundamental difference between what Peters argues for and what I am arguing for within the bounds of this work. Where Peters was seeking to wade against the tide of progressivism in his time, I do not consider such an agenda the remit of this book. To be clear, progressivism is undermined as a *result* of much of what is posited in these pages – but that is not what I am setting out to achieve, despite the ominous onslaught of progressive ideology within education in *this* time.

Nevertheless, despite our difference of remits and intentions, there are various striking similarities between what Peters writes and what you will go on to read in this book. His take on educational authority, in particular, in his book *Authority, Responsibility and Education* (1973), resonates with the authority that I so vehemently defend here. Moreover, the structure of how Peters argues *for* authority is similar to how I proceed – namely, he outlines what authority is and what its 'nature' is, and goes on to describe what our world (both educationally and generally) is like *without* it. My motivation for taking a similar tack is to show in what ways authority can be misunderstood (hence the requirement of a strict definition of the concept) and what results from its absence (to demonstrate the lamentable and worrying consequences of a lack of it).

What I might say, however, before proceeding to examine some of what Peters says in brief, is that Peters' approach, although intuitive and accessible, seems to lack the academic rigour to command any serious philosophical consideration. Indeed, it is a feature of educational philosophizing in general that what constitutes philosophy within education would hardly make the grade in most other disciplines. For this reason, Peters' work – which I believe to be largely anecdotal and which deals with particulars rather than generality – is often held as one of the pioneering philosophical cases for authority in educational discourse. Moreover, the ideas that are put forward in, for example, *Authority, Responsibility and Education* are in drastic need of modernization, to be brought forward to fend off a series of other educational challenges to authority that have arisen since Peters' contribution to the debate.

With such striking similarities between this book and that of Peters, the reader could be forgiven for assuming that everything that this book seeks to say has already been said elsewhere. Nothing could be further from the truth. Certainly, much of what I argue for has had significant groundwork laid down within the literature from some major educational philosophers and thinkers. However, significant amounts of what is contested qualifies as little more than sloppy philosophy, and simply does not carry the same clout as the philosophies of writers such as Polanyi, Oakeshott and Wittgenstein. A firm, sound and irrefutable case for authority within education must be made, and the philosophical foundation must be set on safer ground. I would encourage the reader to digest Peters' arguments, particularly those made in his first (Peters, 1973: 13–21), second (Peters, 1973: 22–32), fourth (Peters, 1973: 43–55) and eighth (Peters, 1973: 81–107) chapters. They will be of certain value when one reads this book – particularly the connection between Peters (1973: ch. 8) and Chapter 6 of this book.

Let me give you here, however, just three striking passages, which seem to capture the value of Peters' work as a preamble to the arguments that I make in subsequent chapters. First, of children, Peters (1973: 104) contests that:

> They start off in the position of the barbarian outside the gates. The problem is to get them inside the citadel of civilization so that they will understand and love what they see when they get there. It is no use concealing the fact that the activities and modes of thought and conduct which define a civilized form of life are difficult to master.

Furthermore, Peters (1973: 100) contests that the culmination of education is that the person responsible for such initiation (the teacher) and the person who undergoes the initiation (the pupil) eventually become almost indistinguishable in their shared ideals: 'At the culminating stage of education there is little distinction between teacher and taught; they are both participating in the shared experience of exploring a common world. The teacher is simply more familiar with its contours and more skilled in handling the tools for laying bare its mysteries and appraising its nuances.' And, finally, on the notion that education is an initiation, Peters (1973: 97–9) makes several pertinent remarks:

> 'Education' involves essentially processes that introduce people to what is valuable in an intelligible and voluntary manner and that create in the learner a desire to achieve it, this being seen to have its place along with other things in life.
>
> A child is born with an awareness not yet differentiated into beliefs, wants and feelings.

Gradually the child comes to want things. ... He learns to name objects, to locate his experience ... He creates pools of predictability by making promises and stating his intentions. In the beginning it was not at all like this. Such an embryonic mind is the product of initiation into public traditions enshrined in a public language, which it took our remote ancestors centuries to develop.

To have a mind is not to enjoy a private picture-show or to excise some inner diaphanous organ; it is to have an awareness differentiated in accordance with the canons implicit in all these inherited traditions. 'Education' marks out the processes by means of which the individual is initiated into them.

Initiation is always into some body of knowledge and mode of conduct which it takes time and determination to master.

The relevance of these points will be made clearer over the course of much of what I argue for in this book. I will make a conclusive argument for viewing education as a process of initiation. Furthermore, I will demonstrate the fundamental role that knowledge plays and how the process of initiation is a process that encourages us to grasp our knowledge inheritance. And I will show that such initiation begins with the initial submission to an authoritative master expert, who, as Peters contests, is simply more familiar with the 'contours' of the landscape that our educational journey is likely to trace. What other option do we have than to follow him or her?

The challenge of progressivism: Right problem, wrong solution

One of my concerns, as author of this book, is that it has the potential to be misunderstood. I suppose that the controversy that tends to circulate the debate on authority in any walk of life, let alone in education, gives rise to a host of potential problems in how the argument for authority might be interpreted and understood. In truth, I seek not to convince others of the validity of these arguments – although I am, naturally, convinced and concerned with their truth, but only for my own sake; rather, I seek to ensure that the case for authority is given a fair hearing and to reopen a debate that has long lain dormant, for the betterment of education. I passionately believe in what I write, and I am convinced of its truth and validity within educational discourse. But passion is an overrated commodity in modern-day life, entirely irrelevant in convincing others of the worth of one's arguments, and the fact that I am convinced by the arguments that I put forward hardly means that you ought to be.

One of the main concerns about a potential misunderstanding in relation to the arguments made in this book is that they be interpreted as a case against progressivism. To be clear, much of what I put forward in these pages is, by consequence rather than design, anti-progressivist. The form of education that I support and for which I argue so vehemently here is, undoubtedly, largely traditional, which by default means that it is largely anti-progressivist. But before the arguments can be articulated, it seems important that I inform the reader what the book seeks to achieve in relation to the progressivist debate.

My issue with progressive ideology is threefold. First, I consider progressivism to have identified a serious problem within education, but to have put forward the wrong solution to it. The problem is, of course, that education should liberate those who are fortunate enough to experience it. This is often painted as the entire essence of progressive ideology: that education ought to free an otherwise inhibited learner. Who could disagree with this sentiment? Education should, indeed, be a process of liberation, emancipation and freedom. It should equip a pupil to be the best that he or she can be in life and to have a thirst for fulfilling his or her potential. However, rather than spend extended amounts of writing space delving deeper into the axiology of education, let me state simply and clearly that I agree that education should, as a final result, liberate the pupils who are exposed to it. Moreover, any teacher worth his or her salt should consider himself or herself fortunate to play such a central role in the liberation of the pupils under his or her charge. However, rather than undermine the case for traditional teaching, I seek to show, as a result of some of the arguments that I will make later, that such a liberating education is built only on the basis of an authoritative foundation.

This is where progressivism has provided us with the correct problem, but the wrong solution. Education should enable us to *do* and to *act* in a manner that is informed. It should liberate us from the inhibitions infringed on us by an ignorance that would prevent such doing and acting. However, I take particular exception to two core elements of the progressivist solution to this problem, which are a feature of almost all forms of progressive ideology ever to have been expressed in print. These two exceptions comprise the second and third elements of my disagreement with progressivism: what I have called the 'anti-authority campaign' and the 'anti-knowledge campaign', each of which I will outline briefly over the next two sections.

Proceed, however, with a dose of realism in mind about what progressivism often (wrongly?) posits to be the problem of traditional education. It is often contested, as we have seen so far – in relation to Furedi's work, for example, in Chapter 1 – that traditional education focuses only on facts and rote learning, which inhibits rather than enables one to 'act out' or 'do' anything. Keep in mind, therefore, the following dismissive comments on such a criticism of traditional education as we proceed:

> Now every teacher knows that only a vanishingly small fraction of his teaching-day really consists in simply reciting lists of ... snippets of information to pupils, but very unfortunately, it happens to be the solitary part which unschooled parents, Sergeant Majors, some silly publicists and some educationalists always think of when they think of teaching and learning.
>
> [...]
>
> As you all know, most teaching has nothing whatsoever in common with this crude, semi-surgical picture of teaching as the forcible insertion into the pupil's memory of strings of officially approved propositions; and ... [the] small and of course indispensable part of instruction which is imparting of factual information is grossly mis-pictured when pictured as a literal cramming.
>
> (Ryle, 1970: 107–8)

Let it be clear, then, that any educator who has any kind of experience in the classroom will attest to the fact that little of what is taught is taught as 'lists' of facts merely to be memorized. This is *not* the education that I seek to defend, for rote learning of facts certainly does not constitute any form of what learning really is. Facts are inert and cannot, by definition, offer any guidance beyond their initial memorization. Something else must be the lifeblood of learning and education if it is to be considered a success – and that is, precisely, a judgement that can be applied, an ability to act, and a freedom to do. Going *beyond* the information is the remit of education; teachers should empower their pupils with information and liberate them with the judgement to apply it. Freedom, it seems, comes only when both of these elements of our knowledge structures are developed. This will be made entirely clear in Chapter 6. For the moment, however, let it be said clearly that progressive ideology has simply undermined its own case by solving a problem that never existed within education (the idea that traditional teaching focuses only on fact memorization) and also by outlining that the best way in which to liberate the learner is to take an anti-authoritative, anti-knowledge approach to education.

Let us dispense of this fable now: true traditional education is not now – nor has it ever been – driven by fact memorization only. This was therefore a problem that never existed, but which progressivism set out to solve nevertheless. There may, however, have been a time when the most dogmatic of traditionalists would have neglected the importance of an education that seeks to liberate the learner. I am not a supporter of such forms of traditionalism. I am also not, however, a supporter of the progressivist solution to this issue. If nothing else, let this book demonstrate that an education that is steeped in authority and in knowledge development is, in fact, the liberating education that the progressivists sought. Liberation need not be a 'free for all' concept, and freedom does not require capricious behaviour in order to be truly 'free'. These things can be gradual and responsibly managed, housed inside the framework of an overtly traditional educational model.

A fact without judgement is useless. A formula without an insight on how to use it is inert. However, this does not render valid the claim that facts are useless; rather, they are largely useless *on their own*. On the basis of this claim, it seems entirely unusual that the progressivists would want to rid education and learning of authority and of knowledge – in particular, of facts and information. These two valuable cornerstones of education – authority and knowledge – therefore need to be reinstated to their rightful place: at the heart of teaching and learning, forming a structure for a successful and responsible educational experience.

The anti-authority campaign: When chaos ensues

One of the most significant concepts inherent in the onslaught of progressivism that this book seeks to undermine is what I call the 'anti-authority campaign'. It is widely accepted that this anti-authority approach that is intrinsic to progressive approaches to education is one of the defining differences between progressivism and traditionalism. It will come as no surprise to the reader that I take exception to this campaign; that much is surely clear from the title of the book alone.

So why might the progressivists seek to cast aside authoritative approaches to education? Well, it seems that this anti-authority campaign goes hand in hand with the twisted understanding of 'child-centred' education that progressivists seek to transmit. In this view of education, with the child supposedly at the centre, the child creates his or her own meaning of the world, based on his or her own experiences and interactions with the environment. There is no place for any form of authority and no belief in what authority represents. Where does this leave the teacher? As a facilitator: someone who prepares the environment in which little explorers will stumble around, seeking to make sense of their own world. This version of education casts authority aside as a restrictive force, a force that infringes on the learner's right to freedom and his or her thirst to explore and create. It seems, therefore, that the belief that underpins the castigation of authority within progressive ideology is one that contests that the child can learn better when he or she is free to explore and discover, rather than being constrained and guided by any kind of authoritative master. We have seen already, from a sociological perspective, how Furedi (2009) considers such a view of education to be irresponsible. I consider such a view of education simply to be incoherent. Furthermore, the belief that being 'child-centred' is synonymous with letting the child do as he or she pleases seems absurd. I will demonstrate why later in the book. Let it be clear that I do consider myself to be a 'child-centred' educator – but this does not manifest itself as an educational 'free for all', within which the classroom is chaotic, and discipline and habitual practice are removed from learning. The progressivists have been more than a little canny in labelling their education 'child-centred', for who in their right mind would contest that education should not be focused on the learner? Nevertheless, what they posit as 'child-centred' is in fact nothing more than an empty vessel of drivel, which serves little purpose other than to undermine the teacher and to create a raft of 'self-centred' children. Let us therefore be 'child-centred' in a manner that makes responsible sense – that is, let us acknowledge the importance of educating the child and consider it our duty to do so, but not by encouraging them to make misinformed choices, all in the name of freedom; rather, let us command their respect and guide them, steering them towards success.

Rousseau, one of the fathers of progressivism, contested in his book *Emile, or On Education*, first published in 1762, that the child learns best when authority is removed and nature is given its place to educate in the way in which things were intended. In Rousseau's world, the only authority from which we can learn is the authority of the environment. Consequently, the role of the educator – the one who sought to facilitate the learner in his or her endeavours – was to create an environment that was more likely to educate, so that nature could be maximized in its operations. Rousseau contested, for example, that should the protagonist Emile break a window in his bedroom, there was no place for the authoritative master to 'correct' such behaviour. Moreover, it was not the place of the educator to outline pre-emptively that breaking windows was not acceptable; rather, he ought to let nature teach the naughty Emile a lesson. He would do this by leaving the window broken and, on the cold nights, Emile would experience the wrath of nature and would learn never to break windows again. Nature was the authority and the educator was to focus his efforts only on making Emile's environment more likely to educate. Certainly, in this case, I would concede that Emile would be unlikely to break any more windows if he were to be subjected to the bitter cold of a winter night. But I cannot help thinking that, had the educator explained this to Emile prior to his breaking of the window, Emile would have been saved from the bitter wrath of Mother Nature and the educator would have been saved the expense of replacing a window.

Bantock (1970) concurs that this 'naturalistic' education – pioneered in the work of Rousseau, Froebel and Pestalozzi, according to Bantock – is an unusual path to pursue. He captures the feel for such educational approaches, outlining what they hold as their core precept as that 'a child's education ought to permit its freedom of development in accordance with the laws of its own nature' (Bantock, 1970: 59). He concludes, however, that these ideas are 'romantic':

They push the notion of 'creativity' (a key word) of the individual mind to its uttermost limits so that development is seen as the result of the spontaneous activity of the inner being rather than of the formative power exercised by any outside authority. The child is to grow, not to be moulded. . . . Hence the exercise of outside authority, in whatever form, is to be reduced to an absolute minimum.

(Bantock, 1970: 59–60)

In a similar manner, Peters (1973: 199) outlines the overhyped nature of the progressivist argument against authoritarianism:

> The progressive protest against authoritarianism goes too far in the opposite direction of individual discovery and inventiveness. The teacher, on this view, is regarded as a mere facilitator of learning who tends the garden in which children can grow, 'do their own thing', and find out everything for themselves. ... It neglects ... the fact ... that the tools of discovery, the conceptual schemes of science, morals, mathematics, and so on, are a public possession into which children have to be initiated. They do not spin them out of their own heads like spiders.

It seems, therefore, that the progressivist take on education has deep-seated confusions about the role that authority ought to play. Consider what Rogers (1983) – an ardent supporter of non-authoritative education – contests in his recital of anecdotal evidence shared by a teacher whom he encountered. The teacher claims to have quit his position because he felt that he was 'being paid to be authoritarian, a disciplinarian' (Rogers, 1983: 11). First, I would ask why, if you seek not to be authoritarian or a disciplinarian, you would choose teaching as your career? More importantly, however, Rogers' own confusions on authority are made abundantly clear in this piece of almost useless anecdotal evidence: he downgrades the role of an authoritative master to someone who merely focuses on negative processes, and he paints a picture of that master as a power-driven force – someone intent only on punishment, discipline and inhibiting the will of the pupils under his or her charge. These confusions, frankly, serve only as an indictment of Rogers' misunderstanding of what it means to be an authority in the classroom. I intend to dispense with this blinkered view of authority throughout the course of this book.

Consider, also, the 'Rousseau-ian' claim that Rogers (1983: 19) offers in defence of so-called 'significant, meaningful, experiential learning': 'When the toddler touches the warm radiator, she learns for herself the meaning of a word *hot*; she has learned a future caution in regard to all similar radiators; and she has taken in the learnings in a significant, involved way that will *not* soon be forgotten.' Permit me, for one moment, to be overtly pernickety and point out that one need not burn oneself to learn the word 'hot'. I, for one, have never been burned and yet know entirely well what 'hot' means. I recall my mother reminding me as a young boy never to touch the fire because it was 'very hot' and ushering me away from the oven whilst she was baking, lest I be burned; I believed her and never felt the inclination to test her warnings. Words are not learned in the way that Rogers suggests. Indeed, in the above extract, Rogers only demonstrates a lamentable inadequacy in his own understanding of what learning a language entails. In the example, the child would acquire an *understanding* of the word 'hot' only if an adult were to equip him or her with the language that is associated to the situation. In the child's moment of crying for help, the concerned parent might say: 'We don't touch that – it's hot!' Better still, any sensible parent would do that *before* the child touches the radiator. Furthermore, if words and their meaning are acquired only through 'experiential' and 'meaningful' learning endeavours, how could the young child come to learn how to use words such as 'it', 'the' or 'and'? The child cannot experience such words in a meaningful way and yet somehow manages to use them appropriately. I will outline in the second part of this book precisely how language is developed, since it serves as a paradigmatic example of how authority is relevant within learning. For the moment, however, simply note that language acquisition is intricate, complex and delicate to explain. In any case, we can *never* acquire the *meaning* of a word through experience alone, nor can we acquire the insight required for its appropriate *use*; such an explanation would require us to have a pre-existing grasp of an internal 'word bank', along with an insight into the appropriate times at which the word fits the context.

Nevertheless, I wonder what it is, precisely, that makes this learning significant and meaningful, according to Rogers. For all intents and purposes, one of the most glaring similarities between this ridiculous story and Rousseau's abuse of Emile is that both the young girl and Emile end up being punished for making a misinformed choice. Why should we be surprised if Emile breaks the window or if this young girl burns herself on the warm radiator if we have not considered it our duty to show either any different? This does not constitute learning of a meaningful kind; it constitutes only what can be described as 'correction' – that is, letting destructive events take their natural course to teach the child a lesson. Does this not serve only to demonstrate further the justification for *informing* our children in order to *avoid* the broken window and the burnt hand? That is, whenever Rousseau, Rogers and the like put forward the case for children to be given the 'freedom' to learn for themselves, are they not, in fact, demonstrating the importance of a responsible guiding master? Indeed, if 'personal meaning' and 'experiential learning' come only at the cost of a cold night's sleep or a burnt hand, perhaps they are better avoided! Moreover, what kind of freedom is there in learning in a manner that is misinformed, misguided and lacking in judgement?

Rogers (1983: 18) rather unusually asserts that '[t]he primary task of the teacher is to *permit* the student to learn, to feed his or her own curiosity'. Consequently, he concludes that '[i]n true teaching there is no place for the authoritarian, nor the person who is on an "ego trip"' (Rogers, 1983: 18). In what way is a responsible educator egotistical? Should we criticize the educator who tries to inform his or her pupil as being caught up within his or her own agenda? Or should we celebrate the fact that, in the guise of the teacher, the process of education provides the learner with an expert master to guide him or her towards informed decisions, with a judgement and an insight that will likely remain with that learner throughout his or her life? Rogers' conclusion that there is no place in 'true teaching' for an authoritarian is deeply troubling. It shows a worrying failure to grasp what the concept of authority represents, and it shows a blinkered understanding of the impact that authority has within education. The authoritarian teacher, however, does not impose his or her *own* way upon the child; rather, as Peters (1973: 119) observes, he or she enlightens the learner to a manner of acting that is a 'public inheritance, not a private possession'.

We could encourage educators to wash their hands of their *duty* and their *responsibility* to those whom they should be teaching, in the pursuit of some misguided understanding of creativity. Indeed, if it were an environment that teaches, there are a host of nervous teachers who would escape the anxiety associated with constant inspections of the quality of their teaching. If a child fails to grasp that things are 'thus and so', perhaps we can simply pin that failing on the environment or suggest that nature had an off-day? I prefer to think that the role of a teacher is to teach, not to facilitate. It is entirely clear that an environment can be used to foster a feel for learning – that is, that an environment can be created in which learning is more likely to happen. Environments cannot, however, teach; rather, the teacher is to use them to help him or her to teach more effectively. This is why the role of the teacher cannot be undermined or underestimated. His or her authority is absolute, and his or her role is indispensable:

> This 'finding out for oneself' which is contrasted with being instructed is of a peculiar kind. No sane person really supposes that children are

going to rediscover the whole of what they need to know quite apart from the teacher's agency; if that were possible we should not need schools at all. In other words, it is not by chance that these discoveries are made but as a result of the teacher's deliberate contrivance, in 'structuring the environment' for example, or in practising discovery 'methods'. Both in the case of instruction and in the case of learning by discovery, then, the teacher's agency and influence are present, though admittedly they are present in very different ways.

(Dearden, 1970: 135–6)

The different types of learning will be examined throughout the book, in particular in Chapter 4. In any case, it will be shown that the role of the authoritative master remains undiminished in *any* definition of learning, should it be by instruction, inquiry or research. Bantock (1970: 59) concurs, claiming that 'in all cases, . . . I believe that education should be primarily deterministic, i.e. that it should be much more in the hands of the teacher to determine the nature of what is learnt'.

The salient point for the moment, however, is that the anti-authority campaign that is rife within progressivism seems odd to the point of incoherence. Each of the arguments put forward within these pages will further serve to undermine the position that authority can ever be dispensed with within educational practices. Teaching requires authority and learning is housed inside it; knowledge development is constructed within the framework it provides and so education, in general, is in chaos without it. In *On Certainty*, Wittgenstein (1969: 22e) asked: 'Must I not begin somewhere?' I propose that pupils begin with a humble submission to the authority of the master expert. Hopefully, by the end of the book, you will be convinced that such initial submission is not only sensible, but also necessary.

The anti-knowledge campaign: The epistemology paradox of progressivism

The other strand of the progressive ideology that this book seeks to undermine is the 'anti-knowledge campaign' that is rife within it. The core belief is that knowledge is no longer of any value in a world that is changing at a frightening pace – so much so, that knowledge quickly becomes obsolete. Where the progressivist would seek to cast aside authority by claiming, as we have seen, that it stifles creativity and infringes upon the pupil's freedom to learn, the anti-knowledge campaign seeks to overthrow knowledge development with so-called 'learning how to learn'. Discovery methods are therefore favoured, as opposed to instruction or teacher-led activity. In a world in which knowledge is valueless, the teacher's role quickly becomes the role of a facilitator: someone who must let the student learn, but never stand in the way of the student who seeks to make sense of the world in his or her own way.

In this view of education, knowledge must give way to understanding, and learning *how* or *what* must step aside to be replaced by *learning how to learn*. Indeed, as Rogers (1983: 18) argues, citing Heidegger: 'Teaching is more difficult than learning because what teaching calls for is this: to let learn. The real teacher, in fact, lets nothing else be learned than – learning. ... The teacher is ahead of his students in this alone, that he still has far more to learn than they – he has to learn to let them learn.' So our schools are to be filled with educators who have more to learn than those whom they seek to educate. Our teachers should consider themselves more susceptible to change, and they should permit their students absolute freedom to learn whatever it is they seek to grasp. Does this view of education not undermine the very essence of what schooling is all about? That is, in the absence of a teacher who considers it his or her duty and responsibility as an educator to guide those under his or her charge, are our classrooms not thrown open to the whims of the misinformed, misguided intentions of so-far-uneducated students?

Rogers (1983: 18), however, seeking to add weight to Heidegger's claim, outlines that the mere absorption of facts is 'of only slight value in the present, and usually of even less value in the future', and therefore concludes that '[l]earning *how* to learn is the element that is always of value, now and in the future'. In this claim, however, two things should be apparent. First, education is not now – nor has it ever been – about the mere absorption of facts. There are deep-seated confusions in this view of knowledge: that it merely equips students with a raft of inert facts to 'carry around' with them in their daily lives. Indeed, had education ever been about the development of mere facts, it would never have been able to pass these facts from one generation to the next, and nothing new would ever have been discovered. Our facts now would have been the same as those facts available at the beginning of time. The truth is, however, that education has never been solely focused on the cultivation of facts *alone*. Good teachers have never been driven by forcing facts upon their students; rather, the very best educators acknowledge the importance of facts and seek to pass them on to their students in such a way that their students can make contributions to them, can engage with them, and can develop an insight and a judgement into their application in other areas of their life picture. Had this never been the focus of a good educator, facts would never have developed, new things would never have been discovered, and our entire knowledge edifice would have remained fixed and stagnant.

The second lamentable element of Rogers' claim is that learning how to learn should replace mere learning. Be under no illusions: talk of 'learning how to learn' induces such a profound paradox that one wonders how such a claim could ever have been made. Indeed, either we *can* learn or we *cannot* learn. If we can learn, we need not learn how to learn; if we cannot learn, we cannot learn *at all*, never mind learn how to learn. That is to say, learning how to learn *presupposes* an ability to learn, which renders useless the learning *how* to learn. This can never be the focus of education. When the proponents of such drivel came to realize that it was a paradox – a paradox that Chris Winch clearly defined in his 2008 keynote lecture *Learning How to Learn: A Critique* – they relabelled 'learning how to learn' as 'metacognition', in the hope that it might be permitted a stay of execution within education. Let us do the honourable thing now and recognize that this idea is steeped in paradoxical foundations – and let us give it the execution it deserves. Learning how to learn is not the core aim of education; it cannot be, given its incoherence.

Another prominent trend within much of the progressivist literature – as I have already made clear – is the notion of *freedom*. The learner's right to freedom, it is contested, overrides the need for authority within the learning process. As Rogers (1983: 186) argues, within authoritative approaches to education, '[d]emocracy and its values are ignored and scorned in practice', and he goes on to outline that students have no choice in educational goals, the curriculum or teaching methods, nor do they control or influence the appointment of new personnel. Such a criticism is highly irregular. It seems intuitive that students would be deprived of such choice for a number of reasons. First, with such choice comes responsibility. In the appointment of a teacher, for example, headmasters and school governors make decisions, so that if mistakes are made in the appointment, someone can be held to account. Moreover, these people are more likely to be able to make an informed judgement about who is right for the job. Likewise, the development of a curriculum is surely the role of a curriculum expert. Indeed, should errors be made in the development of a curriculum, someone is required to answer for such errors. Is it right that we would thrust such responsibility upon an ill-informed or misguided student? We strip the learner of some of his or her choices to lift from his or her shoulders the problems of responsibility. Rogers (1983: 186) regards this as a 'mistrust' of the learner; I regard it as a sensible and responsible approach to educational politics and policy. Freedom and choice come at a cost: the cost of responsibility. Therefore, in some cases, it is the sensible thing to do to ensure that such responsibility for potentially erroneous actions is not thrust upon the young learner, whose primary focus ought only to be learning. This process is not an undervaluation of democratic precepts, but rather a responsible intergenerational transaction between the informed 'adult' generation and the potentially misinformed or misguided 'younger' generation.

Secondly, as Bantock (1970: 68) observed, choice and freedom are bound up with an understanding that such concepts come *after* a process of discipline and initiation has taken place:

> No child is free to choose by the light of nature alone. His capacity depends entirely upon the choices that have previously been made for him by other people to enable him to be free to choose anything. Thus no child is free to choose until he is already sufficiently disciplined to see the implications of his choice. And, in such prior disciplining it is our duty as educators to shield him from harmful impulses that may later militate against his freedom of choice.

Educators are responsible for informing the choices that their students make. Without such information, choices are more likely to be harmful. It is the duty of the educator to show the child how to be disciplined, in the first instance, so that the child's choices are informed, insightful and sensible, and so that his or her eventual freedom is true and absolute. That is, if 'the standard is to be freedom, then freedom itself implies the initial restraint and discipline inherent in the process of becoming free to exercise the required skill' (Bantock, 1970: 69).

The 'choice freedom' conundrum of education gives rise also to what I call the 'epistemology paradox'. The claim is that, in the modern world, given that we have the concept of 'free speech' and the right to an individual opinion free from oppression or coercion, children must be taught in a manner that respects these basic human rights – that is, there must exist a 'freedom of a choice in learning' (Rogers, 1983: 14). This 'choice' emphasizes the underlying feeling that individual 'understanding' is more important than any version of collective knowledge. The young learner must be free to reason for himself or herself, to arrive at the conclusions with which his or her learning experiences have presented him or her. Process trumps fact, and viability replaces correctness. This view of education, however, gives rise to a paradox of epistemology. Indeed, what might it mean for one to *understand* a concept without any *knowledge* of it? Moreover, is a process not, generally speaking, underpinned by an informed way of acting? Is it not true, therefore, that superseding knowledge by process gives rise to a paradox – namely, that in order to be able to *act* one first requires an ability to grasp what one seeks to act about? Knowledge rests at the core of action, and processes are informed by the information and the insight that are a feature of the knowledge edifice. Action without knowledge is chaotic; it bears no hallmarks of a process that ought to be developed or acquired. In the same way as freedom and choice must be underpinned by discipline and trust, process and understanding must be underpinned by facts, information and insight. This is precisely what D. W. Hamlyn (1970: 26) meant when he asserted: 'No one could be said to have come to understand a subject, to have learnt it, without some appreciation of general principles, some idea of what it is all about. But knowing and reciting general principles is not just a matter of being able to recite the relevant general propositions.' It seems that the confusion here lies in the failure to grasp the indispensability of information and facts in the fullest development of knowledge, and the truest and purest version of learning. To be clear, facts and information *do not* and *cannot* be all that there is to learn. This much will be emphasized in great detail when we examine Oakeshott's contribution to this debate. However, this does not render useless the informational and factual elements of knowledge, nor does it undermine the importance of information and facts within the process of learning. The fundamental principles of any learning endeavour are pivotal to its fullest development – but there is obviously more to learning than the recital of mere facts and information.

As Furedi (2009: 148) notes, there are also deep-seated confusions about knowledge and information in such contestations that knowledge is irrelevant and that educational processes are more important than content:

A society's knowledge gives meaning to new information, by allowing people to interpret new facts and by helping society to understand what significance to attach to them. Knowledge itself develops through the appropriation of new experience. But the latest knowledge is linked organically to that which preceded it. Implicitly scepticism towards the authority of knowledge calls into question the meaning of education itself. Once the knowledge of the past is rendered obsolete, what can education mean?

Knowledge is indispensable in *any* educational process. I seek to convey this message throughout the book. Understanding and knowledge are not mutually exclusive; rather, they are mutually compatible, interrelated and interdependent. Without knowledge, understanding is meaningless. Without facts and information, processes are misguided and misinformed. It is an inescapable fact that learning depends on knowledge development and that knowledge development itself depends on the submission to authority.

In this chapter, I hope to have convinced you that there is much reason to read on. We have seen how some previous arguments *for* authority in education have set the tone for what is to follow in these pages. Similarly, I have demonstrated that anti-authority approaches seem to be rife with inherent difficulties. To be clear, though, this book is not, by design, anti-progressivist; rather, many of the arguments put forward in the book are, *by consequence* of their nature, contrary to much of what progressivists would argue *for* in education. Education should be a liberating process; however, the manner in which progressivism posits that this is attainable is questionable. I am fundamentally opposed to anti-authority, anti-knowledge approaches to education. This book will therefore henceforth be dedicated to proving why teaching and learning, and education, should be founded within an authoritative framework in which knowledge takes pride of place.

3 A DEFINITION OF AUTHORITY

As we have already seen, the concept of authority is at the core of many educational and, on a wider scale, political and philosophical debates. It has become an increasingly unappealing notion in the post-modern philosophical era. Indeed, many post-modern philosophers encouraged a dissent from authority into the realms of rationality, individual reasoning and doubt, challenging predetermined ways of thinking and philosophizing. Pre-modern concepts such as trust, belief, practice, tradition and so on were rejected in favour of the promotion of the individual's right to doubt the knowledge imposed on him or her from on high. It is this challenge to which I am taking exception, and it is this challenge that I aim to demonstrate results in unappealing consequences. As a result of this refutation, I aim to show that authority is an indispensable facet of learning, of knowledge and, subsequently, of education. With references to the main works of Michael Polanyi, Michael Oakeshott and Ludwig Wittgenstein, along with other key thinkers and philosophers, I aim to demonstrate that to dispense with authority so willingly is to reduce ourselves to a state of chaos and disarray. In essence, we require authority to save us from causing the destruction of an education that cannot survive without it.

It seems sensible to begin this part of the discussion with a definition of what 'authority' is and what it encompasses. Indeed, in many so-called 'anti-authoritarian' arguments, it seems that there exist deep-seated confusions about what authority is and the role that it plays in educational processes.

To begin with, the *Oxford English Dictionary* sheds some light on what we might mean by authority, but also gives useful insight into why the notion of authority may seem unappealing. 'Authority', first, is defined as the 'power or right to enforce obedience' and 'an influence exerted on opinion because of recognized knowledge or expertise'. 'Authoritative', on the other hand, is defined as 'being recognized as true or dependable', whereas 'authoritarian' is defined as meaning 'favouring or enforcing strict obedience' and 'tyrannical or domineering'. These definitions seem to set the notion of authority in a certain context and also outline why the notion of authority may seem to be a concept worth avoiding. Indeed, anything described in such strong language as 'tyrannical' and 'domineering' can rarely be interpreted in a positive manner. However, in examining the first definition of authority – described as an influence over opinions, substantiated by *recognized* knowledge or expertise – it seems rather natural that this might feature in learning, knowledge and education. Indeed, as I will outline later in reference to the works of Polanyi and Wittgenstein, a submission to such an authority is the very thing that seems to make learning, knowledge and subsequently education possible.

For the purposes of our discussion, it is important to extend our definition of general authority to an understanding of how authority might apply to education, specifically in its application to learning and to knowledge development. In scholarly circles, it is commonplace to hear of a leading academic being described as a 'leading authority in the field'. This description of such an expert might place the concept of authority within an educational context. To be described as a 'leading authority' is to be acknowledged as someone who has experience, expertise and knowledge of a certain discipline or field. In this sense, we can see how an authoritative figure might be viewed – as outlined in the general definition – as true or dependable. Indeed, a 'leading authority' in any discipline is someone who can be taken seriously and who has strong credentials supporting any claims that he or she might make. Authority therefore involves an element of *legitimacy* – that is, a *right* to act in such-and-such a manner.

It also appears that authority is something that is either submitted to or rebelled against, even in terms of the general definition provided in the previous paragraph. It also seems that being 'in' authority is to have a certain power and perhaps even a mandate to act. Authority, in this sense, has to be earned. Thus, if a person is to claim to be 'in' authority, he or she must have to go through some initiation process. Such an initiation also seems to require widespread support from other people. Indeed, it would make no sense to ascribe authority to oneself without foundation or justification. This justification appears to be ascribed, generally speaking, by a collection of people, perhaps best described as a 'community'. The relationship between authority and a community that commits to the cultivation of authority will be discussed in more detail later.

For the moment, however, we appear to have a loose definition of authority that can be applied to education, learning and knowledge. Generally, 'authority' is the justification for acting in a certain way, on the basis of a mandate issued by a community. It is to be submitted to or rebelled against. The consequence of submitting to educational authority is accepting what is taught by the authoritative figure in question. Alternatively, to rebel against educational authority is to question and subject to doubt at least some – if not all – of what you are taught. If someone 'has authority', he or she has the power to act and to influence those in his or her charge, within reason, on the basis of the authoritative credentials ascribed to him or her by a community.

It is also important to note that authority appears to have an unappealing side, should it be abused. Indeed, the use of the words 'tyrannical' and 'domineering' demonstrate that, should authority be abused or misused in any way, the result is someone who can go beyond the scope of his or her authority. As such, it is important to emphasize that authority is a commodity to be treated with respect. It must contain a level of accountability and mechanisms within its framework to prevent its abuse and misuse. Perhaps, as I will show later, this is the role of a responsible community: to ensure that authority is respected from the bottom up and from the top down.

On the basis of this definition of educational authority, I intend to outline why authority simply must be submitted to if learning and the development of knowledge are to be regarded as coherent processes within education. I will outline that the apparently unappealing consequences of submitting to authority are nothing more than overhyped propaganda, created and disseminated by political influences within the education system. Moreover, I will demonstrate how the leading – if not the only – candidate for the authority figure in the classroom is the teacher: the trained expert and representative of the community. In this way, I will show that submitting to one's teacher – as the representative of the community and practice – is an inescapable facet of any successful cultivation of learning and knowledge development. I will also show how a submission to authority allows us to sidestep some major philosophical concerns in relation to learning and the foundations of knowledge. Rebelling against educational authority, it will be shown, is not an option, lest we descend into unstructured teaching and learning, baseless knowledge and the chaotic education that would naturally follow.

The distinction between authority and power

It is important to note the confusions that are inherent in much of what is written about authority within educational discourse to date.[1] Indeed, as I have already shown in my critique of Rousseau and Rogers, for example, there are parts of their respective arguments that seem to confuse the notion of authority with the notion of power. Akin to these confusions, there are also problems with distinguishing between discipline and punishment, as well as respect and fear.

Let it be clear now, therefore, that I am an ardent supporter of an education driven by authority, discipline and respect, as opposed to one focused on power, punishment and fear. The teacher, for me, should be in authority, should have the ability to *instil* discipline and should therefore command respect. He or she should not, however, be driven by power and should not have an interest in the punishment of those under his or her charge, nor should he or she aim to instil fear in his or her pupils.

For the sake of clarity, then, let me briefly demonstrate the differences between these two views of education. Consider, first, the distinction between authority and power. Be under no illusions: these concepts are easily confused, and many writings on authority – particularly in education – are guilty of the confusion. In fairness, however, the confusion is an easy one to which fall prey: the concepts seem to differ only in the fine details, and there are striking similarities between them.

I must confess that, while writing, I watched a programme on television that concerned me greatly in relation to what I was writing about authority, to the extent that I wondered whether what I was writing may have been a mistake. The programme concerned the delicate matter of child abuse within schools and appealed to evidence from some of the victims of this abuse. It was a common trend in this programme to highlight that the abusers had taken advantage of the position in which they had been placed and that they had been driven by their own obsessions with power. It concerned me deeply, because I began to question whether or not the authority that I was so vehemently arguing ought to be reinstated to the teacher ought ever to be ascribed to one person, given the potential problems associated with the abuse of such a position. This concern got me thinking, then, about the distinction between what I was arguing for and how it differed from what had been exploited in these tragic cases of abuse.

The most pertinent thing that came to mind was the concept of *exploitation* and *abuse*: where power can be exploited and abused, authority – by its very definition – must have inbuilt safeguards to prevent its exploitation or abuse. In these troubling cases about which I now found myself thinking, the problem was an abuse of *power* rather than an abuse of *authority*. In this way, I concluded that authority is a legitimacy to act in such-and-such a manner, whereas power need not be. That is not to say that power is always exploited or that it is never legitimate; rather, it need not have any safeguards structurally inbuilt to prevent these things from happening. Authority, on the other hand, is ascribed on the basis of merit and, in this way, it must be earned. It is not bestowed on someone who is likely to abuse it, and it does not permit someone to act beyond his or her scope. In such cases – that is, in cases of the abuse of authority – the authority of the person in question is undermined, to the extent that his or her authority might be removed. The safeguards built into authority must therefore be constructed by the community that is responsible for the ascription of authority to those who are entrusted with it. Failure to uphold these safeguards undermines the community itself and serves only to detract from the message that the community seeks to convey. If the safeguards are not upheld, then there can be no claim to be authoritative; there can be only a claim to be *in* power. Therefore, whereas power *dominates*, authority *convinces*. Moreover, whereas authority entails a *legitimacy* to guide, power is the ability to instruct those under you, regardless of legitimacy or fairness. Authority is *earned*; power is *attained*.

This distinction between authority and power, then, leads to further distinctions between discipline and punishment, as well as respect and fear. Discipline is a counterpart to authority, whereas punishment is a feature of power. In the case of discipline, there is an element of habitual practice, as well as a requirement of correctness – that is, discipline is used in an authoritative manner to ensure that the correct course of action is chosen in the fitting circumstances. Punishment, on the other hand, has no such goal in sight; rather, it seeks, forcefully or otherwise, to emphasize that a certain course of action was not correct, while making no attempt to point towards a solution. Thus discipline is focused on steering towards correct behaviour, whereas punishment is focused only on making clear the consequences for misdemeanours. What Rousseau put forward in *Emile*, therefore, was punishment: he left the window broken to demonstrate that a poor choice had been made, but no insight was given as to what would have been the correct choice or why the original decision was a poor one. Rousseau's solution focused solely on the consequences of a poor decision, which ought not to have been a surprise to us, given the lack of guidance given to the unfortunate Emile, who was punished despite his lack of guidance. The authoritative master seeks to use discipline and habitual practice as tools to ensure that the notion of correctness is instilled in his or her pupils; the power-driven master seeks only to punish those who disobey him or her.

In a similar manner, an authoritative master commands respect, whereas a powerful master is focused only on instilling fear in his or her understudies. The respect that is a feature of an authoritative master is a part of his or her fabric and a facet of his or her being, due to that master as someone who is more knowledgeable and insightful than the pupil. We fear the one who is powerful, however, only because that person has it in his or her ability to punish us if we choose to ignore instructions.

These definitions are particularly important given the concerns that I articulated a few paragraphs ago. Indeed, in the case of the authoritative master under these definitions, we come to realize that such authority has safeguards structurally inbuilt to prevent its abuse or misuse. An authoritative master does not seek to abuse his or her position, but to use it for good to educate those under him or her. Should that master ever step outside of his or her remit, however, he or she is pulled back into line by the community that he or she seeks to represent – and if the master yet fails to conform, he or she is stripped of responsibilities, for he or she will then have failed in his or her duty. The authoritative master instils discipline and habitual practice in his or her pupils, and uses these methods to encourage the learners for whom he or she is responsible to have an appreciation for correctness. These pupils do not fear the master, but have respect for his or her intellect and manner. Power, punishment and fear are not a feature of such an authoritative master, and we would do well to discard such confusions.

4 AUTHORITY: WHY ALL THE FUSS?

The next natural question, now that I have outlined some of the definitions of authority and its derivatives, is: what is the appeal of authority in relation to learning, knowledge and education? Perhaps the most efficient and effective way in which to demonstrate the importance of authority in learning – in the foundations of knowledge and in education – is to consider the consequences of an authority-deprived approach to each of these concepts. I will therefore give a brief description of each of these concepts now, and will discuss them further in relation to key thinkers and philosophers later in the book.

The implications for learning

The first point for consideration is the notion of an authority-free, or an authority-deficient, approach to learning. For the purposes of this discussion, it is essential, first, to establish what learning is, what learning should *do*, how learning is achieved, and what occurs in these processes in the absence of authority. First, adopting a rather broad definition of learning, I will consider learning to be the development of knowledge and skills, information and judgement (which I will discuss more later in relation to Oakeshott's writings) that can be used and applied to assist the learner in solving future problems that are of a similar nature to the examples seen in the learning process. Learning, in this way, seems to be a deliberate restructuring of our approaches to solving problems in light of acquiring some new knowledge or skill.

What, then, should learning *do*? That is, what is the purpose of learning? It seems that learning has, as its main priority, an interest in equipping the learner with the ability to *do* or to *act* correctly, in accordance with what way in which they are expected to act, given a certain type of problem. Indeed, the motivation for learning, for the learner, seems to be an avoidance of ignorance in the hope that he or she can go beyond the information given to him or her in the learning process. The notion of 'correctness' is of particular interest in this instance; I will return to discuss it in more detail later in this chapter.

Finally, for the moment, how should and how can learning be achieved? Although there are many ideas on how learning is possible, it seems that there are three irrefutable notions in any understanding of in what way learning can occur: learning can follow from teacher-led activities (and all that they encompass); learning can be a consequence of research-led activities, such as reading reliable resources or studying textbooks and the like; or learning can follow from inquiry-led pursuits – that is, from searching for answers in our worldly experiences. The final question therefore, before we open this discussion fully, is: what role might authority play in each of these understandings and forms of learning?

Let me begin, however, with a discussion of some of the definitions and expectations of learning outlined in the previous paragraph. I want to take each of the forms of learning in turn – namely, teacher-led learning, research-led learning and inquiry-led learning – and examine briefly what each entails and how authority seems to be needed in each of these forms of learning. I will begin by coupling the notions of teacher-led and research-led learning, since the respective authorities to which they adhere can be considered similar in their nature.

If learning follows, in some instances, from being taught or through private study or research, there must be an acceptance of the authority of the teacher who is doing the teaching or in the resources that are being studied and researched (provided, of course, that these resources, such as textbooks, are reliable). Indeed, to doubt one's teacher or to question the content of a reliable resource is to undermine the very essence of what makes each of these things what they are. A teacher, by very definition, should be an expert in his or her subject and a master at conveying his or her ideas. He or she represents a practice and a discipline, and has earned the right to be trusted. A faith in one's teacher is therefore not unfounded. The teacher, in this way, commands authority. Similarly, reliable resources and textbooks command the authority of the practice and discipline from which they come. They have been subjected to continual scrutiny and have been considered to be fair representations of the message that their discipline seeks to convey to the learners who choose to read such resources. For a learner to pick up a reliable resource and subject it to continued scrutiny would be to question the reliable nature of such a resource. Such reliability is founded in the peer-review process that is a feature of a reliable resource. Faith in the teacher or in reliable resources seems to be *required* in such instances of learning – that is, the teacher (in teacher-led learning) and reliable resources (in research-led learning) command an authority that is to be adhered to in the pursuit of successful learning. It is in this way that Polanyi talks of faith in one's teacher – and textbooks for that matter – preceding one's ability to reason for oneself. However, as Polanyi discusses extensively in his considerations of the roles that authority, traditions, practices and communities play in learning, this faith in one's teacher and one's textbooks is not foundationless. The foundation of such a faith is established in the fact that the teacher and the reliable resources have the approval of the community that they represent to disseminate the message that they portray through their teaching and writings, respectively.

Let us consider the specific case now of one's teacher. On the basis of the above argument, it is safe to have this faith in the teacher, the representative of the community. Conversely, to reject the authority of the teacher, which is grounded in the community and practice that he or she represents, is to turn one's nose up at an accepted way of working. In this way, authority is an indispensable facet of learning, and to rebel against it is to rebel against an entire community and practice, who have accepted ways of working within their discipline.

Consider now the definition of learning founded in inquiry-led activities.[1] Learning, of course, is not always the consequence of teacher-led or research-led activities, or, for that matter, a result of what happens in the classroom or in schools. In a discussion that I had with a colleague, a point was raised in objection to former Education Secretary David Blunkett's claim that 'a child not in lessons is a child not learning' (Grice and Judd, 1999). My colleague suggested, to the contrary, that children will learn regardless of whether they are at school or not. This is, of course, irrefutable. It is a fact of life that children learn; in many cases, they learn too much. We have all come across instances in which parents talk of their own children being 'impressionable' and 'picking things up so quickly'. This is because children pay close attention to those people in their lives who they trust without question – for example parents and older siblings – and copy what they do. After all, as I will discuss later, this is how children learn how to use and speak a language: through imitation of those with whom they are in close contact and who they trust unquestionably.

So, if – as it has been argued – children can learn *outside* of the teacher-led and research-led activities to which they are exposed, it could be argued that the teacher and reliable resources are luxuries rather than necessities within the process of learning – that is, of course, if the notion of inquiry-led learning is *even possible* in the absence of a teacher or in the absence of a guiding reliable resource (which I will prove over the next few sections is *not* the case).

The Meno paradox: A learning conundrum

It is a bold – yet justified – assertion at this stage that inquiry-led learning can be regarded as incoherent. Indeed, the notion of inquiry-led learning, in the total absence of any other guiding or authoritative faculty (such as a teacher or reliable resource), results in a long-standing conundrum in learning known as the 'Meno paradox'. In *Meno*, one of Plato's Socratic dialogues, the main speakers (Socrates and Meno) discuss whether it is paradoxical to think of learning as an inquiry-led concept. Indeed, as Waterfield (2005: 113) asks in his account of *Meno*:

> And how will you search for something, Socrates, when you don't know what it is at all? I mean which of the things you don't know will you take in advance and search for, when you don't know what it is? Or even if you come right up against it, how will you know it's the unknown thing you're looking for?

Socrates' response is to claim that 'it is impossible for a man to search either for what he knows or for what he doesn't know' (Waterfield, 2005: 113). To be clear, then, the Meno paradox is essentially demonstrating that there needs to be some *other* constraint placed on inquiry before one can go in search of knowledge, or ever hope to learn. It is a conundrum of an authority-free form of learning, resolved only in the acknowledgement of the authority of the guiding master expert: the teacher.

Consider, for example, how the young child learns the concept of colour (in general), as well as how he or she learns each individual colour in relation to the general concept. First, however, note that there are two main versions of so-called 'inquiry-led learning' that disregard the role of the teacher's authority in learning: one underpinned by Piagetian constructivism; the other, by Vygotskian constructivism. Both of these strands of constructivism – or 'genesis without structure', as we might call it – posit that it is possible for the child to construct his or her own meaning of concepts without the guidance of an authoritative master expert. We call this 'genesis without structure' since this theoretical standpoint contests that it is possible for the child to originate his or her own interpretation of his or her experience of the world, without the restriction of a guiding force other than his or her own perceptive and reasoning faculties. So how might this 'genesis without structure' apply to how young children acquire the concept of colour, both in terms of each constituent colour as well as the concept of colour in general?

It is widely accepted that children learn their colours by ostensive definition – that is, learning by pointing. The teacher points at a red cube and utters the word 'red', after which the child will be able to identify the colour 'red' in a host of non-cube, red items. In such a primitive form of learning, we seem to arrive at a mutated version of the Meno paradox. Indeed, either the child has pre-knowledge of the super-concept 'colour' (in general), prior to learning the concept 'red', or he or she does not. If the child does have the pre-knowledge of the general concept 'colour' prior to learning 'red', then we can hardly say that he or she has learned the concept 'red' – that is, to have mastered the general concept 'colour', the child must have mastered all of the particular sub-concepts of each constituent colour in its own right. So, perhaps, on the contrary, the child does not have pre-knowledge of the general concept 'colour' prior to being introduced to the concept 'red'. However, in this case, without the super-concept as pre-knowledge, how is it that the child is able to recognize that he or she must attend to the 'redness' of the cube? Why not attend to the angles inside the cube, or the fact that it is a cube? Keep in mind, in this case, that the child has no prior grasp of the concept 'colour' and yet he or she seems able to associate the sub-concept 'red' with the 'redness' of the cube.

It appears that we have our paradox – and it has occurred in the simplest form of learning: a particularly strong indictment of the inability to learn by inquiry only. The child cannot inquire about a concept of which he or she has no prior knowledge, since he or she would be unable to recognize it even if presented with it before his or her very eyes. The child's inquisition in such an instance would be futile. However, should he or she be privy to any prior knowledge of the concept about which he or she seeks to inquire, then we can hardly claim that he or she has learnt anything at all. What seems to be the cause of this paradox? Simply: the assumption that one can go in search of what one wants to know without the guidance of a master arbiter, whose very definition gives intelligibility to the concept of correctness. This arbiter – who must be the authoritative teacher, given his or her superior expertise and judgement – is the person who helps the young child to develop the power to discriminate between 'right' and 'wrong'.

Various attempts have been made to circumvent this paradox, most notably in interpretations of Vygotsky (in his version of constructivism, which incorporated the social aspect that Piaget neglected) and also by Plato, in his attempt to solve the problem with his 'theory', Platonism. However, Vygotskian – or so-called 'social' – constructivism is recognized as failing to circumvent the Meno paradox, and the details of the failings of this attempt can be found in Bereiter (1985), examination of which will be left as an exercise for the reader. As for Platonism, or the belief that we have the answers in an infinite index list and can access them when we inquire? The idea seems so outlandish that it is often rejected on the basis of the fact that what it posits could never be verified or denied – that is, that it is a 'theory' based on supposition and unverifiable claims.

Where constructivism is genesis without structure, Platonism is structure without genesis: if we adopt Platonism as the solution to the Meno paradox (which was put forward as a potential solution by Plato in the *Meno* dialogue itself), we are subsequently adopting a belief that there exists a Platonic realm in which all possible answers to all possible questions simply hang in limbo, awaiting our ethereal connection when we seek them out. Such a view of things renders the very notion of learning redundant, since if we each have access to this Platonic realm (which, presumably would either be 'stored' inside the confines of the skull, or would be retained somewhere in the ether), which contains all possible facts, then we have nothing to learn at any point in time; all things that can be discovered must already, by definition, be part of the Platonic realm that is either held within the confines of each of our individual minds or stored in some non-spatial, ethereal realm which exists outside of the material world. Furthermore, if each of us has the same infinite index lists of all of the possible answers to all of the possible questions that man could ever seek to understand, why is it that everyone does not give the same answer to the same question? That is, suppose that A and B have each had the same list of examples given to them in their respective learning experiences: why is it, if a Platonic realm exists, that A and B are not guaranteed to give the same answers to questions that are designed to test their grasp of their learning? If learning is simply a process of connecting to a realm that pre-exists either inside the mind or in some ethereal realm, then surely everyone who received the same teaching and learning experiences would provide the same answers to the same questions? Being incorrect would cease to be possible once one had connected with one's own Platonic realm.[2] Furthermore, if this Platonic realm exists independent from the real world, somewhere in the ether, then it remains altogether unclear how we are to connect with it, or why there should exist any access to it at all. If all the answers to all the questions reside outside of the world in which we inhabit, it seems like a leap of faith to suggest that we come to realize these answers and that we come to know things only by connecting with a world whose existence rests outside the real material world. Moreover, in this view of things, it is left unexplained how the real world and the Platonic world connect, or how a world governed by physical causal laws (the real world) could be determined by a world where causality seems not to apply (Platonic world). These are big questions, and Platonism seems to leave them all unexplained and unanswered.

Where constructivism is entirely *non-deterministic*, Platonism attempts to find *determinism* in a system that will not yield. A path must be steered between these two extremes. This conundrum, it seems, can be solved only by accompanying inquiry-led learning with an authoritative teacher. Indeed, in instances of inquiry, the teacher can steer a path towards correctness. We move between genesis without structure and structure without genesis towards genesis *with* structure: a system that permits inquiry and creativity, housed inside the structure that is offered by the guidance and leadership of the authority of the master expert. Socrates was famous for using such teaching techniques: the 'Socratic method' was used to direct and (perhaps unintentionally) to influence the learner towards what he or she was expected to see. This inquiry required a teacher to lead the activity and to ask pertinent questions to guide the learner towards the correct answers in the learning process. That is, even in the cases of inquiry-led learning, it seems that the authority of the teacher and the practice are still required to point out that successful learning has taken place. The teacher and the practice, therefore, act as boundaries and parameters to constrain and direct the learning through the authority that their respective positions naturally command. To create an individual version of learning – that is, a version in which the learner is encouraged to consider himself or herself capable of searching for answers *on his or her own*, without any intellectual guidance – sees learners encouraged to wander around aimlessly searching and inquiring for answers in their ultimate quest for successful learning, and naturally leads to the Meno paradox, a damning review of inquiry-led learning.

Therefore, for the moment, we have our justification for requiring the teacher as the authority figure in *any form* of learning: to provide learners with an expert-constrained framework in which to learn – a process that can occur as a result of teaching, researching or constrained inquiry, but which is unlikely to be fruitful without the guidance of an authority to which the learner is to submit. (I will discuss this notion in more detail later in the text, in relation to Polanyi's so-called 'fiduciary framework'.) The motive for having the teacher, the practice or the reliable resource as the authority within *any form* of learning is therefore to provide a voice of reason and sense to a process that would be unsuccessful in their respective absences.

Moreover, to fulfil the remit of successful learning – namely, to ensure that the learner can move on from his or her learning in the *correct* manner – an acceptance of the practice's way of working is essential. The very concepts of 'right' and 'wrong' with respect to learning are founded within an acceptance of the community and the practices that the community fosters. 'Correctness' is an action that accords with the practice, in as much as 'if there was no *we* – if there was no agreement among those who have had the same training, as to what are the correct steps ... then there would be no *wrong* steps, or indeed any *right* ones' (Malcolm, 1986: 156). The 'we' to whom Malcolm is referring is the community and the 'agreement' is found in the acceptance of the authority that emanates from the community. As Malcolm points out, without this accepted way of working – the community to foster these ideas, and the authority that is ascribed to representatives and reliable resources on behalf of the community – we simply wander aimlessly into a world in which the concepts of 'right' and 'wrong' are lost in a learning wilderness.[3] Learning, in this way, can be expertly constrained under a process of authoritative training, which takes an indeterminate being (the learner) to the cusp of determinacy, to provide 'correct' answers to future problems in accordance with the practice that his or her training will have equipped him or her to provide.

It seems, therefore, that I have arrived at my first point of note: that learning as a process, whether it is regarded as a teacher-led activity, a research-led activity or as some form of constrained inquiry, requires the submission to an authority – namely, the authority of the teacher or another reliable resource accompanied by the underlying authority of the practice that they respectively represent. The consequences of rebelling against such an authority seem problematic at best and catastrophic at worst in relation to the possibility of learning. And given that learning clearly is possible, it appears that it requires, as an indispensable facet of it, a component of expert authority to which the learner must submit. Such an expert authority seeks only to constrain the actions that will occur naturally in its absence, to ensure that learning can be successful. In the absence of such authority, learning is chaotic, unstructured and potentially misguided. Without the authoritative arbiter, the expert opinion, there is no one or nothing to guide learners towards what they must see for learning to be successful. In this way, the notion of 'correctness' in learning loses its meaning, since 'correctness' is established in accordance with an accepted way of working, grounded within practices, traditions and communities – that is, *correctness* is a feature not of the individual, but of the collection of like-minded experts who share justified ideals. That is not to say, for example, as Reuben Hersh did, that mathematics is what mathematicians 'do', nor is true of any other discipline, for that matter. The community of mathematicians certainly adopts the precepts and core principles of mathematics as its working tools – but that does not mean that what the community *adopts* as mathematics is what mathematics *is*; rather, it takes time to establish and embed into a tradition the *community's* accepted way of working. Correctness is entangled with a communal, justified ideal – a *practice* – for without the community and the practice, correctness is lost. The Meno paradox is circumvented – and, subsequently, the paradox of inquiry-led learning is prevented – only in the presence of an authoritative arbiter, to judge in conformity with the practice from which he or she comes. This arbiter is the teacher, the master expert, who is chosen to represent his or her practice given his or her own credentials as an expert in his or her subject – and his or her authority seems to be indispensable in successful learning.

The implications for the foundations of knowledge: The Aristotelian problem

In Aristotle's text, *Posterior Analytics*, he describes a system of knowledge development that he believed outlined how knowledge was formed and developed from the foundations up. The system that Aristotle proposes is a form of foundationalism, which essentially argues that everything within a 'belief-system', a 'truth-system' or a 'knowledge-system' is either self-evident (known in Aristotle's system as 'first-principles'), demonstrable from self-evident premises, or demonstrable from propositions that themselves have already been demonstrated. The 'first-principles' in such a system are clearly of a different nature (or category) from the propositions that they are required to demonstrate. Aristotle was insistent that this had to be the case. Indeed, if we suppose that there was no such an object as a 'first-principle' or a 'self-evident truth' that required no demonstration itself, it is possible then to induce an infinite regress of knowledge founded in knowledge *ad infinitum* – that is, without a foundation that is of a different nature from knowledge itself, the process of founding knowledge within prior knowledge will inevitably endure forever. This, of course, would suggest that either one cannot demonstrate one's own knowledge – that is, that the process of demonstration is incoherent – or that knowledge cannot be developed. It seems intuitive to reject any such claim that knowledge cannot be developed and also to reject any notion that we cannot demonstrate – or simply justify – the nature of how our knowledge is constructed. Therefore, to avoid any such unappealing claims, Aristotle pre-emptively separated the concepts of 'first-principles' and 'knowledge' into different categories, with different properties and which must be developed differently.[4]

Aristotle gave his account of what makes 'first-principles' different in nature from knowledge itself. I will argue, however, that the component that Aristotle forgot to include in his account of knowledge development was a component of what I will call 'authoritative foundationalism', or 'training foundationalism'. Later in the book, I will demonstrate how Wittgenstein has solved the Aristotelian problem of foundationalism. For the moment, however, I will simply outline the problems that Aristotle encountered in attempting to explain what lies at the foundations of knowledge.

Within Aristotle's claim that the foundations of knowledge must be different in nature from the knowledge that emanates from them, there is a pertinent question that any sceptic of foundationalism would raise and which, indeed, Aristotle raised pre-emptively himself. Avrum Stroll (1994: 143–7) outlines the problem with foundationalism that Aristotle himself articulated millennia before: First:

> From at least the time of Aristotle many philosophers have asserted that some of the knowledge human beings possess is more fundamental or basic than the rest. If we call such primordial knowledge F and the remainder R, we can roughly express their intuition by saying that R depends on F but not conversely and that F depends on nothing.

This therefore means that 'According to the model, foundational F does not depend on anything and is said to be more fundamental than any R. But the skeptic will ask, How do we know this? How can you be sure there isn't something more fundamental than F upon which it depends?' This is the conundrum that faces any foundationalist, including Aristotle – namely, what allows us to distinguish between the foundations and the knowledge that is demonstrated from and developed within these foundations? As Stroll argues, it seems impossible to fend off the foundationalist sceptic who demands that the avid foundationalist provide evidence for the claim that he or she has reached the foundations. Indeed, unless there is some form of evidence or criteria with which to distinguish coherently between the foundations and the knowledge that is purported to be demonstrable from these foundations, it is irrefutable that what may seem to be foundational may well be another form of knowledge that requires further justification in its own right. That is, the foundationalist might think – and indeed may seem justified in thinking – that he or she is at the foundations when, in actual fact, he or she is still in the realm of demonstrable and justifiable (that is, not indubitable) knowledge.

Aristotle attempted to solve this problem by claiming that the foundations of knowledge were attainable only through perception and the memories of these perceptions:

> He says that we come to know the foundations of knowledge, or 'first principles', differently than we come to know other propositions. They do not require demonstrative proof; rather we arrive at first

principles through a process that begins with perception. We perceive particular things and form memories of them. Particulars, on Aristotle's view, are not objects of knowledge *per se*. Nevertheless, when we form enough memories about particulars of a certain type, we thereby attain experience. Through experience we finally arrive at universals, which, for Aristotle, are the first principles.

(Dempster, 2008: 21)

Aristotle's attempted solution was to develop knowledge within what he believed to be an indubitable foundation, a foundation that would not be subject to doubt in the same way as knowledge could be. He did, however, fail in this quest. Indeed, according to Dempster (2008: 21): 'Aristotle's first principles depend on the faculties of perception and memory. However, our senses can deceive us, and memory is not always reliable. It follows that first principles are subject to doubt. Thus, first principles are not indubitable.'

Aristotle's failure, I will show, emanates from his incorrect selection of the foundations. He bases his first principles – his foundations – in perceptions and memory. His deep-seated confusions emanate from his belief, expressed in the first line of *Posterior Analytics*, that '[a]ll teaching and learning of an intellectual kind proceed from pre-existent knowledge' (Aristotle, 1994: 1). From this point onwards, Aristotle was destined to fail in his solution of a problem that he had created for himself: for if all learning was to be founded inside pre-existing knowledge, how did the pre-existing knowledge get there? Attempts to solve this with memory and perception were futile. Wittgenstein, however, chooses a different candidate at the foundations: training and certainties. This training and these certainties, unsurprisingly, are founded in an acceptance of the authority of one's teacher. I will return to this discussion of Wittgenstein's solution to the Aristotelian problem later in the text.

For the moment, however, I have provided a preamble of philosophy that is relevant to our discussion about the requirement for authority within knowledge development and the spin-off concepts associated with authority, such as traditions, training, belief and trust. I have highlighted that, since the respective times of Socrates, Plato and Aristotle (a trio of successive masters and students), there have been difficulties with the foundations of knowledge. Finding a foundation eluded even Aristotle himself, and Plato's solution (Platonism) was no more favourable. I will show later in the book, with particular reference to Wittgenstein's foundationalism (and Avrum Stroll's discussion of it), that the philosophically coherent candidate for the indubitable foundations that Aristotle sought is an acceptance of one's training, founded in the authority of the teacher, accompanied and supported by the community and traditions from which the teacher comes.

The implications for education

So far, I have outlined the implications of a lack of authority for learning, and for understanding the nature of what knowledge is and how it is developed. I showed, briefly, that, in the absence of authority, learning is forced into a situation in which the notion of 'correctness' becomes unintelligible and meaningless. In essence, the implication for authority-deficient learning was the rather worrying replacement of correctness with viability – that is, in the learning environment, with no or little authority, the student is free to form meaning for himself or herself, forcing a situation in which there are no correct answers, since the very notion of correctness is inexorably linked to the understanding that the teacher is the arbiter of correctness in the classroom. I made the argument therefore that, should we believe correctness to be an important notion in learning, a submission to the teacher's authority was the only option to salvage this notion.

Furthermore, I also outlined that the student should not be permitted to 'wander off' into the learning wilderness under the impression that inquiry-led learning is achievable. Indeed, inquiry-led learning results in the Meno paradox, which proved to be a damning indictment of inquiry-only learning. I made the argument, therefore, that the teacher, once again, was required as an authority figure, to guide and direct learning to ensure that the student does not stumble into confusion and error. Consequently, I concluded that the teacher is an indispensable figure of authority within the learning process.

Secondly, I considered the implications of an authority-deficient or an authority-free approach to knowledge. I discussed the Aristotelian problem of knowledge founded in knowledge and outlined my discontent that Aristotle had solved this potential problem with knowledge foundationalism in his discussion of so-called 'first-principles', which were founded in the faculties of perception and memory. I asserted that, should we ever hope for knowledge to have an appropriately coherent construction and should we also hope for knowledge to be developable, there must be an indubitable foundation that is not subjected to the same levels of doubt as the knowledge that rests upon it. For me, Aristotle failed in this quest, and I noted that the aspect that he appeared to be missing was a foundational submission to authority – perhaps to one's teacher, or to the traditions and practices from which the teacher comes – in order to ensure that knowledge can be developed upon this submission.

Therefore I have outlined the importance of authority within teaching and learning, and within understanding how knowledge is constructed and developed. What, then, are the subsequent implications for authority – or a lack of it – within education in general? The answer to this lies, first, in what is understood by the complex term 'education'. To define the term 'education' is an altogether more difficult task than it first appears. However, for the purposes of this preliminary discussion, it seems that the term need not be *precisely* pinned down; rather, it is sufficient for me to give a pseudo-definition of the term, to outline what *any* version of education must encompass. Regardless of your educational dispositions, it seems irrefutable that education, in the formal sense, will have to engulf the processes of teaching and learning at its core, and also that it will have to encapsulate some form of knowledge development. Indeed, an education that does not include teaching and learning as its fundamental processes, or an education that has no provision for the development of knowledge, is not an education at all. Therefore, although there are grounds for debate about the degree to which knowledge and its development should be considered within education, it remains irrefutable that education must have, as at least some of its components, a provision for teaching, learning and knowledge development.

This definition is all that seems necessary for the moment. Indeed, it permits me to answer the question: what are the implications for an education lacking in authority? Well, in the absence or deficiency of authority, education is an arena in which – on the basis of the previous two sections – teaching and learning are impossible, the notion of 'correctness' has lost its value and meaning, and knowledge is potentially foundationless. Indeed, if education (under any definition of the term) is to be understood to involve an element of teaching, learning and knowledge development, then an education bereft of authority induces a situation in which teaching, learning and knowledge are bereft of authority. Thus, on the basis of arguments already made in the previous two sections, education falls foul of the conclusions established in those sections. It seems intuitive also that an education starved of authority is an education in which there will be chaotic pedagogy and learning, major discipline issues and the potential of motivational issues.

If the reader is comfortable living in a world in which the education system sends out the message that children are to make decisions on the basis of 'what works for them' – an education system that favours the child over the practice and under which teachers have been stripped of any authority that they used to possess – I implore you to reject authority in all of its forms. However, if the reader is uncomfortable with the message of education being that the 'child is all that matters', to the point at which everything else is deemed unworthy of note – if the reader is uneasy with a world in which education is no longer seen to be an arena in which children are expected to set high standards for themselves and are challenged to reach them, and if the reader is restless about the continual undermining of adult authority and the increasingly apparent lack of respect for adults and teachers – then I encourage you to read on and take notice of the arguments put forward in the ensuing sections.

A conclusive argument will be established for why authority is required in education (as though such an argument should ever be required) and why learning is possible only in the initial submission to such authority. The teacher must be restored as the agent of civilization, the school must be reinstated as an institution and the pupil must be reminded that he or she has much to learn. Education has lost its way – but its potential remains undiminished. All that is required is a rejuvenation of the authority that keeps the educational machine well oiled.

PART TWO

THE ARGUMENT

5 POLANYI ON AUTHORITY

A brief philosophical history of authority and doubt

The history of the philosophical considerations of authority is outlined in Mark T. Mitchell's account of Polanyi's approach to knowledge development, subtitled *The Art of Knowing* (2006). At the core of the arguments that Mitchell puts forward in this text are Polanyi's accounts of the importance of the pre-modern concept of authority, in relation to other concepts such as traditions and the communities that cultivate and give justification to this authority. It is an interesting account of the history of authority and tradition, focused around the pivotal role played by St Augustine, whose philosophy was founded in a submission to authority and an acceptance that faith was at the basis of knowledge. As Polanyi (2009: 266) argues: 'He taught that all knowledge was a gift of grace, for which we must strive under the guidance of antecedent belief: *nisi credideritis, non intelligetis*.'[1] That is, Augustine asserted all knowledge to be formed out of accepting certain premises that were founded in faith. This led to the eventual conclusion that knowledge was formed by what Augustine called 'inner illumination', a process whereby we come to 'know' things under the inner guidance of God. I will not adopt this version of 'illumination' as I develop these ideas in this book; the importance of faith as a central component of knowledge development is, however, essential. This dependence on faith was to overturn the ancient Greek practice of absolute reasoning and rationality. Mitchell (2006: 61) summarizes the philosophical history of faith succinctly thus: 'For the ancient Greeks, reason was primary. Augustine overturned that tradition by arguing that faith preceded reason. Modern philosophy, in turn, rejected the Augustinian primacy of belief with its rejection of all forms of tradition.' Therefore we find ourselves subject to the constant oscillation of what Mitchell (2006: 62) describes as a 'pendulum': 'Greek rationalism represents the pendulum at one extreme ... rejected by Augustine ... Modern rationalism, in turn, rejected Augustine and returned the pendulum hard in the direction of rationalism.'

In the post-modern philosophical era, we have therefore returned to a state of rationalism – a state that must, according to Polanyi, oscillate back towards an Augustinian approach to knowledge, founded in faith and authority. In the modern philosophical age, the pre-modern concepts such as tradition, authority, faith and trust were rejected in favour of reasoning for oneself, on the basis of one's own faculties. Perhaps one of the most prominent examples of such philosophical thinking is found in Descartes' so-called 'method of doubt', outlined in his first two *Meditations*. *The Oxford Dictionary of Philosophy* outlines what the 'method of doubt' entails:

> It attempts to put knowledge upon a secure foundation by first inviting us to suspend judgement on any proposition whose truth can be doubted, even as a bare possibility. The standards of acceptance are gradually raised as we are asked to doubt the deliverance of memory, the senses, and even reason, all of which are in principle capable of letting us down. The process is eventually dramatized in the figure of an evil demon ... whose aim is to deceive us, so that our senses, memories, and reasonings lead us astray. The task then becomes one of finding a demon-proof point of certainty, and Descartes produces this in the famous 'Cogito ergo sum': I think therefore I am.
>
> (Blackburn, 2008: 232)

Descartes concludes 'on this slender basis that the correct use of our faculties has to be re-established' (Blackburn, 2008: 232). However, as Blackburn (2008: 232) outlines, 'it seems as though Descartes has denied himself any materials to use in reconstructing the edifice of knowledge'. In a sense, therefore, Descartes' doubt took him to a foundation from which his initial assumptions do not permit his return. Descartes' rationalism/foundationalism will be discussed briefly again later in Chapter 8. For the moment, however, it is important to note only that the Cartesian doctrine survived, in the main part, until Wittgenstein's arrival in the early twentieth century. Ray Monk (2005: 88), a prominent Wittgensteinian scholar, asserts that 'Wittgenstein's greatest achievement, it is often said, was to have undone 300 years of Cartesianism'. Rationalism in general attracted interest and support from various other prominent philosophers of the time, such as Leibniz and Spinoza, who remained committed to the idea that rational thought and reasoning were the sources of knowledge.

Polanyi, on the other hand, uniquely offers a framework in which to house such a rethinking of knowledge development and subsequently a return to Augustinianism, founded in faith, authority and traditions:

> We must now recognize belief once more as the source of all knowledge. Tacit assent and intellectual passions, the sharing of an idiom and or a cultural heritage, affiliation to a like-minded community: such are the impulses which shape our vision of the nature of things on which we rely for our mastery of things. No intelligence, however critical or original, can operate outside such a fiduciary framework.
>
> (Polanyi, 2009: 266)

Polanyi cleverly sets out a framework – his so-called 'fiduciary framework' – based in the acceptance of authority and a faith in one's master. He is, however, cautious not to pull away entirely from the notions of rationality and reasoning, preferring to permit reasoning *within* this fiduciary framework. Indeed, as Mitchell (2006: 62) argues, 'Polanyi's call for a return to Augustine is not a call to reject all appeals to reason or to deny the importance of science or other secular pursuits; instead, it is a call to recognize the indispensable role belief plays in knowing'.

It is this so-called fiduciary framework that I shall discuss now in relation to Polanyi's work on authority, traditions and communities. Polanyi's efforts were dedicated to providing a detailed 'theory' of knowledge on the basis of a return to Augustinian faith. It is this theory that Polanyi argued finds its roots in authority, traditions and communities. This is the essence of our interest in Polanyi's literature and its contributions to the discussion of authority: that knowledge – and its development for that matter – is founded in an acceptance of authority, in the hope of learning something that was previously unknown to us. I will show in the next section, in keeping with Polanyi, that a rebellion against authority is simply not an option should one ever hope to develop one's knowledge.

Polanyi has made significant contributions to the understanding of how knowledge can be developed within an expert-constrained framework and how learning seems to be possible only when the learner submits to the authority of the expert in such a framework. Polanyi coined the phrase 'fiduciary framework' to describe a framework that he claims is a suitable house within which learning and knowledge development can take place. This framework, by its very definition, is a framework within which the learner submits with a trusting nature to the superior knowledge of the expert master – within which the learner acknowledges that he or she can learn only through such a submission. Indeed, '[i]n learning by submitting to the authority of the teacher, the pupil seeks to grasp what he initially does not comprehend' (Mitchell, 2006: 64). Mitchell's account is demonstrating that at the basis of any hope for knowledge and its development is a submission to an authoritative figure: the teacher.[2] It is this fiduciary framework, proposed by Polanyi, which I shall examine in more detail now, with reference to Mitchell's account on the same discussion, *The Art of Knowing* (2006).

Polanyi's fiduciary framework

In Mitchell's account of Polanyi's theory of knowledge, he illustrates that Polanyi attributes central roles to the concepts of tradition and authority in the development of knowledge. In keeping with this analysis, I will outline the importance that tradition and authority have in relation to a paradigm for knowledge. As I have already discussed, a submission to such an authority and the traditions into which the authority seeks to inculcate others seem to be pivotal concepts in the notion of knowledge development. While Aristotle sought to found knowledge in 'first-principles' – which he argued were attainable through perception and memory – Polanyi proposes that there is a demand for authority at the foundation of any knowledge system. It is this structured, authority-founded framework that I shall consider now.

The subtitle of Mitchell's book, *The Art of Knowing*, raises an interesting thought – namely, what is involved in 'knowing'? What does it mean to 'know' or to have 'knowledge' and, in a similar vein, how does one acquire or develop it? Moreover, what might the *art* of knowing entail? I have already discussed the notion of how knowledge is constructed from a foundationalist point of view earlier in the text in relation to Aristotle's foundationalism. Mitchell (2006: 63) himself, in his analysis of Polanyi, outlines that 'knowing is an art, and any art is learned by apprenticeship and practice'. It is by referring to knowing as an 'art' that one finds the need for an authority. Indeed, Polanyi talks of practical knowledge forming a basis for the knowledge of rules, whereby this practical knowledge itself is dependent on a submission to an authority – that is, the natural order of developing the 'art' of knowing is, first, to accept the master's authority, then to attain practical knowledge through this submission to authority, and finally to attain the knowledge of the rules that are related to this practical knowledge. As Polanyi (2009: 50) claims: 'Rules of art can be useful, but they do not determine the practice of an art; they are maxims, which can serve as a guide to an art only if they can be integrated into the practical knowledge of the art. They cannot replace the knowledge.' Mitchell (2006: 63) develops this claim about the progression of practical knowledge:

> Practical knowledge precedes the knowledge of rules … one must possess a degree of practical knowledge in order to properly apply rules. … One acquires practical knowledge through doing … how can one practice an art if one does not yet know how to do so? The answer lies in submission to an authority in the manner of an apprentice. We learn by example.

It is in this sense, as I outlined earlier, that the student *must* submit to the authority of the master in the hope of learning something that he or she does not, as yet, understand. To reject this authority is to turn one's nose up at the possibility of being exposed to the accepted traditions and practices of the community that the master represents. It is these traditions, practices and communities that delegate the authority to their representative. Should a student rebel against this authority or have no faith in this authority, that student is subjecting to doubt something that simply has to be accepted in the pursuit of knowledge: the authority of all that is encompassed by Polanyi's fiduciary framework. As Polanyi (2009: 53) himself argues:

> To learn by example is to submit to authority. You follow your master because you trust his manner of doing things even when you cannot analyse and account in detail for its effectiveness. By watching the master and emulating his efforts in the presence of his example, the

apprentice unconsciously picks up the rules of the art, including those which are not explicitly known to the master himself. These hidden rules can be assimilated only by a person who surrenders himself to that extent uncritically to the imitation of another.

The submission to this authority, therefore, is a means to an end in attaining for oneself, eventually, the ability to understand and reason beyond what has already been taught. It is a case of '*fides quaerens intellectum*, faith in search of understanding' (Polanyi, 1946: 45), in the hope that this understanding will one day permit the student to become part of the community from which the authority comes.

It seems that Polanyi is providing a framework – this coveted 'fiduciary framework' – which deliberately constrains the students in its charge, under the guidance of a legitimate master expert, in the hope that they will *engage* with the practices and traditions set down within the framework in such a way that they will ultimately *contribute to* and *participate in* these traditions and practices. That is, the traditions and practices do not stand at a distance from the students, who are engaging with and participating in them; rather, they are *brought to life* by this constant interaction with each other, always guided by the master to ensure that their integrity is not compromised. Indeed, this is a process to be handled responsibly, and Polanyi (1946: 45–6) argues that there is no one better suited to handle this responsibility than the expert master:

[N]o one can become a [scientist] unless he presumes that the [scientific] doctrine and method are fundamentally sound and that their ultimate premises can be unquestionably accepted.

Thus the authority to which the student ... submits tends to eliminate its own functions by establishing direct contact between the student and the reality of nature. As he approaches maturity the student will rely for his beliefs less and less on authority and more and more on his own judgement. His own intuition and conscience will take over responsibility in the measure in which authority is eclipsed.

This does not mean that he will no more rely on the report of other[s] – far from it – but it means that such reliance will henceforth be entirely subject to his own judgement.

Submission to authority will henceforth form merely a part of the process of discovery, for which – as the process as a whole – he will assume full responsibility before his own conscience.[3]

It should thus become clear what Polanyi is proposing through the acceptance of this fiduciary framework to which much of his writings about knowledge are devoted: he is talking of a foundational acceptance by the student, in the authority of the teacher and the doctrines that the student hopes to assimilate. As a result of this, the student will become accustomed, initially, to imitating the expert master, on the basis of the authority that he or she commands – an authority that was issued to the master by the traditions and community that he or she represents. Subsequently, once the student has developed his or her own judgement – a concept about which I will talk more later in relation to Oakeshott's writings on authority – that student will rely less on the authority to which he or she initially submitted and more on his or her own conscience, which will have been trained and developed to guide the student into the same practices and traditions from which the master came. In this process, however, the master should not oppress originality:

> The student will therefore practice a measure of criticism even during this period of study, and the teacher will gladly foster any signs of originality on the part of the student. But this must remain within the proper limits; the process of learning must rely in the main on the acceptance of authority. Where necessary this acceptance must be enforced by discipline.
>
> (Polanyi, 1946: 46)

In the end, the student will achieve his or her goal of quasi-independence[4] from the master, but only because the student has become a master himself or herself, having been inculcated into the practice from which that master came. In this case, it will be the student-turned-master's responsibility to protect the traditions and practices towards which he or she is now entitled to make serious and significant contributions, depending now on his or her sense of inner guidance[5] to make such contributions. It is an organic process of recycling knowledge through traditions, practices and the authority that is inherent in both of these concepts: a process that constantly regenerates itself in such a way that traditions need not be static and inert, however difficult they might be to change – and traditions simply *should* be difficult to change. And in this overall process the master–student relationship is at the core.

We see how pivotal the teacher or master is in guiding those in his or her charge towards quasi-independence in a responsible manner. It is the master, therefore – and the institutions, traditions, practices and communities that he or she represents – who holds the key to the chest of knowledge. However, the process begins with the acknowledgement of that fact that 'faith precedes reason' (Mitchell, 2006: 61). This 'faith' on which Polanyi seems to be constantly focused is manifested in the student's submission to the authority of his or her master: a submission that is the indication that the student trusts the master, because of what the master represents. Indeed, the student will align himself or herself with the master initially – and consequently will also align himself or herself with the practices and traditions that the master holds dear – but will begin, eventually, to exercise a degree of scepticism, albeit only once the student has developed his or her own 'knowledge-conscience'. In this sense (Polanyi, 1946: 45): 'At every stage of his progress towards this end he is urged on by the belief that certain things as yet beyond his knowledge and even his understanding are on the whole true and valuable, so that it is worth spending his most intensive efforts on mastering them.'

The importance of traditions and communities within the fiduciary framework

Another underlying theme in virtually all of Polanyi's work is the role that the tradition plays in knowledge development. He links, rather uniquely, the concepts of authority and tradition to fit inside the fiduciary framework that we have already encountered. The concept of a tradition is controversial in most disciplines and education is no different. Some critics talk of traditions as dogmatic and restrictive, and see them as nothing more than controlling mechanisms from which those under their control are to be set free. Polanyi talks of traditions in knowledge, which seem to have natural analogies for education in the purposes of this discussion.

A tradition is an accepted way of working, something that has stood the test of time, and – most importantly – it is something that *is* and *should* be difficult to change. It is handed down from one generation to the next and is responsibly reshaped when necessary. As we will see, Polanyi demonstrates that traditions need not be static and unchanging; they are dynamic and plastic, but only when change is required and when the change can be overseen by the community that protects the interests of the tradition. Indeed, as Mitchell (2006: 68) points out, 'we cannot participate in tradition without changing it'. Moreover, 'each person who participates in a tradition contributes to the further development of the tradition' (Mitchell, 2006: 68). This is why traditions must be passed on, like a baton, to the next generation. I will discuss this notion of the plasticity of traditions later in this section.

Such plasticity of traditions comes to life when the 'passing on' of traditions is viewed as a responsible intergenerational transaction between the 'learned' and 'non-learned' communities. Let us begin, however, with a look at why, according to Polanyi, traditions are an indispensable component of any knowledge system.

I have already laid the foundations of knowledge within the submission to a master's authority, in keeping with Polanyi's fiduciary framework. This submission to a master's authority, however, should be seen only to be the stepping-stone towards Polanyi's final solution – a solution that introduces students into a practice and a tradition founded in their initial submission to authority. Polanyi (1983: 61) talks of how this step is achieved, through a process to which he refers as 'indwelling': 'In order to share this indwelling, the pupil must presume that a teaching which appears meaningless to start with has in fact a meaning which can be discovered by hitting on the same kind of indwelling as the teacher is practising. Such an effort is based on accepting the teacher's authority.' In this sense, the student is expected initially to accept the teacher's authority, in the hope of attaining a glimpse of the traditions that dwell within the teacher. That is, the teacher is the carrier of his or her own indwelling – an indwelling that is already aligned with the traditions and practices with which the teacher is accustomed – and, through submission to this teacher's authority, the student has a bridge to align *himself or herself* with the traditions and practices via his or her own version of this indwelling. This concept of 'indwelling' therefore provides a route via which the student can navigate the labyrinth of potential confusion, towards a tradition that provides all of the answers for which he or she could ever hope.

Therefore, so far, we have a sequence of events that begins with the acceptance of authority of a master, in an effort to align oneself with a tradition and a practice, via a process of indwelling. Let us remind ourselves that the final quest is to become skilled in the *art of knowing*. This is where the notion of a tradition becomes ever more pertinent, because 'if knowing is an art, and if learning an art requires dwelling in the practices of a master, then it follows that there must exist a tradition by which the art is transmitted' (Mitchell, 2006: 64).

This places a major responsibility into the hands of the tradition. If, as Mitchell points out, the tradition is to be the transmitter of the *art of knowing*, then it is to be regarded as the hub from which the knowledge emanates. Precisely how this knowledge can be transmitted is in the hands of the authoritative teacher to whom I have already referred. However, Mitchell, in keeping with Polanyi, is assigning a pivotal role to the tradition in the development of knowledge – namely, the role of a font from which students are to drink should they hope to become 'knowledgeable'.

Traditions therefore seem to be given pride of place; from such a stronghold, they have been given rank that is almost equivalent to the knowledge itself. Indeed, as Mitchell (2006: 64) goes on to say: 'Any attempts categorically and systematically to reject tradition must be logically incompatible with knowing.' That is, should we choose to reject traditions, we will be choosing also to reject an insight into the *art of knowing*. Traditions are an indispensable component in knowing. Indeed, as Polanyi (1969: 41) himself points outs: 'No human mind can function without accepting authority, custom and tradition: it must rely on them for the mere use of a language.' This example of acquiring the knowledge and mastery of a language is something to which Polanyi constantly refers as a paradigmatic example; it will be discussed later in its own right. The relevant point for the moment, however, is that authority and traditions have been established in Polanyi's philosophy as indispensable facets of the *art of knowing*. Regardless of the nature of the knowledge to be acquired and regardless of what the motivation for acquiring such knowledge might be, authority is at its foundations, and traditions emanate and disseminate the knowledge itself.

This process of founding knowledge development in authority and traditions is subject to further scrutiny by Polanyi, and subsequently Mitchell. Continuing the discussion on how young children acquire the knowledge and use of a language, analogies can be drawn for other forms of knowledge development, as well as how these notions relate to the development of one's skills: according to Mitchell (2006: 65) 'any skill must first be acquired through submission to the authority of a particular tradition'. In this way, we 'rely on the guidance of tradition' (Mitchell, 2006: 66). This guidance is what makes the lure of a tradition so strong;

in fact, it makes it *essential* to knowledge development. To reject traditionalism within the development of knowledge is to reject the guidance that accompanies such a traditional approach. This guidance is sustained over years of consistent scrutiny through which all traditions must pass before they can be regarded as traditions. As I outlined earlier, traditions are difficult to change – and so they should be. To change a tradition whimsically is to destroy the intrinsic properties that constitute what a tradition is by its very definition. It is a way of working, handed down through generations and shaped along the way, in a gradual process that permits only small changes to the tradition in any instance and radical changes in only the most extreme instances. Traditions are not to be dumped or cast aside; they are to be fought for and protected, viewed as an inheritance[6] from previous generations and cherished as such.

This version of Polanyian traditionalism is so appealing because it is dynamic and regenerative in its nature. Where traditionalism is often criticized of being static and inert, Polanyi cleverly devises a form of traditionalism that 'is in no way static' (Mitchell, 2006: 67). As Mitchell (2006: 67) goes on to argue, we must 'comprehend tradition as an orthodoxy that enforces a kind of discipline on those subject to tradition; but the orthodoxy is a dynamic one'. This element of plasticity of traditions is essential should we wish to prevent the traditions from being unchallenged, from becoming totalitarian dictates. However, we must remain steadfast in our claim that traditions should be changed *slowly* over a period of time and only when change is required. We must not be flippant or careless with our traditions. This is not an 'anything goes' culture, in which traditions change and become obsolete before they can be reshaped and recycled. Such 'flippancy' is reserved for overt and radical forms of progressivism, the natural counter-argument to traditional approaches. Polanyi (1969: 70) argues that, by its very nature, a tradition 'implicitly grants the right to opposition in the name of truth' – that is, a tradition *must* be contested if it purports to convey anything other than the purest version of truth and knowledge that is accessible at that moment in time.

Polanyi's motivation for this 'progressive view of traditionalism' – an oxymoron if ever there were one – finds its basis in his consideration of the contrasting views of Tom Paine and Edmund Burke. Their dispute was over the French Revolution and its effectiveness in achieving its aim of radical social, political and religious reform by overhauling the predetermined, static, inert traditions in favour of supposedly more dynamic, progressive social, political and religious approaches. Burke was an opponent of the French Revolution, claiming that it was carried out in an irresponsible manner, casting aside traditions without a second thought, in favour of a new start founded in pure reason and rational thought. Paine, on the other hand, argued that the Revolution was necessary to overthrow dogmatic approaches that had long been in need of changing. Polanyi references this example to demonstrate that traditionalism need not be a 'one or the other' approach. He proposes a structure in which traditions are upheld – and, indeed, form the foundations of our intellectual pursuits – but are subjected to scrutiny in the name of truth. Polanyi therefore pioneers the construction of a dynamic and fluid traditionalism 'in that it encourages a degree of dissent' (Mitchell, 2006: 68). This view of tradition, Polanyi (1969: 71) argues, 'transcends the conflict between Edmund Burke and Tom Paine. It rejects Paine's demand for absolute self-determination of each generation, but does so for the sake of its own ideal of unlimited human and social improvement. It accepts Burke's thesis that freedom must be rooted in tradition, but transposes it into a system cultivating radical progress.'

In this mutated form of authoritative, yet progressive (and indeed pragmatic), traditionalism that Polanyi proposes, there is a collision and subsequent coalescing of traditions and their rejuvenation through a process of input that Polanyi – and Mitchell – argues is an inescapable part of the nature of traditions. As I outlined earlier in the text, it seems impossible to engage with a tradition without making a contribution towards its perpetuation, dissemination and, consequently, its renewal. We make contributions to these traditions in the way in which we embrace them and interpret them. They are handed over to us through a submission to an authority – an authority that itself has been generated within a fiduciary framework, founded in traditions and communities who are focused on its promotion. Indeed, 'traditions are transmitted to us from the past, but they are our own interpretations of the past, at which we have arrived within the context of our own immediate problems' (Polanyi, 2009: 160). However, these traditions are developed and continued through a process of constant engagement with them by the people who are most focused on their protection:

> The major principles of science, law, religion, etc., are continuously remoulded by decisions made in borderline cases and by the touch of personal judgement entering into almost every decision. And

apart from this silent revolution steadily remoulding our heritage, there are massive innovations introduced by great pioneers. Yet each of these actions forms an essential part of the process of carrying on a tradition.

(Polanyi, 1946: 58–9)

The other major component of Polanyi's so-called 'fiduciary framework' is the component of the community and the subsequent role that the community plays in knowledge development. The notions of 'belief' and 'tradition' – notions that have already been shown to be at the core of this authority debate – are founded well and truly within the community from which they come. Indeed, it is this community whose entire *raison d'être* is to cultivate and protect the traditions and beliefs that emanate from it. Moreover, it is the community, as I have already outlined, which ascribes the authority to its expert representative – the teacher – in the pursuit of knowledge. And perhaps most importantly, it is the community that is the steadfast cornerstone of knowledge, committed to its dissemination and rejuvenation whenever necessary.

Mitchell outlines how the concepts of tradition, belief, practice and community are inextricably linked to one another in a series of connections that ultimately results in the art of knowing. On the concept of the connections between the tradition and the community, he argues that a 'tradition, of course, requires the presence of a community committed to its perpetuation' (Mitchell, 2006: 68). It is in this way that we come to recognize that traditions and communities must be linked. The community fosters a tradition and communicates the message. Traditions and communities are undoubtedly two of the cornerstones of knowledge, and of what Polanyi and Mitchell call the 'art of knowing'. The role of the community in knowing leads Mitchell (2006: 68) to conclude that knowing is a social construct: 'Since knowing is an art that requires one to enter into its practice through submission to the authority of a master, and since traditions are embodied and transmitted through practices, knowing is fundamentally social.'

This conclusion is particularly important, since it leads to pertinent realizations about the role that authority plays in knowledge development, as well as far-reaching conclusions for the central role of traditions and communities in how knowledge is formed and passed on through time. Mitchell (2006: 68) observes that 'knowing is rooted in submission to tradition and authority'. This is the fundamental undertone in all of the arguments surrounding authority and knowledge: there is simply no escaping the fact that knowledge is generated inside a framework based on a submission to authority – what Polanyi himself labelled the 'fiduciary framework'. In the context of what 'knowing' entails, trust comes before doubt, submission comes before emancipation and 'belief precedes knowing' (Mitchell, 2006: 69). The connection between believing and knowing is found in the role that the community plays in generating belief in the message that it seeks to convey (Mitchell, 2006: 69): 'Belief, of course, cannot exist except within a community.' This clearly shows that the connections between traditions, communities, trust, authority, and intellectual emancipation (that is, knowing) are found in an initial rejection of doubt, resulting in the eventual membership of a community. This membership entitles one to full initiation into a knowledge inheritance – a tradition, a way of acting that is passed on throughout time – which is otherwise inaccessible.

It seems, therefore, that Mitchell, in keeping with Polanyi, argues that the community is the catalyst of the perpetuation of traditions and practices, as well as that it assumes the responsibility of disseminating the authority to the representatives whom it sees as fit for purpose. In this sense, a community is a social convention committed to protecting traditions and practices, and it allocates authority to experts in order to control this process responsibly. It does this, however, with honourable intentions, and it always exercises a degree of responsibility and accountability, ever aware not to permit the oppression of genius or originality, even should it result in dissent from within its own ranks. The student, however, is expected to exercise a belief (or a trust, within Polanyi's fiduciary framework) in the community's representative: the teacher.

A community, under this definition, is a silent partner in the business of knowledge – a relationship that involves several other big players to make it possible. Indeed, the community requires traditions and practices that it seeks to portray. It requires a master teacher to control responsibly the flow of knowledge emanating from the practices and traditions in which the master himself or herself will educate those under his or her charge. It also needs a learner – a student: someone who is willing to *engage with* and *participate in* the traditions, under a submission to the authority of the master, aspiring to emulate the master and to become part of the community himself or herself. The community, however, is silent in the sense that it steps in only if the business is failing. Should its representative – the teacher – not be fulfilling his or her remit, that representative is contested accordingly. If truth is not pursued in its purest form and if the master oppresses originality in his or her teaching, he or she risks losing that status as a representative – and rightly so. If learners dissent without good cause, the community intervenes to protect its investment. It will shield its representatives from misinformed criticisms, and it does so with a collective and ominous battle cry. Its investment was in knowledge, traditions and practices, and its trust was in its representatives to protect this investment. The community will therefore protect its representatives in order to preserve itself. And this process all begins with *authority*.

The paradigmatic example: Learning how to speak

In preparing to write this part of the text, before I had undertaken my literature review, I considered the same example that Polanyi (and indeed others) had analysed himself many times throughout his literature. At the same time as being slightly disappointed at my naivety in thinking that I had considered a novel idea, I was pleased to read the work of an acclaimed scholar outlining the same concept that I had subjected to consideration myself.[7]

The paradigmatic example in question is the simple example of how a child learns to speak and use a language. The reason why I considered this example, as I am sure was the same for Polanyi, was the fact that language is developed, without questioning the foundations upon which it is acquired and used, in a way that does not permit doubt or reason – that is, it permits only *instinct* in its development.

Language, it seems, is something that children learn through close imitation of those whom they trust unquestionably. They do not, for example, question every word to which they listen; indeed, they would not have the requisite tools to do so, unless they were to accept the language to which they were exposed. Rather, children begin to use the language in the same way as they have heard it used either to them or around them. Indeed, according to Polanyi (1946: 43): '[T]he process of acquiring speech offers a good example for the principles by which the premises of thought are in general transmitted from one generation to the next. Speech is learned by intelligent imitation of the adult.' This notion of learning through trust is at the core of much of what I have discussed so far; the paradigmatic example of such a trust is found in language acquisition, development and use.

Polanyi founds the basis of language acquisition and development – in the same way as he founds the development of knowledge – in the learner's initial acknowledgement that there is something of worth to be learned and grasped. Indeed, Polanyi (1946: 44), speaking generally about knowledge, claims that 'any effort to understand something must be sustained by the belief that there is something there that can be understood'. This point is emphasized by the appeal to the paradigmatic example of language acquisition and development, to enforce the requirement of submission to authority in the *pursuit* of knowledge (Polanyi, 1946: 44): 'Its effort to learn to speak is prompted in the child by the conviction that speech means something.' In essence, therefore, the submission to authority finds its motive within the understanding that there is something of worth to be learned. If there were no such understanding, there would be no requirement for the student to submit to the master's authority.

However, in the example of learning to speak and master a language, the 'something of worth' is the requisite language skills that can be accumulated and acquired by an initial acknowledgement that the language to which the student is exposed is of worth to him or her. This acknowledgement, however, seems instinctive – that is, it is not subject to doubt or reason. Indeed, the child does not seem to question the usefulness of the language used by the language users around it; in fact, the child is, initially at least, incapable of doing so. Rather, the young child will examine closely, and tacitly, the language behaviours of the people to whom it is most exposed, and instinctively acknowledge the importance of mastering the language that they all seem to use. Initially, as a non-language-using being, this must be a peculiar process for the young child. However, the fact that almost all children learn how to speak – eventually – would suggest, if not prove, that such an acknowledgement must take place in the first instance.

The young, undeveloped child, as a human being who places survival as one of its primary aims, acknowledges that learning to speak is vital in being able to demand the things that it requires from those around it. This motivation gives language a worth, and it is this value of language to the child that ensures its undivided attention to the master (in this case, parents, guardians, older siblings and teachers, among others) in learning to speak this language that has assumed importance.

However, this understanding of the fact that there is something worth learning is only the beginning; there must also be an understanding, instinctive and intrinsic to a human being in his or her nature, which encourages the student to choose his or her masters carefully. That is, the choice of the master is not a random one: there is a trust upon which such a choice is based, and this trust is founded in *who* the master is. In the example of learning to master a language, the natural choice of such a master – indeed, perhaps the only choice – is the people to whom the student is most exposed in his or her early years: parents, older siblings and perhaps teachers during the early stages of formal schooling.

A rebellion against such authority would result in the child never developing the requisite language skills to engage with notions of doubt, reason and rationality further into its knowledge career; the student, rather unusually (indeed, perhaps inexplicably), seems to be aware of this. In developing language, the student is not equipped to reason and doubt, because the very notions of reason and doubt are open only to those who have the skills to articulate them in language that can be understood by others.[8]

Therefore the child instinctively submits to the master's authority in the development of language, aware – perhaps even certain – that it has no other option. The child does not subject the basis of the master's language to scrutiny, simply because it cannot. There is a belief that, because of the language that the master uses, there is a requirement that the child master the language itself. Indeed, as Mitchell (2006: 69) asserts: 'When a child learns a language, he believes (trusts) that the language-speakers who surround him are not uttering gibberish. Likewise, all skills require submission to a master because the novice does not yet comprehend what he is practicing.' Thus there is an instinctive understanding on the student's behalf that he or she must place trust in the authority of the master and in the practice of the language that the student seeks to learn, lest he or she face a situation in which the mastery of the language is forever beyond his or her ability. The master's actions and utterances implore his or her students to follow his or her lead in a process of close imitation and instinctive reaction. Polanyi (1946: 44) tells us that, in this way: 'Guided by its love and trust of its guardians, [the child] perceives the light of reason in [its masters'] eyes, voices and bearing and feels instinctively attracted towards the source of this light.

It is impelled to imitate – and understand better as it imitates further – these expressive actions of its adult guides.' That is, the child initially submits to a form of imitation in order to master what it initially does not comprehend in terms of language skills.

In this way, we can see the attraction of the paradigmatic example of language acquisition for our overall understanding of how knowledge can be developed. Polanyi uses this example effectively to emphasize the importance of a submission to authority, in that without such submission the student would fall into a quagmire of disarray and incomprehensibility.

As I have already outlined earlier in the text, Polanyi talks of a submission to authority as being the initial requirement for a student who seeks to pursue further knowledge. These notions seem always to be linked to our paradigmatic example of speech and language, by way of illustration. The attitude required for a student to develop knowledge, says Polanyi (1946: 45), 'is the same attitude as that of the child listening to its mother's voice and absorbing the meaning of speech. Both are based on an implicit belief in the significance and truth of the context which the learner is trying to master.' Indeed, as Polanyi (1946: 45) argues, 'a child could never learn to speak if it assumed that the words which are used in its hearing are meaningless'.

It seems, therefore, that there are two vitally important lessons to be learned from our paradigmatic example of language and speech development, and the analogy with knowledge development. First, language development requires an initial submission to authority of a master in a quest to understand what is initially incomprehensible to the student. Language, perhaps more than any other example, requires such a submission because the alternative – a rejection of the authority – would result in a situation in which the student attempted to question the master without the requisite language skills to do so. It is in this way that Polanyi talks of faith preceding reason, a claim that is irrefutable in the example of language development.

Secondly, Polanyi makes the point that, in developing the language just as in developing knowledge, there is an acknowledgement that the language (or the knowledge, generally speaking) is of worth, and the initial submission to the master's authority is the only choice if the student is to become accustomed to the practices that the master offers. Just as an innocent child listens to its mother's voice in the hope that, one day, it will be able to converse with her, the student must submit to the authority of his or her master in the hope that, one day, he or she will be able to contribute to the knowledge that the student hopes to develop under the master's supervision and guidance. In this way, trusting one's master seems to be the *only* option.[9]

Polanyi's 'theory of knowledge': A critique

So far, I have outlined precisely how Polanyi views knowledge development – that is, precisely how knowledge is built and constructed by an individual. This process, I have shown, is a process that begins with a submission to the authority of a master expert: a teacher. Knowledge is then, according to Polanyi, developed in such a way that any challenge to the authority of the master, and the practices and traditions from which he or she comes, is encouraged only in the name of the purest version of truth and knowledge. In this way, there is always a need for the student's submission to the authority of the master, even into the university years, although quasi-independence is the eventual aim – that is, an independence that requires the student to submit only to the authority of the tradition with which he or she will, at the final stage of his or her education, be aligned:

> School ... imparts a facility ... to indicate the established doctrine ... The University tries to bring this knowledge to life ... It also imparts the beginnings of ... judgement[10] by teaching the practice ... But a full initiation into the premises ... can be gained only by the few who possess the gifts for becoming independent ... and they usually achieve it only through close personal association with the intimate views and practice of a distinguished master.
>
> (Polanyi, 1946: 43)

Thus far, however, I have said nothing about what Polanyi discusses in relation to the nature of knowledge itself – that is, I have not outlined what Polanyi suggests knowledge is made of or what its constituent parts are. There is a subtle distinction between how knowledge is acquired and what knowledge actually is. Of course, the nature of knowledge and how it is constructed will play at least some part in how one proposes that it may be successfully developed and eventually acquired. Indeed, the converse of this statement seems also to be true: the way in which knowledge may be successfully developed may well tell us a certain amount about how knowledge is constructed.

Polanyi dedicated significant amounts of his time and effort to developing a 'theory of knowledge'. In this theory, he considered both of these questions – namely, what is knowledge and how is it constructed, and what is the best way in which to develop knowledge? I have dealt sufficiently with Polanyi's accounts of knowledge development in the text so far; I need now to consider the question of what knowledge is and how it is constructed.

Polanyi seems to have developed – perhaps even pioneered – a new brand of knowledge theory that encompasses two main aspects: so-called 'tacit knowledge' and 'explicit knowledge'. As I will outline in more detail later in this section, tacit knowledge seems to be the bedrock upon which explicit, articulated knowledge is built. This concept of explicit knowledge founded in tacit knowledge is the basis upon which Polanyi (1983: 4) claimed that 'we know more than we can tell'. Indeed, by founding articulated knowledge within a setting of knowledge that cannot be spoken of – so-called 'tacit knowledge' – we grasp the setting of which Polanyi is speaking in making such a claim.

At first glance, Polanyi's claim seems intuitive. Indeed, we do appear to have more knowledge at our disposal than that of which we can possibly speak. Even in considering the notion of our paradigmatic example of language, a child learns to speak the language before it has mastered the rules of the language itself. Furthermore, many extremely successful language users – people with extreme articulacy – may, in fact, have only a comparatively limited grasp of the linguistic rules of their language. In this sense, they know more than they can tell. Should a strange sceptic request an explanation of such a person's articulacy and linguistic ability, that person would be stumped. Even in my own case, as a vaguely accomplished mathematician, were I to be asked to provide articulated evidence of my ability to solve a certain problem in an area of mathematics – say, in the simple case of a simple addition – I could offer little other than some examples of addition that I may recall as paradigmatic examples and thereby display to my challenger that I was able to complete them without difficulty. I could offer no explanation other than that 'I know' how to complete the sums. In precisely this way, I know more about addition than I can ever possibly articulate.

In terms of Polanyi's theory of knowledge, I can be said to have a bedrock of tacit, inarticulate knowledge of addition, which has permitted the building of explicit, demonstrable knowledge on top of it. In relation to such a view of how knowledge is constructed and developed, I find myself agreeing with Polanyi's sentiment, but remain uncomfortable with his choice of knowledge structure and his choice of words used to describe such a structure. By positioning tacit knowledge as the bedrock, Polanyi fails to resolve the foundationless knowledge problem, outlined earlier in the book – that is, rather than creating a dichotomy of knowledge that comprises tacit and explicit components, Polanyi seems to create a knowledge *hierarchy*, which induces the same problems as Aristotle created by means of his foundations of perception and memory. Polanyi is right to distinguish between knowledge that can be articulated (explicit) and knowledge that cannot be articulated (tacit) – but he is veering down the same path as many of his predecessors by placing tacit knowledge at the foundation of explicit knowledge. We do, indeed, know more than we can tell – but this does not mean that what we cannot 'tell' rests at the root of all other knowledge.

However, setting aside this minor disagreement, let us proceed on the grounds that we accept Polanyi's distinction between tacit and explicit knowledge, and share his belief that we know more than we can tell. The argument that tacit knowledge rest underneath explicit knowledge and acts as its foundation is questionable, in that it does not serve to bring us any nearer to a solution of the Aristotelian problem. Nevertheless, this problem will be dealt with later in the book, and it is precisely the reason why I must cite Oakeshott and, eventually, Wittgenstein. We must, however, find a way of refuting our knowledge sceptic, who might contest that what we think is tacit knowledge is, in fact, a collection of concealed, innate rules, stored within the skull, which, despite being beyond our articulation, are accessible to an omniscient being who has access to the inner workings of our minds.

Tacit knowledge or guided by rules?

To be clear, a sceptic might contest that Polanyi's attempt at constructing a 'theory' of knowledge is insufficient. Indeed, Polanyi posits that tacit knowledge cannot be articulated by definition, because of its very nature as 'tacit' – that is, that such knowledge cannot be written in the form of rules or rule-like propositions. But the natural contestation to such a claim would be: 'What makes tacit knowledge "tacit" and how can we be sure that what we think is tacit is in fact so?' This challenge by our 'tacit' sceptic is tough to avoid – that is, it is indeed a legitimate point to note that even if *I* cannot articulate *my* tacit knowledge foundations, this does not point to the fact that I am not being guided by some internal mechanism. In other words, perhaps what Polanyi offers as 'tacit' knowledge is nothing other than a collection of innate inner rules that guide us towards knowledge development. In such a view of things, perhaps the omniscient being, who has access to the inner workings of my mind, could find an inner rule or rule-like proposition that guides my practice and explains my ability to solve mathematical problems, or my ability to use language, despite *my* being unable to explain how I can do these things. In Polanyi's take on 'tacit' knowledge foundations, my being unable to articulate such knowledge does not mean that it is *unintelligible* to think of this knowledge as beyond articulation; rather, it is beyond *me* to articulate such knowledge. In such a view of knowledge construction, the sceptic might contest that there needs to be more stringent philosophical evidence that, in fact, such tacit knowledge is beyond articulation – that is, that it is beyond being put into rules or rule-like propositions.

To ensure that we are justified in adopting Polanyi's claim that 'we know more than we can tell', we must establish that tacit knowledge does indeed exist. To prove its existence, it suffices to show that not all knowledge can be written in the form of rules and rule-like propositions. Indeed, if not all knowledge can be written as rules, then there must exist some kind of knowledge that cannot be written as a rule and such knowledge would be by definition tacit knowledge. So we must set about proving that not all knowledge can be written in the form of rules or rule-like propositions.

A proof by contradiction

The proof that we require for the existence of tacit knowledge is most easily articulated using 'proof by contradiction'. A description of this proof technique can be found in any basic logic text or any text about basic propositional calculus. Essentially, we will begin by supposing that the hypothesis we want to prove (that tacit knowledge exists) is, in fact, *not* true. We will then show that, on the basis of this hypothesis, we arrive at a contradiction. We will then conclude that the only point at which there was a flaw in the logic that resulted in a contradiction was in our original hypothesis itself, and so it must have been a flawed premise. We will use this technique later in this section to prove that tacit knowledge does indeed exist.

The fabric of tacit knowledge means that we cannot put such knowledge into the form of rules or rule-like propositions – that is, knowledge that is 'tacit' is so because it is demonstrated (in our actions, for example) rather than articulated. This led Polanyi to contest, as has already been outlined, that we know more than we can tell. As I have already argued, I concur that we do indeed know more than we can tell, but I reject Polanyi's attempt to delve further into the knowledge picture, pulling apart tacit knowledge to rest beneath the explicit knowledge that can be articulated and reasoned. To be clear, Polanyi did little to fend off the sceptic who would contest that tacit knowledge is an illusion; I aim to do that over the next few sections. Furthermore, whatever knowledge *is* housed inside cannot itself be another form of knowledge, tacit or otherwise. Indeed, what Polanyi posits seems to be based on one fundamental error: he creates a hierarchy of knowledge, by distinguishing between 'tacit' and 'explicit' knowledge in such a way that one is rooted inside the other. Such a hierarchy gives rise to the infinite regress problem inherent in other accounts of knowledge development.[11]

We do not disagree with Polanyi that we know more than we can tell. Therefore, as a consequence, we concur that there are elements of knowledge that *we* cannot articulate. In essence, there are parts of our knowledge that cannot be 'propositionalized'. But this does not mean that we can conclude, as Polanyi does, that 'tacit' knowledge is the foundation of 'explicit' knowledge. Nevertheless, in exposing the true extent of the inadequacy of Polanyi's hierarchy of knowledge construction beyond that for which I have already argued, I beg the reader's patience. Indeed, the details of why we should depart from Polanyi at this stage are made clear when I invoke Oakeshott's take on knowledge development, and Wittgenstein's distinction between knowledge and certainty. The concept of 'tacit' knowledge as the bedrock of explicit knowledge is marked as 'read' and rejected on the basis of subsequent arguments.[12]

For a brief prelude to these arguments, note that the shortcoming in Polanyi's knowledge theory is that tacit knowledge is at the basis and that it remains unclear how tacit knowledge is developed or how it can be distinguished from explicit knowledge. It is insufficient to outline, as Polanyi does, that tacit knowledge is simply knowledge that we cannot articulate in the same manner as we can explicit knowledge – that is, that whereas explicit knowledge can be reasoned and built using rules and propositions (together with inductive and deductive reasoning), tacit knowledge, according to Polanyi, lacks this construction. It is tacit simply because it is beyond reason, and because it requires faith and imitation. There is no doubt that this model is appealing and intuitive, and indeed it has some merit – but it fails to sidestep the problem of foundationalism in that it cannot distinguish between the knowledge foundation and the building that rests upon it sufficiently well to fend off the sceptic who claims that tacit knowledge is, for example, simply a collection of innate rules. Indeed, tacit knowledge is, for all intents and purposes, still knowledge; the fact that I cannot articulate such knowledge hardly makes it a sufficient candidate for the foundations of all *other* (that is, explicit) knowledge. Knowledge is knowledge is knowledge; describing it as 'tacit' and arguing that it cannot be articulated needs more detailed philosophical analysis.[13]

Let us return, then, to proving that tacit knowledge does, in fact, exist. We need to prove that tacit knowledge is, in fact, beyond being put into the form of rules and rule-like propositions. In doing so, we will dispense with the knowledge sceptic, who might argue that what Polanyi thought was 'tacit' knowledge is instead a collection of innate guiding rules that hide somewhere in the skull (the mind or brain?), and the tacit nature of which is simply a problem for us as inarticulate beasts, but the details of which can be accessed by the omniscient being.

There is a standard argument against such a view of things, which is captured by various authors throughout the core and secondary literature on this discussion. This argument is generally labelled the 'rule-following paradox', pioneered in the first instance by Wittgenstein and commented on in a raft of secondary literature that would merit a book in itself. Rather than retell a story that has been told many times over, I will offer the reader a glimpse of the core elements of the rule-following argument, to ensure that the integrity of the arguments put forward in this book is not compromised. The applicability of the rule-following paradox to this discussion, however, is clear: it dispenses with the notion that we are guided by rules (innate or otherwise) *in their own right* – that is, that even the omniscient being looking into our minds can find no reason or rule that explains our 'tacit' knowledge.

The rule-following paradox

The statement that best captures Wittgenstein's paradox is found in his *Philosophical Investigations* (2009: §201): 'This was our paradox: no course of action could be determined by a rule, because every course of action can be brought into accord with the rule.' This paradox is pertinent for the purposes of our discussion since it makes clear the difficulty in holding the view that a rule *in itself* can guide. Wittgenstein's paradox consequently highlights the inevitable and inherent difficulties with adopting that knowledge can be made up entirely of rules. Indeed, if all knowledge is constructed of rules and rule-like propositions, and rules in themselves cannot guide, then we would never be able to move beyond the information that we are given at point of origin. However, since it is clear that we can go beyond information that is provided to us in the first instance (the genesis of our knowledge, so to speak), to apply it and to use it in different contexts from those that we have previously encountered, it follows that there is an element of knowledge that is not contained in rules and rule-like propositions.

The salient points of this argument are made clear in various accounts of the so-called 'rule-following argument', of which I will consider but a few. Once again, the details of this argument can be found in various items of secondary literature,[14] as well as in Wittgenstein (2009: §§134–242). Consider, for example, Kripke (1982: 14), who invokes the omniscient being, as I have earlier in this chapter, when he claims that 'whatever "looking into my mind" may be, the sceptic asserts that even if God were to do it, He still could not determine [why I can go beyond the information given]'. This leads Kripke to conclude that we follow rules at random. This is not the conclusion of this book; rather, as I will show in the next few paragraphs and over the remainder of the book, we are constrained by our training and the authority of the master whose manner we have decided to imitate – and this constraint gives rise to *an impression* of determinism. We are constrained to the cusp of determinacy by our training and our submission to the authority of the master expert, whose judgement we hope to assimilate. Whatever the 'contents' of my mind might be, such judgement cannot be propositionalized or put into rule form, and so it can never be found there. Judgement is found in interactions and in the learner's imitation of his or her master. As I will conclude later, the consequence of this argument is that to remove the teacher as the guiding arbiter of correctness is to remove the intelligibility of moving beyond the information that we absorb from the transmission of facts, rules and propositions. That is, without a judgement, a rule is inert, static and essentially useless – it cannot guide and it permits no movement – whereas judgement, developed through close imitation of the teacher, creates a freedom and breathes life into the information that we amass throughout our engagements in life.

To be clear, a reasonable question to ask would be: 'How can pupils take a finite list of examples from their teacher and go on in the same way?' One of the most prominent philosophers to argue that a rule is underdetermined by a finite list of examples was Leibniz. He argued that any finite number of examples can be *interpreted* in an indefinite number of ways to accord with any rule. In some sense, he argues that, given a finite list of examples, there is no rational way in which to separate a 'correct' manner to 'go on in the same way' from an 'incorrect' manner. This, as an idea, would surely make teaching and learning impossible. Anscombe (1985: 342–3) outlines this difficulty by way of example:

> Although an intelligence tester may suppose that there is only one possible continuation to the sequence 2, 4, 6, 8, . . ., mathematical and philosophical sophisticates know that an indefinite number of rules (. . .) are compatible with any such finite initial segment. So if the tester urges me to respond, after, 2, 4, 6, 8, . . ., with *the* unique appropriate next number, the proper response is that no such unique number exists.

Consider the difficulties that this provides for the teacher who is intent on teaching the concept of even numbers to the class. When he or she asks for the students to 'go on in the same way', the teacher must concede from a purely rational point of view that any number the pupil provides as the next term in the sequence 2, 4, 6, 8, . . ., is correct under *some* interpretation of his or her instruction. No *unique* rule can be made to fit the finite list of examples that the teacher provided in his or her teaching. The problem, however, appears to arise when the process of learning is considered to be purely rational. As Panjvani (2008: 307) outlines: 'The idea here is that instructions for following a rule underdetermine the correct way to follow the rule.' If rule-following is regarded as a rational activity, it would follow that the pupil must have some process for eliminating the infinite array of 'incorrect' answers if he or she is to provide the 'correct' answer as the teacher requests.

In the example of the even numbers, if a pupil is asked to 'go on in the same way', but there is no apparently logically sound way in which to evaluate the 'correct' next term, how is teaching – even in its simplest of forms – possible? It cannot be argued logically that there is any one connection between the teacher's instructions and the child arriving at the answer that the teacher 'expects'. As Wright (2001: 98) outlines: 'Finite behaviour cannot constrain its interpretation to within uniqueness.'

As I noted earlier, Malcolm (1986: 156) suggests why this logical loophole rarely raises its ugly head by offering the following observation: 'If there was no *we* – if there was no agreement among those who have had the same training, as to what are the correct steps in particular cases when following a rule – then there would be no *wrong steps*, or indeed any *right steps*.' That is, without consensus, teaching is impossible, and since there is a general way that is accepted to be the 'correct' way to follow given rules, it is rarely an issue when the teacher tells the class to 'go on in the same way'.

It is also strangely tempting to suggest that students more often than not interpret the finite list of examples in the same way as does the teacher, because the student in some way selects the 'simplest rule' to fit the examples provided. There are, however, glaring difficulties even with this simple attempt to salvage 'theories' of learning. For example, Turing's 'halting algorithm' and Gödel's 'incompleteness theorems' prove that, in fact, a 'simplest rule' does not exist (Chaitin, 2007). The argument here is also related to the previous section: if a 'simplest rule' were to exist – and, indeed, if it were possible for students somehow to select this 'simplest rule' – this would infer that the pupil had compared the infinite list of possible rules that fit the finite examples provided by the teacher, eliminated all of the 'more complicated' rules and settled on what the pupil deemed to be the 'simplest rule'. This, of course, invokes a result that is contradictory of what was refuted in the previous paragraph and therefore the error in the logic must have occurred with the assumption that a 'simplest rule' exists. Chaitin (2007: 120–1, emphasis original) outlines this idea succinctly in his account of algorithmic information theory:

> Let's say I have a particular calculation, a particular output, that I'm interested in, and that I have this nice, small computer program that calculates it, and I think that it's the smallest program, the most concise one that produces this output. Maybe a few friends of mine and I were

trying to do it, and this was the best program that we came up with; nobody did any better. But how can you be **sure**? Well, the answer is that **you can't be sure**. It turns out you can **never** be sure! You can never be sure that a computer program is what I like to call *elegant*, namely that it's the most concise one that produces the output that it does. **Never, ever!**

In summary, the rule-following paradox invoked in this instance outlines one glaring problem that is pertinent to the argument that will follow – namely, that rules *in themselves* do not guide a pupil beyond the information given. Moreover, a finite list of examples can be made to accord with any rule, and so, unless there were *some other* facet of knowledge that is transmitted during teaching, then it would be impossible ever to move beyond the information that is given to us at point of origin. Given that this is not the case and that we are able to move beyond a finite list of examples to yield highly 'determined' outputs, the explanation must lie elsewhere – that is, there must be some other guiding feature that does not exist in the locality of the learner.

Concluding the proof by contradiction

Let us return, then, and use this rule-following paradox in our proof by contradiction to demonstrate that tacit knowledge does indeed exist. Let us assume, in aiming towards finding a contradiction in our assumption, that tacit knowledge does not exist. It follows, then, that all knowledge can be articulated – that is, that all knowledge can be written in the form of rules or rule-like propositions. Note that this means that, for the moment, we are assuming that even the things that *seem* to be beyond *our* articulation are, in fact, a collection of rules that are stored, say, in the mind or brain and which could be accessed by the omniscient being. Now that all knowledge has been propositionalized, we reach our conceptual conundrum: if all knowledge comprises rules or rule-like propositions, and rules cannot guide *in themselves* (owing to the rule-following paradox outlined in the previous section), how can we ever go beyond the information transmitted to us at point of origin? That is, rules do not guide, and we have assumed that all knowledge can be written in terms of rules and rule-like propositions; therefore we must conclude that it is never possible to go beyond the information to which we are exposed. But this is clearly absurd and thus we have reached our contradiction; it therefore follows, by contradiction, that not all knowledge can be articulated in the form of rules and rule-like propositions – that is, that there exists some knowledge that is indeed tacit.

This conclusion is pertinent for the purposes of this book, because the development of what Polanyi calls 'tacit knowledge', as I will demonstrate later, is entirely dependent on the authority of the master expert, whose *judgement* and guidance leads towards the construction of tacit knowledge. To truly develop an element of knowledge that is beyond articulation (what Oakeshott might call 'judgement', as I will show later), the pupil is required to submit to the authority of the master teacher, to imitate his or her ways, and to adopt his or her mannerisms. Such insight is precisely the nature of tacit knowledge: insight that is beyond articulation and which cannot be propositionalized, but which is key to enabling the pupil to go beyond the information that he or she is given. This is why *following* a rule and *acting in accordance with* a rule are different. Following a rule requires judgement and insight; acting in accordance with a rule does not. This led Wittgenstein (2009: §202) to conclude: 'That's why "following a rule" is a practice. And to *think* one is following is rule is not to follow a rule. And that's why it's not possible to follow a rule "privately"; otherwise, thinking one was following a rule would be the same thing as following it.' Rules *in themselves* cannot guide. The fullest development of knowledge requires the development of a form of tacit knowledge, a judgement, which opens the pupil's eyes to a world of applications of the information that is at his or her disposal.

Back to Polanyi

To return from this minor digression, it appears that, for the purposes of our discussion, this is all that we require from Polanyi's theory of knowledge – although he does go on to explain precisely how he believes such tacit and explicit knowledge is constructed, and outlines in explicit detail of what knowledge is constructed.[15] For the moment, however, the discussion of tacit knowledge and explicit knowledge permits us to go in search of alternative answers, because it is here that I pull away from Polanyi's explanations of knowledge.

By founding explicit knowledge inside tacit knowledge, Polanyi has once again induced a crypto-version of the Aristotelian problem. In Polanyi's theory of knowledge, the only stage further that he seems to have progressed than Aristotle himself is to replace Aristotle's 'first-principles' with tacit knowledge. Where Aristotle founded his 'first-principles' in the faculties of perception and memory, Polanyi founds his notion of tacit knowledge in the faculties of so-called 'subsidiary' and 'focal' awareness. However, this is an unappealing solution to the problem, because the only distinction between tacit knowledge and explicit knowledge is that one can be articulated and one cannot. However, aside from this difference, knowledge is still knowledge, tacit or explicit. In failing to make a more distinguishable (that is, categorial) contrast between what is at the foundations of knowledge and what is built upon the foundations, Polanyi has reverted to type. Rather than solve the problem of knowledge founded in knowledge, his theory redresses it in a crypto-version of the same problem, still crippled by the same inadequacies. Indeed, Polanyi's theory of knowledge, no matter how intuitive or appealing, still seems to fail to draw a distinguishable difference between the foundations and the building. Although his claim of 'knowing more than we can tell' seems to be intuitively true (and has now been proven to be conceptually true, following the proof by contradiction), the apparent deduction from this claim that tacit knowledge is at the base of all knowledge seems far-fetched and unappealing. Indeed, the problem still arises that tacit knowledge is still knowledge and seems only to be different in *kind* from so-called 'explicit knowledge'.

Perhaps the foundations of our knowledge edifice are the components that simply cannot be articulated. This idea will be discussed later in the book, in Chapter 8 in particular. To be clear, however, Polanyi seemed to be working towards a solution in noticing that there are elements of the knowledge edifice that are beyond explicitness – that is, that there are clearly elements of knowledge that we 'know', but which we cannot express. Not everything in our knowledge repertoire can be put into words, rules or propositions. So tacit knowledge has its place – but it is not at the foundations of the knowledge picture. As we will see in the next chapter, Oakeshott makes Polanyi's attempts at describing the construction of knowledge somewhat clearer by developing a dichotomy – rather than a hierarchy – of knowledge components, both of which are needed to avoid ignorance, but only one of which is explicit and propositional. As for the foundationalist problem that is still a feature of Polanyi's attempted solution (and to which Oakeshott makes no contribution), it is for this reason that I will cite Wittgenstein later in the text, because Wittgenstein seems to have found a solution that avoids the potential of foundationless knowledge in his famous 'knowledge–certainty' categorial distinction.

6 OAKESHOTT ON AUTHORITY

Next in line for consideration is another major commentator on the notions of authority and training within education: Michael Oakeshott. In many of his writings, Oakeshott is an author who strikes a chord with the issues most important to the discussion at hand; his handling of educational issues is no different. His most significant contribution to the matters within educational discourse appears in his book *The Voice of Liberal Learning* (2001), a text in which Oakeshott outlines many of the components of education that he believes to be instrumental in delivering a high-quality education system.

For the purposes of this discussion on authority, however, it is Oakeshott's views on two main concepts in which I am particularly interested: first, on the collective concepts of teaching and learning; and secondly, on the role that these processes play in the development of knowledge, founded in an understanding of how knowledge is constructed. It will become clearer later in this chapter – a chapter dedicated to Oakeshott's writings – precisely why these two concepts are of concern to us. To begin with, however, I need to outline the key definitions of familiar terms as they appear in Oakeshott's writings – particularly, the concepts of 'teaching', 'learning', 'information', 'judgement' and, subsequently, 'knowledge'.

Teaching and learning: Oakeshott's definition

Oakeshott sets out definitions of teaching and learning in typical fashion, using unapologetically restrictive language. He discards the nonsense that at times engulfs an understanding of the terms 'teaching' and 'learning', and restricts these notions to typically deflationary definitions. In doing so, he makes clear why there is an inherent need within the processes of teaching and learning for the learner to act under the guidance of the more learned teacher.

Let me begin by setting out the terms of what is encompassed under the term 'learning' according to Oakeshott. First, Oakeshott opens the chapter of *The Voice of Liberal Learning* dedicated to teaching and learning with a rather broad and sweeping definition of what he suggests learning entails:

> Learning is a comprehensive engagement in which we come to know ourselves and the world around us. It is a paradoxical activity: it is doing and submitting at the same time. And its achievements range from merely being aware, to what may be called understanding and being able to explain.
>
> In each of us, it begins at birth; it takes place not in some abstract world, but in the local world we inhabit; for the individual it terminates only in death, for a civilization it ends in the collapse of the characteristic manner of life, and for the race it is, in principle, interminable.
>
> (Oakeshott, 2001: 35)

This definition of learning encompasses a wide range of concepts. Learning is an engagement that happens, according to this definition, on three levels of any society – namely, the individual level, the civilization level and the race level. That is, individuals engage in learning themselves, but there is also an allowance for entire groups – and indeed the entire race – to engage with learning as a process. It seems important, also, that Oakeshott makes a distinction between 'doing' and 'submitting' in his definition of learning, while also pointing out that these activities, paradoxically, seem to happen at the same time within the learning process.

The 'doing' to which Oakeshott is making reference in this instance is related to the idea of an active engagement with the practices to which we are hoping to become accustomed. Learning in this manner encourages the development of a type of knowledge that Oakeshott calls 'judgement'. This judgement, however, is accompanied by another equally indispensable facet of knowledge that Oakeshott calls 'information', which seems to be linked to the other aspect of learning, 'submitting'. It is this submission that is inextricably linked to the notion of authority and training. In this version of learning, a submission to the authority of the teacher – an indispensable partner of the learner – along with a submission to the practices and traditions that the learner hopes to grasp are inescapable facets of the learning process.

Finally, and perhaps most importantly in this definition, Oakeshott outlines that learning as an activity is an 'interminable' feature of the human race – that is, it can *never* be dispensed with. Indeed, it seems intuitive that the human race will never reach a day on which there is *nothing* else to learn. In this way, learning can never be made completely redundant.

Moreover, inherent in any form of learning seems to be an element of practice – that is, of repeated action under the guidance of a teacher. Conversely, Oakeshott argues, almost every performance worth mentioning involves some form of learning. Indeed (Oakeshott, 2001: 35): '[L]earning itself often entails practicing what we have in some sense learned already, and there is probably a component of learning in every notable performance. Moreover, some activities, like intellectual inquiries, remain always activities of learning.' Therefore, for Oakeshott, learning is an important activity that is at the core of all pursuits and performances worth a mention. Furthermore, this definition of learning is something that he believes distinguishes human beings from other animals. Oakeshott (2001: 35–6) argues that learning is 'an activity possible only to an intelligence of choice and self-direction in relation to his own impulses and to the world around him. These, of course, are pre-eminently human characteristics, and, as I understand it, only human beings are capable of learning.' It is in this way that I have described Oakeshott's definition of learning as 'restrictive'. Indeed, many might disagree that only human beings can learn. However, under Oakeshott's definition, true learning is an activity that is restricted to the domain of human beings, given their superior intellectual capabilities. Moreover, it is under this definition that learning acquires a new significance in terms of its requirement that there be a teacher under whose guidance learning can take place. Perhaps this is the reason why Oakeshott is so restrictive in his definition and understanding of what is meant by 'learning' in its purest of forms.

It is interesting, then, how Oakeshott (2001: 36) develops this definition of learning as 'conduct' as opposed to learning as mere 'behaviour': 'Learning concerns conduct, not behaviour. In short, these analogies of clay and wax, of receptacles to be filled and empty rooms to be furnished, have nothing to do with learning and learners.' In subjecting this definition to my own consideration, I initially struggled to distinguish what Oakeshott might have meant by invoking such a contrast, particularly with reference to how conduct and behaviour apply to the notion of learning. It is, however, clear within the subtleties of Oakeshott's definition why that contrast is required; these subtleties manifest themselves when one considers the difference between what 'conduct' and 'behaviour' mean in their applications to learning. Behaviour is an action focused only on doing; conduct, on the other hand, seems to focus on two dimensions in equal measure – namely, what is done and the reason for doing it. It is therefore Oakeshott's contention that learning is concerned not only with doing, but also with *why* one might *choose* to act in this way. Learning as conduct therefore involves not only an action, but also an understanding and justification of one's actions. And this understanding is founded in a trust in one's teacher.

Furthermore, learning as conduct requires the teacher as the leader to set a foundation if the learner is to be justified in pursuing a certain action. In contrast, learning as behaviour requires no teacher, since it is an action without any moral implications. Perhaps most significantly, in defining learning as conduct as opposed to mere behaviour, Oakeshott subtly induces the need for a educationally moral agent, the teacher, for who else is better placed to ensure that there is a moral accompaniment for the pupil's actions, to rebrand learning from mere behaviour into behaviour founded in appropriated constructs – that is, to ensure that learning is *conduct*? It is the definition of learning as conduct, therefore, which forces the need for such a moral agent, a teacher, who can guide behaviours into appropriately constructed conducts. In this way, Oakeshott also disregards the notion that learners are pliable entities who can be described by means of analogies with 'clay and wax' and 'rooms to be furnished'. Such analogies describe behaviours and the pliability of behaviours, and, as such, are not befitting of the nature of learning as conduct rather than behaviour.

On the basis of this definition, we can found a definition for the accompaniment to learning – namely, 'teaching'. Rather loosely, Oakeshott (2001: 36) defines teaching as 'a practical activity in which a "learned" person (to use an archaism) "learns" his pupils'. This definition, for me, is a particularly poignant definition of teaching that inextricably links the activities of teaching and learning. It highlights also the intrinsic need for a teacher – the 'learned' person – and, of course, the need for a pupil in these two processes; through the connections between the teacher and the pupil, this definition sets the boundaries for teaching and learning as linked processes.

Such a definition of teaching may seem overtly traditional in its educational nature. Indeed, teaching in the modern day seems to have encompassed an entirely larger remit than the one outlined in this instance by Oakeshott. However, such an extension of the remit of teaching as an activity in the modern day is only to undermine – and, indeed, potentially damage – the process of teaching in its purest form. Teaching simply is as Oakeshott describes it; it is nothing else. This simple definition of teaching permits only the most deflationary understanding of what is meant by 'teaching' and permits no other jargon to infest on the activity, ensuring that the integrity of the process is not compromised. Under such a deflationary understanding of teaching, the process assumes a new significance. Indeed, the definition emphasizes the need for the only two key stakeholders in the process: the teacher and the pupil. Such a definition systematically, yet subtly, removes the need for any other resources within teaching other than the 'learned' person. It places an overwhelming importance on the role of the teacher and a responsibility on the shoulders of the pupil. And it describes the simple, yet beautiful, process whereby the pupil is invited to understand the ways of his or her master, the teacher. It is in this definition that we find where Oakeshott tacitly outlines the need for authority in the teaching process: the pupil must submit to the authority of the 'learned' person under such a definition of teaching if that pupil is ever to hope to become 'learned' himself or herself. But this process, as Oakeshott describes it, is a 'practical' process, inducing the need for an active participation and an active engagement between the 'learned' teacher and the pupil.

It is also interesting to note that Oakeshott does not permit teaching oneself – say, from books or observations or experiences – to be considered true teaching. He does not deny that one can *learn* from such resources or activities, but seems at pains to deny that such resources and activities can be described as being capable of *teaching*:

No doubt one may properly be said to learn from books, from gazing at the sky or from listening to the waves (so long as one's disposition is that mixture of activity and submission we call curiosity), but to say that the book, the sky or the sea has taught us anything, or that we have taught ourselves, is to speak in the language of unfortunate metaphor.

(Oakeshott, 2001: 36)

In this way, Oakeshott is encouraging us not to fall prey to considering teaching as a metaphor at the cost of understanding what teaching really is. He is outlining that teaching and learning do not always overlap. He seems to be suggesting that the activity of teaching is reserved for a special form of learning, which requires a 'learned' teacher to direct the process. Learning, on the other hand, is a process that can take place either as a result of teaching or as a result of some other engagement with a reliable resource, such as a book, or through one's own experience of some worldly event. However, the latter form of learning is not linked in any way to teaching – that is, the resources of the activities or worldly experiences are incapable of teaching. The process of teaching is reserved specifically for the teacher. It is in this way that Oakeshott emphasizes the teacher as a pivotal figure in the teaching process and the learning that comes as a result of this teaching.

Oakeshott (2001: 36) further distinguishes between teaching and learning when he claims that 'the counterpart of the teacher is not the learner in general, but the pupil'. In making such a claim, he distinguishes between a 'learner' and a 'pupil'. A learner seems, quite obviously, to be someone who learns, with no restrictions or stipulations placed on *how* he or she may have learned; the pupil, in contrast, is someone who has been *taught* and who has learned only as a result of his or her being taught. This therefore makes the pupil a special type of learner who has learned from the process of submission to his or her teacher's authority in the hope of becoming 'learned' like that teacher.

In acknowledging the difference between a learner and a pupil, Oakeshott once again places a subtle emphasis on the importance of the teacher, and the authority that he or she simply must command for such teaching and learning to take place. In this engagement with teaching and subsequent learning, the teacher is the person with insight and, as such, is the person with the requisite tools to guide the pupil under his or her charge. Should the pupil choose to accept and submit to the authority of the teacher in this instance, the pupil can hope to become learned himself or herself. However, should the pupil choose to rebel against the authority of the teacher, he or she reverts from the state of pupil to that of learner and will never be taught. Indeed, in such an instance of rebellion, the pupil would consequently reject teaching itself (by rejecting the teacher), and would instead be guided only by books, activities and worldly experiences – resources to which the now-learner would merely attach his or her own 'non-learned' interpretation, without the guidance of a 'learned' master. The teacher, accompanied by the authority that his or her position should naturally command, therefore holds the key to a pupil becoming 'learned'.

The process of learning, for Oakeshott, is a process the essence of which is not to be undermined or undervalued. He gives it a proud place, describing it as an inheritance that is to be embraced by pupils by means of their teacher's guidance and support. He argues that '[e]very human being is born an heir to an inheritance to which he can succeed only in the process of learning' (Oakeshott, 2001: 37). Oakeshott (2001: 37) expands this notion of inheritance, to give a particular significance to the process of learning, in light of what the inheritance encompasses: 'What every man is born an heir to is an inheritance of human achievements; an inheritance of feelings, emotions, images, visions, thoughts, beliefs, ideas, understandings, intellectual and practical enterprises, languages, relationships, organizations, canons and maxims of conduct, procedures, rituals, skills, works of art, books, musical compositions, tools, artifacts and utensils.' In light of this variety of priceless commodities encompassed by the inheritance and given that this inheritance is embraced through the process of learning, this statement highlights the importance of learning. Indeed, to inherit the concepts of feelings, emotions, images, and so on, one must submit to the process of learning them. Thus Oakeshott (2001: 38) asserts: 'This world can be entered, possessed and enjoyed only in a process of learning. A "picture" may be purchased, but one cannot purchase an understanding of it.'

Therefore learning is the process that ensures that we are capable of embracing an inheritance of riches, passed down from previous generations, and true learning follows as a result of teaching. In this way, the teacher plays an important – indeed indispensable – role in the pupil embracing his or her inheritance. This is why Oakeshott has appealed to the rather apt metaphor of purchasing a picture of the world: in purchasing a picture, the individual may seem dissatisfied by his or her lack of understanding of the picture itself. This understanding cannot be bought; it can only be attained through the process of learning. Analogously, to truly embrace and understand one's inheritance, one must submit to the superior mastery of one's teacher, to ensure that one's world picture is accompanied by an appropriate understanding. To acknowledge that we have an inheritance worth embracing 'is the only way of becoming a human being, and to inhabit it is to be a human being' (Oakeshott, 2001: 38). It is our essence – our entire human instinct – to embrace and become part of our inheritance, and we do so through the process of learning.

Oakeshott then develops this idea of inheritance further, referring to the idea of our inheritance of knowledge as a *geistige Welt*, or a 'spiritual world', into which the young child – even in its infancy and early childhood – has a desire to be initiated. It is in this description of the inheritance, however, that Oakeshott reinforces the importance of the role of the teacher in the child's desire for initiation into the spiritual world of knowledge. Indeed, '[i]t is into this *geistige Welt* that the child, even in its earliest adventures in awareness, initiates itself; and to initiate its pupils into it is the business of the teacher' (Oakeshott, 2001: 38). The teacher therefore is the pivotal character in leading the child to fulfil its desire of being initiated into its inheritance. The pupil's initiation into the *geistige Welt* is possible only through the intermediary of the teacher. This notion, once again, reinforces the importance of the teacher and the importance of the child's submission to the teacher's authority should it hope to embrace its own inheritance fully. To reject and rebel against this authority is to reject and rebel against one's own initiation into one's rightful inheritance of knowledge. This inheritance is so important that, for Oakeshott (2001: 38), it is the very essence of what separates us as human beings from other less fortunate animals: 'If, from one point of view, the analogies of wax and clay are inappropriate to learning, from another point of view the analogies of sagacious apes and accomplished horses are no less appropriate. These admirable creatures have no such inheritance; they may only be trained to react to a stimulus and to perform tricks.' That is, the human being is fortunate in the sense that he or she has an inheritance to embrace and with which to become engaged. A rejection of the authority of the one – the teacher – who offers to initiate us into such a privileged inheritance is therefore going against the essence of what makes us human beings. If a submission to the authority of a 'learned' teacher is required for us to inherit what is rightfully ours as human beings, it is at odds with our very own natural order to reject it. Indeed, if the teacher holds the key to the door through which we hope to walk to inherit what is rightfully ours – that is, to seize our inheritance – it makes sense only that we align ourselves with the teacher, as the doorkeeper to the *geistige Welt*.

The role and importance of the teacher in the teaching and learning processes are subjected to further discussion by Oakeshott in light of these initial claims that the teacher is the key for the pupil embracing his or her own inheritance. Indeed, Oakeshott (2001: 39) regards the teacher not only as an authority to which the pupil must submit, but also as a character whose attention every pupil should regard as a privilege – a person to whom each is indebted for widening his or her scope of understanding: 'But initiation into the *geistige Welt* of human achievement is owed to the Sage, the teacher: and this debt is to be acknowledged with the profoundest reverence – for whom can a man be more deeply indebted than to the one to whom he owes, not his mere existence, but his participation in human life?' This 'Sage' – this calm and experienced source of wisdom – is to be held in the highest of regard by any pupil who was under his or her charge, thankful for the role that the Sage has played in initiating that pupil into participation in and embracing of his or her inheritance. This process highlights the importance of the teacher, aptly described as a Sage on the basis of the wisdom and calm judgement that he or she will communicate when offering understanding of an inherited world that would otherwise lead only to confusion. Without the teacher – when considered a Sage – the world is bereft of wisdom, understanding and informed judgements, to which the pupil can hitch his or her learning wagon, and via which the pupil can engage with that inheritance of knowledge to which the teacher is already accustomed. The teacher, as a Sage, assumes a more significant role: a role that involves calming the learning storm, and providing guidance and supervision through a wilderness of ideas and notions. The teacher guides the pupil through a labyrinth of knowledge to ensure that everything is in its correct place and context, so that the pupil receives the appropriate insight into what precisely his or her inheritance entails. In this sense (Oakeshott, 2001: 39): 'It is the Sage, the teacher, who is the agent of civilization. And, as Dr. Johnson said, not to name the school and the masters of illustrious men is a kind of historical fraud.'

The teacher therefore deserves his or her place at the centre of the processes of teaching and learning. The teacher is a beacon of light in the darkness of ignorance. His or her guidance and direction points the pupil towards the correct solution. And the pupil accepts this guidance only through a submission to the teacher's authority, in acknowledgement of a debt to that teacher for permitting the pupil an informed glimpse into his or her inheritance of knowledge.

In light of Oakeshott's prominent role of the teacher, there is, naturally, subsequent significance given to the teacher's activities – namely, the process of teaching. Teaching as a process, remember, was regarded by Oakeshott as attributable only to a teacher and not to reliable sources, textbooks, activities or human experiences. In this way, learning as a by-product of teaching was distinguished from the learning that takes place through experience, and similarly the learner was distinguished from the pupil in that the pupil was seen to be the counterpart to the teacher, whereas the learner had no such requirements or privileged position. Teaching therefore, associated with this significant role of the teacher, 'is the deliberate and intentional initiation of a pupil into the world of human achievement, or some part of it' (Oakeshott, 2001: 39). Given, also, the fact that the teacher is the person responsible for the role of teaching and all that it entails, the teacher is therefore seen to be the one conducting such an intentional initiation.

The roles of the teacher and his or her pupils, as well as the processes of teaching and learning, are thrown open to further discussion by Oakeshott in an effort to tie the processes to the key players involved. As I have already outlined, the subset of pupils seems to be contained within the set of learners, to the extent that every pupil is a learner, but the pupil must demonstrate the added characteristic of being attached to a teacher. Moreover, teaching as a process is possible only in the presence of a teacher; no other resources suffice to deliver the process of teaching successfully, which is considered to be the holy grail of learning. In this sense, Oakeshott ties the processes and the players together, noting that 'a pupil is a learner known to a teacher; and teaching, properly speaking, is impossible in his absence' (Oakeshott, 2001: 40). The teacher is therefore a guide through the learning process, the person who ensures that the pupil under his or her charge is directed to the concepts and notions of a so-called inheritance, which may be of interest or use to that pupil. The structure and delivery of how the pupil is introduced to and embraces his or her inheritance also falls under the remit of the teacher, who decides in what way to construct the learning and how best to deliver the teaching. By understanding the pupil, and similarly by understanding what is right and proper for that pupil to learn, the teacher opens the doors to learning, to provide the pupil with the requisite tools not only to take notice of his or her inheritance, but also to embrace, engage with, and participate in that inheritance. The teacher, therefore, understands that he or she 'is one who studies his pupil, that the initiation *he* undertakes is one which has a deliberate order and arrangement, and that, as well as knowing what he designs to transmit, he has considered the manner of transmission' (Oakeshott, 2001: 40).

In the discourse of education, there has been a long-running debate about what teaching and learning are – or, indeed, what they *should be*. The two popular camps of educational thought are the purists versus the more practical thinkers. The purists, naturally, contest that learning is a process of knowledge acquisition and that teaching is, subsequently, a process of initiating a pupil into the inheritance of such knowledge. In this way, there is a motive of 'learning for learning's sake' within the purist's mindset. In contrast, the practical thinker would contest that learning is about taking a holistic approach to the learner, to develop him or her into a well-rounded being, and that teaching as a result of this should be focused on encouraging the pupil to make the most of himself or herself. Oakeshott (2001: 40) poses, and indeed answers, this quandary himself within his own considerations on teaching and learning:

> With regard to the pupil, there is a famous dilemma which has haunted reflection on education for long enough. Is learning to be understood as acquiring knowledge, or is it to be regarded as the development of the personality of the learner? Is teaching concerned with initiating a pupil into an inheritance of human achievement, or is it enabling the pupil to make the most or best of himself?

In answer to this question, Oakeshott puts forward an ingenious solution, which attempts to fuse together the 'best parts' from purist and practical thinking in terms of teaching and learning. First, the purpose of learning is 'not merely as the acquisition of knowledge, but also as the extension of the ability to learn, as the education and not merely the furnishing of a mind, as an inheritance coming to be possessed in such a manner that it loses its second-hand or antique manner' (Oakeshott, 2001: 40–1). That is, learning must be seen to be a process that encourages not only the acquisition and extension of knowledge, but also some form of understanding of how to apply and further develop any knowledge. In this way, learning is prevented from being a 'stand-still' entity, which stops, for example, in the classroom. There is, of course, the foundational necessity of acquiring knowledge in line with what our teacher guides us towards – our so-called inheritance – and, as such, we are not encouraged to be free with our choices in the first instance, when *beginning* to learn.

However, by accompanying a version of rote learning with a dynamism that extends beyond our initial point of learning contact, Oakeshott ensures that learning is a process that is not passive, but rather a process that encourages pupils to engage with and participate in their inheritance. However, this is encouraged only under the acknowledgement that the teacher *begins* the process by imparting knowledge to the pupils, guiding them towards some form of future independence.[1] The analogy of an inheritance is perhaps most pertinent in this instance, given that an inheritance *changes ownership* once it is passed on. Therefore, under the process of learning, the teacher enlightens the pupil under his or her charge as to what the pupil's inheritance is; after that, it is up to the pupil to embrace it, to care for it and to pass it on in a similar way to that in which he or she received it. Learning, therefore, is intergenerational in nature and finds its intergenerational transactions founded within an authority of the more 'learned' generation, whose task it is to encourage the 'not-yet-learned' generation to take up their knowledge reins.

Oakeshott's understanding of teaching is similarly captivating and, typically, liberating in terms of its consequences. Teaching should be regarded 'not as passing on something to be received, nor as merely planting a seed, but as setting on foot the cultivation of a mind so that what is planted may grow' (Oakeshott, 2001: 41). Such an understanding of the process of teaching discards many of the problems with which other more frivolous definitions of teaching are fraught. This definition of teaching encompasses everything that should be delivered through *any* teaching process. Rather uniquely, however, this definition offers an understanding of teaching as a process for both the short and the long terms. Indeed, there is an acknowledgement of the need for the here-and-now approach to teaching – that is, the necessity for (to appeal to Oakeshott's own analogy) 'planting a seed'. This might be viewed as the static component of teaching, which demands that the pupil accept what is shown to him or her on the basis of the teacher's authority. However, Oakeshott inadvertently acknowledges in his definition that 'planting a seed' is insufficient. In unpacking this analogy, it is clear that 'planting a seed' is merely a passive process. Indeed, to plant a seed into land that is neither ready, nor refined enough to take it, will not result in any growth. But by encouraging the process of teaching to have a component of cultivation, which encourages the seed to 'grow', Oakeshott injects a new dynamism into teaching as a process that, rather cleverly, unifies the passive and active components of teaching, and the subsequent learning that results from such teaching. Planting the seed – to extend the analogy to teaching – is a process that *in itself* is insufficient for teaching to be successful; accompanying this planting process with a preparatory cultivation, however, ensures that teaching can be successful, through an engagement by the pupil with what the teacher has taught. Both processes, however, can be successful only against a backdrop of the teacher's authority to offer guidance towards pre-appropriated actions. That is, teaching can be successful – in both planting and growing – only if what the teacher encourages is understood to be founded in an authority that his or her position naturally commands. Indeed, without such an authority, the teacher could claim *no right* in planting anything, or encouraging it to grow in the way that he or she sees fit. In this way, teaching can be successful only when it is overarched by the guidance of an authoritative teacher, who has the right to impart knowledge through that teaching and, similarly, has the right to impart an accompanying foundation, to ensure that what he or she has imparted to the pupil may one day develop in the manner intended.

In light of these rationales for teaching and learning, I can perhaps answer – in keeping with Oakeshott – precisely what teaching and learning should mean to the teacher and the pupil, respectively. Let me consider the pupil first, with particular reference to what learning should represent to him or her. The two offers open to the pupil were placed within the purist and the practical camps of learning, purporting, respectively, that learning should be *either* acquiring knowledge *or* attempting to be the best that one can be. Oakeshott argues that the discrepancy between these two notions lies not between the pupil and the world, but between the processes of teaching and learning. That is, the remit of learning – and consequently the focus of the pupil – should be the acquisition of knowledge. In contrast, the remit of teaching – and consequently the focus of the teacher – is the encouragement of the pupil to embrace his or her inheritance and to be the best that he or she can be. In this way, the pupil should grasp that 'to learn is not to endeavour to make the most of himself, it is to acquire knowledge, to distinguish between truth and error, to understand and become possessor of what he was born heir to' (Oakeshott, 2001: 41). In grasping the values of learning in this way, the pupil can then claim to have taken ownership of his or her knowledge inheritance, via a process of successful learning. It is not the pupil's concern to be the best that he or she can be; rather, it is to embrace his or her inheritance and to take ownership of it.

From the teacher's perspective, however, Oakeshott (2001: 41) asserts that the teacher is 'an agent of civilization. But his direct relationship is with his pupil. His engagement is, specifically, to get his pupil to make the most of himself by teaching him to recognize himself in the mirror of the human achievements which compose his inheritance.' This therefore distinguishes between the processes of teaching and learning, and subsequently distinguishes between the respective focuses of the pupil and the teacher. The pupil is to be concerned with acquiring knowledge via a process of successful learning to ensure that he or she inherits his or her knowledge entitlement. The teacher, however, is to ensure that the pupil under his or her charge is to be the best that the pupil can be, by encouraging that pupil to embrace his or her inheritance and to engage with it to become part of the human achievements to which he or she is heir. The confusion, therefore, lay in drawing a distinction between the 'pupil succeeding to his inheritance of human achievement and making the most of himself' (Oakeshott, 2001: 41): it need not be one or the other.

The true distinction needs to be drawn between the processes of teaching and learning, and the requisite focuses of each of the people involved – namely, the teacher and the pupil, respectively. By evoking a system in which the pupil focuses on acquiring knowledge and the teacher focuses on encouraging the pupil to be the best that he or she can be, the pupil ultimately sees *no* discrepancy between acquiring knowledge *and* making the most of himself or herself. These concepts become equal partners as by-products of successful teaching and learning. They both begin, however, in acknowledging that the inheritance of human achievements is attainable only through a submission to the teacher's authority, to provide an insight into *what* the inheritance is and *how* it can be claimed.

Within this discourse, Oakeshott contests further that there must be an acknowledgement of the role that is played by previous generations on whatever inheritance is presented to the pupil by his or her teacher. Indeed:

> To initiate a pupil into the world of human achievement is to make available to him much that does not lie upon the surface of the present world. An inheritance will contain much that may not be in current use, much that has come to be neglected and even something that for the time being is forgotten. And to know only the dominant is to become acquainted with only an attenuated version of this inheritance.

To see oneself reflected in the mirror of the present modish world is to see a sadly distorted image of a human being.

(Oakeshott, 2001: 42)

In acknowledging the past and the role that previous generations have played in shaping what is constituted within human achievements, the pupil becomes capable of envisaging a more representative picture of what is encompassed in the *entire* human being. The present – and, similarly, the future – are not the only components that contribute to a holistic view of such a human being, the collection of human achievements and the inheritance that encapsulates them. Indeed, the term 'inheritance' has a distinctive flow of the past coursing through its veins, suggesting that there is something of worth from the past – perhaps lessons to be learned and achievements to be recognized. Indeed, Oakeshott (2001: 42) argues that it is irresponsible – perhaps even arrogant – to suggest that the present trends are all that should be considered in grasping the magnitude of the inheritance of human achievements, or that it can be argued that the beliefs are held as *current* truths have, in any way, adhered to some version of crypto-knowledge Darwinism to dispense with the worse in favour of the better: 'There is nothing to encourage us to believe that what has captured current fancy is the most valuable part of our inheritance, or that the better survives more readily than the worse.' The teacher therefore assumes the responsibility 'to release his pupils from the servitude to the current dominant feelings, emotions, images, ideas, beliefs and even skills, not by inventing alternatives to them which seem to him more desirable, but by making available to him something which approximates more closely to the whole of his inheritance' (Oakeshott, 2001: 42).

In this process, however, the teacher is – perhaps privately – concerned with the worth of introducing his or her pupils to their inheritance. That is, the teacher must himself or herself be convinced in what he or she teaches, for 'if he has no confidence in any of the standards of worth written into this inheritance of human achievement, he had better not be a teacher; he would have nothing to teach' (Oakeshott, 2001: 43). It is in this process of consideration that the pupil finds justification for having faith in the teacher's authority. The pupil has faith – perhaps not explicitly – that the teacher has reasoned on the pupil's behalf, prior to encouraging that pupil to embrace his or her inheritance. Such a faith is established structurally of the teaching community. A teacher's judgement is to be trusted on the basis of the fact that, in his or her entire *being* as a teacher, he or she is convinced of the worth of the message that he or she imparts to the pupil. Better still, the pupil has certitude that the teacher will not teach anything not of worth to the pupil, in the name of *learning*. The value of this may not be apparent at first – but the pupil rests assured that the authority that the teacher commands, by his or her very essence as a teacher, will not lead the pupil to embrace an inheritance bereft of value. The teacher therefore uses his or her authority responsibly (so as not to soil the name of teaching and learning) to encourage the pupil to embrace his or her inheritance with open arms, secure in the certitude that what has been conveyed to him or her is of eventual – if not immediate – worth. Teaching and learning therefore 'always relate to a historic inheritance of human achievement' (Oakeshott, 2001: 44).

Information as 'inert' knowledge

So far, in my discussion of Oakeshott's writings and their applications to teaching and learning, I have outlined the importance of accepting the authority of the teacher and the practices that he or she represents if the process of teaching is to be successful and if, as a consequence of this teaching being successful, the pupil under the teacher's charge is to learn successfully. In this way, the processes of teaching and learning were inextricably linked into a process that begins with the 'learned' person – the teacher – assuming the authoritative responsibilities in his or her relationship with the 'not-yet-learned' person – the pupil. A similar significance is given by Oakeshott – again, rather subtly – to the role that authority plays in how knowledge is constructed and subsequently to how it is developed. I will begin this section by describing how Oakeshott believes knowledge to be *constructed* and, as a result of this description, I will outline precisely why a development of knowledge constructed in this way remains dependent on a submission to the authority of the teacher, should one ever hope to gain access to it.

Oakeshott (2001: 45) contests that knowledge is constructed in combining two separate, yet connected, components: information and judgement. I will consider first what Oakeshott means by 'information'; I shall return to what is encompassed within the term 'judgement' in the next section. Information, for Oakeshott (2001: 46), 'consists of facts, specific intellectual artifacts (often arranged in sets or bunches). It is impersonal (not a matter of opinion). Most of it is accepted on authority, and it is to be found in directories, manuals, textbooks and encyclopedias.' This definition of information, set against the backdrop of the claim that such information captures part of the picture of the construct of knowledge, deals with four rather sweeping elements of what to expect from information.

First, there is a factual element to information – that is, an element of information that cannot be disputed.

Moreover, and secondly, information, by its nature, does not take into consideration any form of opinion in the process of its construction. This is what Oakeshott describes as the 'impersonal' nature of information, meaning that information is brute fact, free from the input of people's personal dispositions.

Perhaps most interestingly for the purposes of our discussion, and third on my list of points worthy of note, is that information is described as being accepted 'on authority'. Oakeshott seems to drop this notion of authority into his understanding of information and proceed without further explanation. However, upon closer inspection, the need for an acceptance of authority in the construction of information is both intuitive and substantiated by evidence in practice. Indeed, as young schoolchildren, we will have been fed masses of information by our teachers and most (if not all) of us will have felt no impulse to challenge what our teachers told us. There was an evidential trust in our teachers, manifested in our blind submission to them and subsequent submission to the information that they transmitted to us in their teaching. This blind submission was the characterization of an acceptance of the teacher's authority in passing on information.

Finally, in this typically deflationary definition of information, Oakeshott outlines a fourth element: where information is to be found, suggesting a series of what could be described as 'reliable sources', such as textbooks and encyclopaedias. Such resources, in their nature, command a certain authority of their own, to the extent that they are the net result of a sequence of continued scrutiny that leaves intact, in 'reliable form', what is true and informative at any particular moment in time.

To reinforce this definition of information, Oakeshott (2001: 46) provides some examples of what such a definition might point towards as information: 'Typical pieces of information are the date of Shakespeare's death or St. Paul's conversion, the average annual rainfall in Bournemouth, the ingredients of Welsh rabbit, the specific gravity of alcohol, the age of consent, the atomic structure of nitrogen, the reasons given by Milton for favouring polygamy, the seating capacity of the Albert Hall.' Such examples manifest the four aspects of information intrinsic to Oakeshott's definition. Indeed, the atomic structure of nitrogen, for example, is factual in essence; it is impersonal to the extent that it takes no account of personal dispositions of people who are aware of such information; it is accepted as information on the authority of the chemists and scientists who claim to know its atomic structure, and this authority cannot be questioned without evidence; and such information could be found in any reliable science textbook.

One aspect of information that as yet has not been mentioned, however, is the usefulness of the information, or what it purports to tell us. That is, it is unclear in the definition given so far what use information is to the receiver of it and why it should be of any value to him or her in the ultimate pursuit of knowledge. Oakeshott (2001: 46) suggests that 'the importance of information lies in its provision of rules or rulelike propositions relating to abilities'. In essence, therefore, information is the component of knowledge that provides the 'knower' with the rules of abilities. Indeed, as Oakeshott (2001: 46) provides: 'Every ability has its rules, and they are contained in that component of knowledge we call information. This is clearly the case with mathematical or chemical formulae.' In the examples of mathematics and chemistry, which Oakeshott offers, he is suggesting that the rules that govern the ability to *do* mathematics and chemistry are contained in the information of these subjects. Being 'informed', therefore, is a platform to being 'knowledgeable', since the information component of knowledge provides the rules that give rise to the abilities in question. Even information such as the seating capacity of the Albert Hall, referred to earlier in Oakeshott's list of examples of information, can be used as a rule that governs the ability to decide on how many tickets may be sold for a performance in that venue (Oakeshott, 2001: 46). Information, therefore, is a precept for knowledge, in as much as information is the component of knowledge that governs its rules, which in turn govern the abilities entailed in the notion of 'being knowledgeable'.

However, a set of rules, or governances, is inert in its nature – insufficient *in itself* to guide the knower towards appropriate actions and abilities. That is, information *in itself* is not knowledge. Being aware of rules does not lead, necessarily, to being able to act out those rules. Indeed, being aware of a recipe does not necessarily ensure that one can cook the dish. Similarly, being aware of mathematical information such as a formula will not *in itself* guide a pupil towards a solution. Something else is needed for each of these actions: there must be an insight – an ability to recognize what the recipe is telling you and when the mathematical formula is applicable.[2]

The fact that Oakeshott defines 'information' as a subcategory of 'knowledge' highlights that there is a component of knowledge that is absent from information, alluded to in the previous paragraph. Within the descriptions of information given thus far, being 'informed' tells only part of the story of being 'knowledgeable'. The description of information as a component in knowledge has outlined to a certain extent that information seems to be the inert, factual, impersonal component of knowledge; to complete the knowledge picture, there must therefore be a natural counterpart to information that is dynamic, open to interpretation and personal in nature, in order to offset the inertness and passive nature of information within knowledge construction. Moreover, information *in itself* is intuitively insufficient in the art of knowing. Indeed, to be informed seems to suggest that one has information that prevents a person from being ignorant. That is, one might have attained information and retained it in its factual nature, but such retention says nothing about whether or not one is able to choose the appropriate situations in which to apply that knowledge. Such choice requires more than information, because information *in itself* will not guide us towards the appropriate application. Therefore, although 'there is in all knowledge an ingredient of information', we are forced into the recognition that 'the ingredient of information, however, never constitutes the whole of what we know' (Oakeshott, 2001: 49). A performance of note is guided by more than inert information, which, as a stand-alone entity, cannot guide.[3] Indeed, mathematical formulae, for example, will not guide towards the correct *application* of such formulae, since a formula is nothing other than inert, rule-like knowledge that relates to the ability to be demonstrated in its correct application. Rules, and rule-like propositions, however, require an accompanying understanding of *how* and *when* to apply them. Such an understanding is absent in being 'informed', in as much as being 'informed' requires one only to know *what* rather than know *how*.

In this way, 'before any concrete skill or ability can appear, information must be partnered by "judgement", "knowing *how*" must be added to the "knowing *what*" of information' (Oakeshott, 2001: 49). This so-called 'judgement' completes the knowledge picture, taking one from being 'informed' to being 'knowledgeable'. Judgement is therefore the natural counterpart of information in the construction of knowledge.

Judgement as 'dynamic' knowledge

It is this notion of 'judgement' that I will discuss now to complete the construction of knowledge. The fact that judgement is the accompaniment to information in the construction of knowledge obviously suggests that there is something that distinguishes these components of knowledge from one another, and also something that makes both aspects indispensable in a full understanding of knowledge. Oakeshott (2001: 49) defines the concept of 'judgement' as 'the tacit or implicit component of knowledge, the ingredient which is not merely unspecified in propositions, but is unspecifiable in propositions. It is the component of knowledge which does not appear in the form of rules and which, therefore, cannot be resolved into information or itemized in the manner characteristic of information.'

From this definition can be drawn several ideas that distinguish information from judgement. First, judgement is implicit or tacit and therefore cannot be articulated in the same way as can information. So whereas information might be recorded in textbooks and other resources, judgement finds its tacit explanation in *doing* and in *acting*. (Notice, at this point, the similarity between Oakeshott's 'judgement' and Polanyi's 'tacit knowledge'.)

Secondly, not only is judgement *not* specified in propositions, but it also *cannot* be specified in propositions – that is, it is *unintelligible* to think of judgement as being written in the form of rules and rule-like propositions. This is the most striking difference between information and judgement: whereas information is constructed into rules and rule-like propositions, judgement cannot be specified in this way.

By its very construction, judgement therefore has a different nature from information. In understanding this, we see not only how judgement and information are different in nature, but also why both aspects of the 'full picture' of knowledge seem indispensable in its construction. Indeed, judgement and information, under these definitions, bring entirely different things to the knowledge table: information brings the rules and the propositions, which are generally inert and static (and as such are incapable of guiding *in themselves*); judgement brings an aspect of dynamism and tacit understanding to knowledge that would otherwise be notable in its absence. Knowledge, for Oakeshott, therefore requires both the dimensions of information and judgement to complete the knowledge picture in such a way that it promotes the use of facts and rules to govern abilities, and offers a dynamic insight to know *how* and *when* such facts and rules apply.

The tacit nature of judgement in comparison to the explicit nature of information is what most distinguishes these two facets of knowledge, but also what make both facets indispensable in the construction of knowledge. Oakeshott, however, is at pains to emphasize that, even in skills and abilities for which the 'knowing *what*' component of the underlying knowledge seems not to be articulated, the notion that judgement and information can be pulled apart is unappealing. Indeed, for Oakeshott (2001: 49–50): 'We may know how to do something without being able to state explicitly the manner of acting involved. This, for example, appears to be the case in swimming, riding a horse, playing a fish, using a chisel and turning a bowl on a potter's wheel.' All of these activities seem to be possible 'to do' when one has an understanding of 'knowing *how*' to do them, even in the apparent absence of 'knowing *what*' is being done – that is, it appears that, in these instances, judgement is required, whereas information is not. Oakeshott (2001: 50) goes on to argue: '[F]urther, that we may recognize an action as being of a known kind without being able to specify how we recognized it; that we are able to discover similarities in things without being able to say what they consist of, or patterns without being aware of the elements they are composed of or the rules they exemplify.' That is, it seems that, in certain cases, we may know *how* to perform a certain action, but our actions may be entirely devoid of knowing *what* it is, precisely, that we are doing.

Oakeshott (2001: 50) further suggests that the paradigmatic example outlined in the last chapter of speaking and mastering a language is just such an example, claiming that 'we may speak a language without knowing the rules we are following and even without those rules ever having been formulated'. These examples are difficult to dispense with and the argument that, in such instances, judgement *in itself* is sufficient in being able to perform the actions outlined is difficult to refute. However, although Oakeshott concedes that these examples are difficult to sidestep, he suggests that any skill or ability that appears to require only a 'knowing *how*' automatically has an element of 'knowing *what*' inextricably linked to it. Indeed:

[W]hat it suggests to me is that there are skills and abilities where what is known may lack certain forms of informatory content (particularly the sort of information we call 'rules'), rather than that there is a 'knowing *how*' which can be divorced from any 'knowing *what*.' Thus I have used 'judgement' to distinguish 'knowing *how*' from the information because I think 'knowing *how*' is an ingredient of all genuine knowledge, and not a separate kind of knowing specified by an ignorance of rules.

(Oakeshott, 2001: 50)

Therefore, even in the instances of abilities and skills that seem not to depend on information as a component in the related knowledge, there still remains a need for both information and judgement in knowledge construction. 'Knowing *how*', for Oakeshott, is not a stand-alone entity in any skill or ability; rather, it is the natural accompaniment to the 'knowing *what*' provided through information, even in the instances in which information *seems* to be absent. Judgement can therefore be seen to be the partner of information in knowledge and 'knowing'. Both aspects are connected, and both are required for genuine knowledge and the abilities that emanate from such knowledge. Furthermore, both aspects are indispensable, to the extent that one without the other is worthless and inaccessible. 'Knowing *what*' to do leads to an inevitable stand-off, in that, without the accompanying 'knowing *how*' to do it, one could never hope to put one's information into practice.

Conversely, 'knowing *how*' to do something seems to be founded – and therefore linked to – an understanding, either explicit or tacit, of 'knowing *what*' is being done. That is, should a person demonstrate an ability to *do* a certain activity, he or she is, in his or her actions, demonstrating a manifested exemplification of knowing *what* he or she is doing, even if that person cannot articulate the underlying rules and rule-like propositions (that is, the information) of *what* he or she is doing.

The need for both information and judgement

Can we dispense with either information or judgement and hope to be knowledgeable? On the basis of the definitions outlined in the previous few sections, it seems not. Indeed, information is required in the construction of knowledge to provide facts that act as rules and rule-like propositions, which point towards – but cannot entirely guide – abilities and skills. Such rules are required to govern the appropriate manner in which to act, but are devoid of any guidance on how and when to appeal to the rules themselves – that is, they tell us *what* we need to know, but tell us nothing about *how* to act on this information and *when* to apply it. That is where judgement is required. Judgement equips us with the understanding of *how* and *when* to apply the information. It is tacitly demonstrated to us by way of example and cannot be outlined in propositions in the same way as information. Oakeshott (2001: 50) summarizes succinctly thus:

> Facts, rules, all that may come to us as information, itemized and explicit, never themselves endow us with an ability to do, or to make, or to understand and explain anything. Information has to be used, and it does not itself indicate how, on any occasion, it should be used. What is required in addition to information is knowledge which enables us to interpret it, to decide upon its relevance, to recognize what rule to apply and to discover what action permitted by the rule should, in the circumstances, be performed; knowledge (in short) capable of carrying us across those wide open spaces, to be found in every ability, where no rule runs.

In this description, we find the connection between information and judgement, and the precise reason as to why neither can be dispensed with in a quest for genuine knowledge.

Oakeshott (2001: 50–1) develops these ideas further, claiming that rules are 'are always disjunctive ... they never relieve us of the necessity of choice. They never yield more than partial explanations: to understand anything as an example of the operation of a rule is to understand it very imperfectly.' The 'choice' to which Oakeshott refers is intrinsically linked to the element of judgement within knowledge. Making the appropriate choice of how to *apply* the information aspect of knowledge is found in one's ability to judge appropriately when and how the information is to be applied. Without this insight – this judgement – information remains inert and inapplicable. Without judgement, the knower is merely a 'carrier' of information, who remains ignorant as to its use. In this sense, Oakesh (2001: 51) proposes: '"Judgement", then, is not to be recognized as m' information of another sort; its deliverances cannot be itemized, remembered or forgotten. It is, for example, all that is contained in what has been called "the unspecifiable art of scientific inquiry" without which "the articulate contents of scientific knowledge" remain unintelligible.' Thus where information constitutes the rules by which appropriate skills and abilities are to be fulfilled, judgement is the key to unlocking the knowledge door, to the extent that, without judgement, the rules are inapplicable and unintelligible. To embrace knowledge fully, in all of its glory, both aspects of knowledge are indispensable. Abilities find their roots in knowledge, and knowledge is founded in information (facts) and judgement (the insight into how and when to appeal to the facts). In this sense, 'in every "ability" there is an ingredient of knowledge which cannot be resolved into information' (Oakeshott, 2001: 52).

Information is the bedrock upon which knowledge is founded. It is inert and static, and not open to personal dispositions. Judgement accompanies such information to encompass a fuller picture of genuine knowledge. And on the basis of knowledge rest abilities and skills – that is, being capable of *doing* and *acting*. Oakeshott (2001: 52–3) suggests why such judgement may seem so appealing, by offering an account of what results in its absence:

> What, then, is significant is not the observation that one may know how to speak a language without knowing the rules one is following, but the observation that until one can speak the language in a manner not expressly provided for in the rules, one can make no significant utterance in it. And, of course, by a 'language' I do not mean merely Latin or Spanish, I mean also the languages of history, philosophy, science and practical life. The rules of art are there, but they do not determine the practice of the art; the rules of understanding are there, but they do not themselves endow us with understanding.

By introducing the practice of 'language', Oakeshott is outlining what we would be missing were we never to develop judgement in using that 'language'. In the absence of judgement, we may have access to the rules, but have no access to participating in the practice of the art that is governed by the rules. We would remain static and utterly incapable of proceeding beyond the information given. In the absence of judgement, our information would never be applied and, as a consequence, we would never liberate ourselves to embrace our true knowledge inheritance.

What, then, are the implications for teaching and learning in understanding knowledge – our inheritance – as a combination of information and judgement – 'learning which is succeeding to the inheritance, and teaching which is deliberately initiating pupils into it' (Oakeshott, 2001: 53)? First, the intuitive answer is that teaching as a process must account for the fact that to encourage the pupil to embrace his or her inheritance is, essentially, to impart information (facts) and to develop judgement (insight). Learning as a process, on the other hand, must therefore take into account that there is both information to be acquired and judgement to be attained. There must be recognition that information is factual and not open to one's personal dispositions, and that judgement requires an engagement in order to develop it fully. In essence, the distinction between information and judgement is in how they are each communicated and acquired, based on precisely of what each component is made:

> It suggests, first, that what I have called the two components of knowledge ('information' and 'judgement') can both be communicated and acquired, but cannot be communicated or acquired separately – at least, not on separate occasions or in separate 'lessons' . . . Secondly, it suggests that these two components of knowledge cannot be communicated in the same manner. Indeed . . . the distinction between 'information' and 'judgement' is a distinction between different manners of communication rather than a dichotomy of what is known.
>
> (Oakeshott, 2001: 53)

This distinction between the manner in which information and judgement are communicated leads to the realization of the fact that teaching 'may be said to be a twofold activity of communicating "information" (which I shall call "instructing") and communicating "judgement" (which I shall call "imparting")', whereas learning may be regarded as 'the twofold activity of acquiring "information" and coming to possess "judgement"' (Oakeshott, 2001: 54). Therefore the teacher is to 'instruct' the pupil under his or her charge to acquire information and is to 'impart' an insight to the pupil that endorses the development of an accompanying judgement for the information that has been acquired. Thus, in ensuring that both aspects of knowledge have been developed, the teacher will have succeeded in leading the pupil towards embracing his or her inheritance of knowledge, and the teacher will have fulfilled his or her remit as such, of encouraging the pupil to be the best that he or she can be. The pupil, on the other hand, is to focus on acquiring the information and developing judgement under the tutelage of the master. Learning is the focus of the pupil, to ensure that he or she keeps his or her end of the inheritance contract in becoming knowledgeable.

By considering the teacher to be the 'instructor', we characterize the teacher as the 'deliberate conveyor of information to his pupil' (Oakeshott, 2001: 54). This information, as I have already outlined, is to be 'impersonal and mostly taken on trust' (Oakeshott, 2001: 54). The motivation for the pupil to follow the teacher's instruction is found in '[the pupil's] desire not to be ignorant' (Oakeshott, 2001: 54). Such a desire ensures that a teacher is a necessity in the teaching and learning processes, because he or she is the *only* candidate who can ensure that the pupil's ignorance is lifted. However, the teacher as the instructor has a broader remit than simply conveying information. First, the teacher is to ensure that the information that he or she instructs to the pupils is the relevant information that should be passed on to them. That is not to say that it is to be practical; rather, it is to be relevant to the pupils grasping the fullest picture of their knowledge inheritance. It may assume no particular practical significance to the pupils in their lives; however, it must be significant in their quest to embrace their knowledge inheritance. In so doing, however, the teacher is not to withhold information from the pupil that is rightfully part of his or her knowledge inheritance; that would serve only to undermine the teacher's message. The teacher must pick his or her moment to introduce such information, however, should it be difficult to understand, to ensure that the message has a greater chance of success. Indeed, as Oakeshott (2001: 54–5) suggests:

> The task of the teacher as an instructor is to introduce the pupil to facts which have no immediate practical significance. (If there were no such facts, or if they composed an unimportant part of our inheritance, a teacher would be a luxury rather than a necessity.) And therefore, his first business is to consider and decide what information to convey to his pupil.

Secondly, the teacher must ensure that the information that he or she chooses to convey to his or her pupils is 'more readily learnable by giving it an organization in which the inertness of its component facts is modified' (Oakeshott, 2001: 55). It seems obvious – to the extent that it is hardly worth mentioning – that a teacher must, at every point in his or her teaching, ensure that what he or she is teaching is learnable. That is not to say that the teacher is to compromise the integrity of the messages that he or she hopes to convey; rather, the teacher must be concerned with the business of making his or her message communicable and understandable. Otherwise, the teacher is not a leader: should he or she lose sight of the 'learnability' of the message, the teacher will lose all of his or her followers – the pupils.

In the instances in which the message is difficult to follow, the teacher is to be concerned with making the message more accessible by means of a series of sensible techniques that open the eyes of the pupils, but which protects the integrity of what the teacher represents. He or she is to remind the pupils that information may be difficult to follow and that, in such cases, the only possible way in which to overcome such difficulties is through hard work and endurance. The teacher must never release false information; that would be to undermine his or her position. The teacher must never endorse the misuse of the information that he or she conveys to the pupil; that would be to discredit his or her subject. And the teacher must never withhold information from the pupils that they are entitled to know because he or she believes it to be too difficult for them to grasp; instead, the teacher must search for ways in which to lead the pupils to a fuller understanding of their knowledge inheritance, lest he or she deprive them of what is rightfully theirs. The teacher might pick a more appropriate moment – perhaps when they are more prepared to grasp their inheritance – to introduce the pupils to their entitlement of knowledge. Such instances are found in the fact that school curricula tend to increase in difficulty, to culminate in the most difficult concepts at the final stages of teaching and learning. However, provided that the moment is correct, the teacher must illustrate even the most complex of concepts to his or her pupil if it is part of their knowledge inheritance.

Finally:

There are ... two other tasks which obviously fall to the teacher as instructor. First, he has to consider the order in which the information contained in each of these somewhat arbitrary organizations of facts shall be transmitted to his pupil ... Second, he has to exercise his pupil in this information so that what has been acquired may be recognized in forms other than those in which it was first acquired, and may be recollected on all the occasions when it is relevant.

(Oakeshott, 2001: 56)

The first of these related tasks for the teacher as an instructor is to consider the appropriate order for the information to be conveyed to the pupil. I have already alluded to why this may be regarded as important. Indeed, the order of the instructions issued in the information stage of teaching is linked to a so-called 'incline of difficulty', which is a feature of any successful teaching process. Indeed, it seems intuitive that instruction would, generally speaking, begin with simple concepts and increase in difficulty towards more complex concepts at a later stage. This is not necessarily the argument that teaching must be constructed in such a way that it promotes super-concepts to be built from sub-concepts; rather, the message that is conveyed by the teacher during the instruction process must be suitable for the level at which the pupil is expected to be. Therefore an appropriate order must be established as to what it is reasonable to expect a pupil at a certain stage in his or her learning to be capable of understanding. For example, it would make no sense for a teacher to attempt to convey the information of how many seats there are in the Albert Hall – to pick up on a previous example – to a child who has no concept of number. Such information would be utterly useless and, indeed, meaningless to that child. The pupil would have no ability to understand the message that was put forth by the teacher and, as such, the message would lose its inherent value. The teacher must therefore ensure that what he or she teaches is appropriate to the pupils' respective levels; otherwise, the message is worthless. If the order of teaching is not thought through, the teacher risks conveying information to a pupil before that pupil has the prerequisites that enable him or her to understand fully what is being taught.

The second task of the teacher was to exercise the pupil in the information that has been conveyed, to ensure that the pupil recognizes how and when to apply it. Such an exercise is the development of judgement, and the word 'exercise' is particularly pertinent in this instance. Indeed, 'exercise' suggests that there is a need for repetition in order to grasp the concept involved. It also suggests that there is an element of hard work involved in the process of developing such a judgement. Therefore, through repeated hard work, the pupil can hope to develop an insight into how and when to recollect a certain item of information and apply it to a problem when presented. This process could be viewed as becoming a librarian in the library of knowledge: the information that the teacher has conveyed is contained in all of the books within this knowledge library, but unless the pupil knows how to find the requisite book to answer a certain problem, he or she will revert to a situation in which he or she has the information, but not the judgement to utilize the information. The facts will remain in the books, but without an insight into how to recall and use the appropriate book for a particular problem, the books themselves will be useless to the pupil. The accompanying judgement, therefore, is similar in this analogy to being equipped with an understanding of how the books in the knowledge library are organized and in what section of the library one needs to search when a problem is presented.[4]

It is therefore one of the tasks of the teacher to ensure that, when a pupil is presented with problems beyond the direct scope of the teaching and learning to which he or she has been exposed under tutelage, the pupil is able to identify the appropriate problem types in order to arrive at the appropriate solution types. That is, if a pupil is presented with a problem of 'type A', that pupil could never hope to solve a problem of 'type A' if he or she were first unable to distinguish between 'type A' and, say, 'type B' problems. The first stage of any solution – that is, the application of information – is to recognize the 'type' of problem that is being presented. Such an ability to recognize the 'type' of a problem finds its roots in the pupil's judgement – the insight acquired and developed through his or her training under the authority of the teacher. Such an insight is reinforced by way of examples that require not only the recitation of information, but also an accompanying judgement of when such information applies:

> [T]he instructor has not only to hear his pupils recite the Catechism, the Highway Code, the Capes and Bays, the eight-times multiplication table and the Kings of England, but he has also to see that they can answer questions in which the information is properly used. For the importance of information is the accuracy with which it is learned and the readiness with which it can be recollected and used.
>
> (Oakeshott, 2001: 56)

The significance of information in the knowledge process is therefore established in the judgement that is developed alongside it, which ensures that the pupil is capable of identifying *when* and *how* to apply the information to a problem in hand. The judgement, in this way, provides the information with its importance and relevance to the pupil.

Without a judgement in application, the information is, in essence, useless and uninteresting to the pupil. Judgement, in this sense, breathes life into the inertness of information, to provide the dynamic twist to knowledge that is missing in its absence. This is perhaps why Oakeshott (2001: 57) suggests that 'something of what I mean by "judgement" has begun to appear whenever the pupil perceives that information must be used' – that is, it is in being aware of the application of information that the information assumes importance. And this awareness is found in the pupil's judgement (Oakeshott, 2001: 57): '"Judgement", then, is that which, when united with information, generates knowledge or "ability" to do, to make or to understand and explain. It is being able to think – not to think in no manner in particular, but to think with an appreciation of the considerations which belong to different modes of thought.'

It is obvious precisely how information may be passed on to the pupil by the teacher. The fact that information is recorded in textbooks and the like means that it can be imparted by means of some form of quasi-passive[5] instruction – that is, by encouraging the rote learning of facts and so on. Judgement, however, seems somewhat more difficult to explain, particularly with regard to how it may be taught. For Oakeshott, however, the first note of importance is that the teaching of a judgement is part of the remit of the teacher – that is, that judgement cannot be self-taught and it cannot be learned without the aid of a teacher. Indeed, '"judgement" may be *taught*; and it belongs to the deliberate enterprise of the teacher to teach it' (Oakeshott, 2001: 58). Moreover, it is acquired and developed through imitation of the teacher's tacit implications, which manifest themselves in his or her actions and words. It cannot be pulled apart from the information that it accompanies to be taught in a separate lesson. Information and judgement are taught in the same lessons, but through different teaching mediums. So where information is passed on by means of lists, examples and exercises, judgement is tacitly imparted through the teacher's choice of actions, words and mannerisms, which subtly encourage the pupil to follow his or her lead. Judgement therefore:

> . . . can be taught only in conjunction with the transmission of information. That is to say, it cannot be taught in a separate lesson which is not, for example, a geography, a Latin or an algebra lesson. Thus, from the pupil's point of view, the ability to think is something

learned as a by-product of acquiring information; and from the teacher's point of view, it is something which, if it is taught, must be imparted obliquely in the course of instruction.

(Oakeshott, 2001: 58)

In essence, therefore, while the teacher is instructing the pupil under his or her charge in the appropriate information, he or she must consider the manner in which he or she does so, because it is this manner that tacitly imparts a judgement in how the pupil is to use and apply the information to future problems when the teacher is no longer visibly present. However, in conducting himself or herself in such a way, the teacher permits the pupils an insight that they may use in their own future problems. The teacher, in this way, will never leave the pupil's side, even when that pupil comes to solve such problems *on his or her own*.[6] This judgement provides the pupil with the ability to think for himself or herself, yet rather paradoxically constrains that pupil's thinking to align with the judgement that he or she received from the teacher at the point of teaching contact. Such constraint in judgement is necessary to prevent radical dissent from appropriated judgements within subject disciplines. In this way, the pupil never truly breaks from the teacher's training, to the extent that all of the pupil's future judgements are conducted in such a way as to align with the judgement that was displayed during teaching. Some would argue that such constraint restricts moments of true inspiration and genius; I would argue that such a criticism is short-sighted and ill-considered. Indeed, rather than restrict genius, such a judgement is instilled in the pupil by his or her teacher to *encourage* a moment of insight that might *generate* genius. Furthermore, such a criticism is founded in the notion that true genius comes only from total creativity and spontaneity – but without a judgement, imparted by one's teacher at point of teaching, one could never recognize an instance of inspiration or originality even if it were looking one straight in the face. Indeed, judgement is the very thing that makes it clear when genius or remarkable insight presents itself. It provides the pupil with an assurance that he or she has cause to believe in a moment of inspiration. Without it, the pupil is lost in a wilderness of ignorance, ever unable to unlock the potential gems that he or she might have harvested under the tutelage of an expert master and the judgement that he or she might have received from such a master.

Furthermore, judgement not only equips a pupil with the ability to know *when* to use the information that he or she has been given at teaching, but also equips the pupil with the ability to decide *how* to put such information to use (Oakeshott, 2001: 58). That is, in any solution that goes beyond the information given to the pupil at teaching, there are two stages at which judgement is required: first, the stage of recognizing that the information is useful in this instance – the knowing *when*; and secondly, the stage of putting the information into practice – the knowing *how*. So, for example, when I was taught the quadratic formula in mathematics, I was given the information – perhaps the formula itself – but I also had to be equipped with an insight into *when* the formula applied to a given problem. To complete the teaching and learning, I had to develop an understanding of *how* – once I had recognized that the formula was applicable – to apply the formula to the problem in question, which went beyond the scope of the examples given in teaching. It is in such an instance that Oakeshott (2001: 59) claims: 'We may listen to what a man has to say, but unless we overhear in it a mind at work and can detect the idiom of thought, we have understood nothing.'

Information without judgement therefore equips the pupil with only a useless form of knowledge. Such knowledge is distorted beyond recognition and can never be used. It is a currency that is of no value in a market dominated by genuine knowledge, which is equipped with the freedom of its use, spurred on by a component of judgement. The 'mind at work' that the pupil is expected to see in the teacher is the tacit understanding of the judgement that the teacher possesses and that which the pupil *hopes* to possess to grasp his or her inheritance fully. Learning, therefore, 'is acquiring the ability to feel and to think, and the pupil will never acquire these abilities unless he has learned to listen for them and to recognize them in the conduct and utterances of others' (Oakeshott, 2001: 59). The pupil is required to submit to the authority commanded by this conduct and these so-called 'utterances' in the belief that what they portray is of intrinsic value to him or her. Developing a judgement is the component of knowledge, therefore, which dispenses with the inertness of information. It is, in essence, 'the real substance of our inheritance – and nothing can be inherited without learning' (Oakeshott, 2001: 60). The teacher therefore must consider it to be the very *raison d'être* in his or her dealings with the pupils under his or her tutelage. The teacher must convey information and 'impart' judgement, to encourage the pupil to grasp a fuller picture of the inheritance of human achievements.

With respect to teaching and learning, judgement cannot be separated from the information that it accompanies. As Oakeshott (2001: 60) argues: 'It cannot be *learned* separately; it is never explicitly learned and it is known only in practice; but it may be learned in everything that is learned.' Judgement, therefore, is distinguishable from information only to the extent that it is not articulated. It lurks beneath the surface of learning, but can be found in all learning that takes place. Furthermore (Oakeshott, 2001: 60): 'It cannot be *taught* separately; it can have no place of its own in a timetable or a curriculum. It cannot be taught overtly, by precept, because it comprises what is required to animate precept; but it may be taught in everything that is taught.' That is, judgement is to be taught using only the manifestations of actions in *particular cases*. It is taught as an insight into the workings of the teacher, in order to give the pupil a view of how to progress in future problems. Perhaps paradoxically, however, it is not taught *in its own right*, but it is taught in *everything* that is taught – that is, it cannot be pulled apart from the information that it provides an ability to apply. It is inextricably linked to such information and stands alongside it in teaching. In this sense, we can perhaps see why teaching by example is the requisite tool for successful teaching, which equips the pupil to proceed in the desired manner, '[f]or "teaching by example", which is sometimes dismissed as an inferior sort of teaching, generating inflexible knowledge because the rules of what is known remain concealed, is emancipating the pupil from half-utterances of rules by making him aware of a concrete situation' (Oakeshott, 2001: 60). That is, by highlighting particular cases to the pupil, the teacher is able to convey the requisite information, but also to display – within his or her 'utterances' – how such information might be applied. The example therefore provides a particular case of a general solution; in this particular case, the teacher attempts within his or her teaching to release the pupil from ignorance by bringing the rules that are encompassed in information to life. The example, in this sense, provides an insight into how future problems might be solved. Moreover, it gives a context to the abstractness of information. This context lies in seeing the master at work. The example provides an opportunity for the pupil to imitate the teacher, and repeated imitation – it is hoped – will lead the pupil to be freed from ignorance, by developing the information and judgement required to embrace his or her inheritance fully. As Oakeshott (2001: 60) puts it: 'In imitating the example [the pupil] acquires not merely a model for the particular occasion, but the disposition to recognize everything as an occasion. It is a habit of listening to an individual intelligence at work in every utterance that may be acquired by imitating a teacher who has this habit.'

The teacher's authority is therefore well founded. He or she is a standard-bearer marching to battle, leading the way for the pupils to follow. He or she provides examples and, in doing so, provides the leadership that is required to initiate the pupil into the inheritance of human achievements. Knowledge – the combination of information and judgement – can be passed on in no other way. The teacher must provide the examples, and the pupil must imitate the master both in the information that he or she has been given and in the way in which it was given to him or her. Moreover, the teacher must cherish the message that he or she hopes to impart, lest he or she risk compromising its value. Indeed, such 'intellectual virtues may only be imparted by a teacher who really cares about them for their own sake and never stoops to the priggishness of mentioning them' (Oakeshott, 2001: 60).

The responsible, 'learned' teacher leads the way and, in doing so, gives his or her pupils no other choice but to follow. The actions of the learned teacher are methodical and authoritative. He or she commands respect through his or her actions; cherishes his or her message, and recognizes that the collection of knowledge for which he or she has been given responsibility is not his or her own to tamper with; and passes this knowledge inheritance on to the pupils, showing them through his or her own actions that this knowledge is to be protected, and demonstrating how and when it is to be used. The leadership of the learned teacher is evident in all of his or her actions – so much so that even when the pupils embark on their own endeavours, the teacher's impact has left its mark. The pupils are never totally free from their teacher's input; they are always constrained by his or her teaching. The teacher's actions always spoke louder than his or her words: as Oakeshott (2001: 60) would have it, '[n]ot the cry, but the rising of the wild duck impels the flock to follow him'.[7]

7 THE NEED FOR AUTHORITY IN KNOWLEDGE, TEACHING AND LEARNING, AND EDUCATION

In the last chapter, I outlined Oakeshott's definition of knowledge as information accompanied by judgement; I also outlined what the implications of such an understanding of knowledge are for the processes of teaching and learning. It now seems necessary to relate these notions back to that of authority, particularly with reference to the teacher's authority in teaching, but also the reasons why authority is necessary in embracing the knowledge that is constructed as Oakeshott has described.

Authority and knowledge

I will begin with an examination of why the authority of the teacher is an indispensable aspect of acquiring the knowledge. Recall that, in all knowledge, there is always a component of information and judgement. Consider first the notion of information: information was inert in nature, factual and impersonal; it took no account of personal dispositions and was to be transmitted by direct instruction. Information of this kind can never hope to be passed on unless the more 'learned' person – the teacher – has the authority to disseminate such information to those in his or her charge – the pupils. Indeed, should the teacher have no authority in this instance, the information that he or she chooses to convey need not assume any importance to the pupils in receipt of it.

Therefore, should a teacher ever hope to convey such a message successfully to pupils, the teacher must be acknowledged as the authoritative representative of the information that he or she chooses to convey – that is, he or she is to be recognized as *an authority* in his or her subject, and in the information that is encompassed in the matter of his or her subject. The teacher's authority in conveying such information is founded in his or her own training – a training that has made him or her stand out as an expert in the subject and the information that it entails as its subject matter.

Inextricably linked to the teacher's expertise is the authority that he or she is entitled to claim as a master of his or her subject. The fact, therefore, that the teacher possesses the information and chooses to convey it to the pupils *in itself* commands an authority that is to be adhered to should the pupils ever wish to attain such information themselves. The teacher's authority is therefore founded in his or her expertise, and this expertise is founded in a mastery of the information that he or she is choosing to convey.

To challenge or undermine the authority of the teacher is inadvertently to challenge and undermine the information that he or she has the expertise to transmit through teaching. As a consequence, to undermine such information is to undermine the notion of ever hoping to be knowledgeable, since information was an indispensable facet of knowledge itself. Therefore, in hoping to extinguish his or her own ignorance, the pupil has no other choice but to accept the teacher's authority, as an expert in the information in which the pupil himself or herself hopes to become an expert. To reject such an authority is to couple arrogance with ignorance, to the extent that it signals not only that the pupil is 'uninformed', but also that he or she has no interest in submitting to someone who is more informed than the pupil himself or herself. Such an arrogance founded in ignorance is inexplicable and inexcusable in equal measure.

Let us consider next the element of 'judgement' in knowledge. Acquiring and developing a judgement could be considered, under Oakeshott's definition, to be grasping the teacher's *way of working* – that is, to develop a judgement is to develop an understanding of how and when to act, in accordance with how and when the teacher might act given similar circumstances. By its very nature, therefore, judgement seems to be attained in but one way: through close imitation of one's teacher and the ways in which he or she chooses to operate in given circumstances. I alluded to this notion of imitation in the last chapter.

The important point of note in this instance, however, is that an imitation of this kind, by its very essence, requires an unshakable devotion to the teacher's chosen methods of working. This unshakable devotion, undoubtedly, finds its justification in the authority of the teacher, and the practices that he or she chooses to adopt and convey in his *own* workings. In the absence of authority in this instance, the pupil has no other option but to form his or her own judgement and to decide what *works for him or her*. Without the guidance that the teacher's authority naturally commands and the judgement that emanates from it, the pupil is to wander whimsically into a labyrinth of potentially unrecognizable and unsolvable quandaries. Equipped, on the other hand, with the judgement that emanates from the teacher's authority, the pupil is able to recognize problems and feel assured in solving them, on the basis of the information and judgement that he or she has at hand as a result of his or her training. That training – that apprenticeship – was a process of initiation into the pupil's inheritance of knowledge. This knowledge was a dichotomy of information and judgement, which provided the pupil with the requisite tools to apply that information to future endeavours. Hence to reject the authority of the teacher's chosen methods is to reject the possibility of gaining an insight to which the teacher is attempting to grant the pupil access. This insight is in the teacher's possession, attained during the course of his or her *own* training. When the teacher shows the pupil his or her ways of working, he or she is permitting the pupil a glimpse of how and when things *should be done*.

A pupil who chooses to reject this insight – an insight that is a privilege to access – is as arrogant as the pupil who turns his or her back on the information that the teacher hopes to share with his or her pupils. The teacher is like a master chef: he or she knows the recipe *and* knows how to apply it. The teacher's authority is unquestionable, the foundations of it rooted in his or her own training. The teacher has served his or her own apprenticeship and has experienced the errors that can befall an ignorant being. He or she has a message worth hearing and seeing; indeed, that message is worth imitation. The teacher has methods worth experiencing. His or her ways are to be closely watched, for these are the ways of the tradition and practice from which the teacher comes. In every lesson, the teacher puts on a show that grants its viewers permission to witness the secrets with which the teacher's training has endowed him or her.

The teacher is a selfless beast, offering his or her own insight to ensure that others might avoid errors. The teacher's judgement commands an authority in its own right, to be adhered to in an effort to avoid ignorance and to be rejected at the risk of the gravest of losses. Indeed, such judgement is never attainable unless the authority of the teacher's tutelage is acknowledged and embraced. And if the judgement is never attainable, then one can never hope to be liberated with an ability *to do*.

In imitating the ways of the teacher, however, the pupil can open the door into a world of action, application and active engagement. That pupil can embrace his or her inheritance and make significant contributions towards it – for he or she has been equipped with the judgement to do so. In essence, the pupil will have become 'learned' himself or herself; will have embraced his or her worth; and will have become the best that he or she can possibly be. Ultimately, the pupil will have acquired information and an accompanying judgement – will have become knowledgeable – and his or her coming into being will have been founded in the acceptance of the authority of the master.

Authority in teaching and learning

The requirement of an authoritative component is equally as evident within the notions of teaching and learning. Consider, first, the notion of teaching as described in the last chapter. Recall that teaching was described as the deliberate initiation of a pupil into his or her knowledge inheritance, through a process that was described as the cultivation of a mind. In answering the question of why authority is needed in teaching, it is therefore sufficient to demonstrate why such processes of initiation and cultivation cannot be successful *without* authority.

Any initiation, first of all, requires a submission to an initiator – that is, the person who is responsible for the process of initiation. To be in receipt of an initiation, one must acknowledge that there is a process of 'following' to which one must adhere – that is, that a successful initiation requires one to lead and one to follow. Indeed, one cannot initiate oneself into an inheritance: such a process sounds contradictory in its very nature. Furthermore, an initiation requires being shown what to do and how to do it. To be initiated into an organization, for example, one must become accustomed to the way in which the organization conducts its business and one must conform to those conducts to complete one's initiation.

Also, an initiation, as a process, sets out to ensure that the initiated candidate will have attained a full membership of the organization in question. To be initiated, therefore, is to be shown *how* to become a member of the organization. To reject the organization's methods and ways of working will result in one's initiation remaining unsuccessful, and subsequently one's membership will not be signed off.

Teaching, therefore, in keeping with this analogy, is the process of setting the pupil on a journey towards embracing his or her knowledge inheritance. And the person who begins – and, indeed, ultimately rubber-stamps – this process is the teacher. In this sense, one can never hope to complete one's initiation into the knowledge inheritance that results from it unless one submits to the authority of the person who leads one through and finalizes such a process. The teaching process requires an authoritative teacher, who can lead and direct the pupil under his or her charge through the initiation process successfully. There is no better candidate for the job than the teacher; indeed, the teacher is the *only* one who can deliver successful teaching, as I asserted in the last chapter. To reject the authority of the teacher, as the agent of a successful teaching process, is therefore to reject the very essence of teaching itself.

Thus, since teaching is a process of initiation into one's own knowledge inheritance, and since this process ensures that the pupil in receipt of such an inheritance receives it and engages with it in such a way that 'it loses its second-hand or antique manner' (Oakeshott, 1989: 41), to reject the essence of the teaching process is therefore to reject the only possible way of receiving this inheritance of human achievements.

Teaching as a process is therefore impossible without authority at its core. This authority is naturally ascribed to the representative of the teaching process – the teacher – who is acknowledged as the *only* candidate capable of delivering the teaching process successfully. To teach, therefore, is to command authority; no further justification is required. The message of such teaching is accepted on the basis of this organic, natural authority, intrinsically linked to the process of teaching itself. In this sense, teaching not only requires authority; rather, teaching *commands* and *demands* authority to the extent that, when regarded as a process of initiation into a knowledge inheritance, its remit could not be fulfilled without it.

Finally, consider the process of learning and why it requires a submission to authority. Learning was described as the pupil's attempt to avoid ignorance through an engagement with and participation in his or her inheritance of knowledge. The definition that Oakeshott gave of learning distinguished between the different resources from which a learner can learn. He suggested that a pupil was the counterpart for the teacher, outlining that a learner was different from a pupil in that where a learner had no necessary attachment to a teacher, the pupil did – that is, the pupil was a learner whose learning followed directly from the teaching that he or she received from the teacher. Moreover, Oakeshott restricted teaching solely to the domain of the teacher, claiming that teaching cannot possibly result from any other activity other than the activities of a teacher. However, learning is *not* restricted under this definition as the result of teaching. For the purposes of this discussion, we can understand learning to encompass the range of activities that, broadly speaking, include learning as a result from teaching, learning from textbooks and other reliable resources, and learning from worldly experiences and activities through a process of 'discovery'.[1]

Under this definition, I can return, almost full circle, to where this discussion on authority began. Indeed, in the first part of the book, I discussed the idea of why authority might be needed within learning by considering the implications of learning in the absence of authority. In light of the definition of learning put forward by Oakeshott, it makes sense to return to this discussion at this point in writing to elaborate on the ideas from earlier in the text. Let me consider first – keeping in mind the definitions that have been outlined since previously dealing with an authority-free approach to learning – the understanding of learning as a direct result of teaching. An understanding of why authority is needed in such a version of learning comes as a natural corollary of the reasons for authority being required for the teaching, which, in this case, serves as the precept to learning. Indeed, to learn as a result of teaching is to acknowledge and submit to the authority of the teaching process; as such, this means to submit to the authority of the teacher, who, in this instance, is the agent responsible for the process of teaching. Thus no further justification for authority is required in this version of learning, since the justification has already been established in the process of teaching, which is the prerequisite process for successful learning in this instance.

The second type of learning is learning that emanates from the learner reading books and other reliable sources. Such learning is sometimes referred to – rather unfortunately and, indeed, rather confusingly – as 'self-teaching'. Oakeshott rejects such a *description* of this form of learning (while acknowledging that learning of this form is possible, he rejects the notion of 'self-teaching'), outlining that to ascribe the teaching process to a textbook, for example, would be nothing more than to use an unfortunate metaphor. Indeed, in this instance, the term 'self-teaching' is rendered incoherent, to the extent that teaching is a process that can be seen as possible only under the tutelage of a teacher. Thus to 'self-teach' is to suggest that one is capable of playing both the role of teacher *and* learner in the teaching and learning processes.

This is not to say that one cannot *learn from* such resources as textbooks; rather, one cannot *teach oneself* using such resources. Reliable resources such as textbooks possess no teaching powers, and it is not sensible to suggest that the learner who is solely dependent on the textbook or reliable resource is *teaching* himself or herself. In such an instance, however, it is still possible for the learner to *learn* from the reliable resource, under the limited guidance that such a resource provides. In this way, the reliable resource commands its own authority. I will allude to this concept later in relation to Wittgenstein's view of textbooks and the like, outlining that what appears in textbooks is largely taken on trust, to the extent that a reliable textbook or resource has been subjected to the scrutiny of the discipline whose content it contains. That is, reliable resources are the product of careful deliberation from representatives of the discipline who decide the content and agree on its manifestation in such a resource. In this way, the resource *has the backing* of the community whose views it is sent out to represent.

A reliable mathematics textbook, for example, is a collaboration of mathematical facts that the writers of the book (who must be accomplished mathematicians themselves in order for the book to be reliable) believe to be pertinent for the task at hand – namely, learning mathematics. The community of mathematicians and subsequently the practice of mathematics, in this instance, have therefore stamped their authority *onto* the book. As such, the reliable resource of this nature commands an authority of its own, given that it is a reliable account of what the community chooses to represent its practices by means of its content. This authority must be adhered to if the book is to be of any use. It would seem absurd if a learner were to scan through a reliable resource, looking for errors and subjecting the claims within the resource to doubt and scrutiny. Such a process has already been undertaken by a group of accomplished reviewers, who will have checked the information contained in the reliable resource prior to its release. Thus the authority in this instance emanates from the content of the book or reliable resource itself, and the subject from which it comes, but remains founded in the community and the practices of this subject or discipline. The resource is unable to teach – but should the learner choose to submit to the authority that the resource commands, in its very essence as a *reliable* resource, he or she can then hope to *learn* from it. Learning therefore, once again, is dependent on an acceptance of authority: in this case, the authority of the community and its practices, manifested within a reliable resource.

The final form of learning outlined was learning through experiences and 'discovery'. The notion of why authority might be required in such an instance of learning is, at first, entirely unclear. An experience or a discovery suggests that one has noticed something of importance and attached *one's own* meaning to it. Such an understanding of learning through experience or through discovery would therefore seem to require no authority, other than some form of self-regulation.

Suppose that a learner has discovered or experienced a *new* concept of which he or she had no prior understanding. Suppose that such a discovery or experience occurred under no guidance and under no authority – that is, that whatever the discovery or experience was, it was *the learner's* discovery or *the learner's* experience. Suppose, next, that the learner tries to attach a meaning to this experience or discovery. There are only two options open to explain his or her actions in this instance. First, the learner can create a meaning of his or her own and attach his or her *own* interpretation of the events to whatever the discovery or experience to which he or she has just been made privy. However, under no guidance towards a correct[2] interpretation, the learner can but offer a *viable* interpretation. Indeed, in such an instance in which the guidance of an authority[3] is absent and there is no prior understanding, viability is the *only* option. 'Correctness' has therefore lost its meaning. Learning, as a consequence, cannot be seen to deliver 'correct' understandings; only 'viable' interpretations of the information provided. In such a situation, *every* solution is viable, because *no* solution is correct. There is no way in which to decide between the correct answer and the infinitely many incorrect ones – unless, that is, authority is permitted. Authority in this instance would permit the learner to attach a meaning to his or her experience or discovery that conforms to the accepted way of working. That is not to say that the learner is to be entirely controlled to the extent that his or her own experiences tell him *nothing* original; rather, the authority in this case is used to constrain the learner's understandings within the confines of correctness.

The second attempt to circumvent the inherent problems in such a discovery system of learning is to suggest that the learner is simply discovering a notion of which he or she already has an inherent understanding and that, as such, the process of learning is nothing other than a 'connection' with the realm in which the set of *all possible solutions* is contained. Such a notion of learning as 'connecting' with this realm is known as Platonism (see Chapter 4). The realm of all 'absolute truths' is the Platonic realm, in which all knowledge exists ready for learners to connect with it. I find such a notion of learning bizarre, bordering on absurd – but it is not the mere ramblings of lesser thinkers: such an understanding of learning has many high-profile supporters, including (self-evidently) Plato and, more recently, Sir Roger Penrose. For me, however, such an understanding of learning soils the very name of learning itself. The concept of 'learning' under such a model assumes a lesser position than that to which it is rightfully entitled. Learning is not a connection with another realm; indeed, it cannot be. If such a realm were even to exist, why should we assume that we would be able to connect with it at all? Moreover, such a realm, in its definition, could belong either (a) to an inner domain, deep within the catacombs of the mind, or (b) to an ethereal world that exists outside of space-time. To learn, therefore, would be either (a) to provoke these hidden depths of the mind into action – to release knowledge to us upon discovering or experiencing it, or (b) to make a strange connection with an ethereal realm that rests outside of the confines of the real world. In case (a), everyone, presumably, would have the same realm 'in mind', although only the privileged few would be able to gain access to its deepest crevasses – and those privileged few would be the most intelligent and most knowledgeable among us. In case (b), precisely how the connection between a material (real) world and an immaterial (ethereal) world might be made is altogether unclear.

In such a world, learning would not be learning at all. Learning would not even be possible, since 'to learn' would assume a meaning of being able to connect with this other world (whether within the mind or existing somewhere in the ether). Even if such a world were to exist and our only hope of connecting with it were through discovery or experience, it would, by definition, contain *all* possible solutions to *all* possible problems. In such a world, upon connection with it, how would the learner distinguish between what was a correct solution and what was an incorrect solution? In the absence of authority, even in this science-fiction abstract world, the learner remains unable to distinguish between correct and incorrect. Learning becomes a 'connection' with an abstract world rather than an alignment with an authority in the *real* world.

Thus, even in the instances of learning through experience or 'discovery', the learner remains dependent on the authority of a master or a practice as the *only* option (since the other options have been rejected) to guide him or her towards the solution that the learner *is expected* to see within his or her experience or discovery. Learning, therefore, is a quest to avoid ignorance – a quest that has but one guide: the guidance of authority.

The inbuilt safeguards of authority

What, then, of the teacher to whom the authority has been ascribed, and what of the practice and community from whom the authority emanates? These are to take their respective authorities seriously. The teacher is to acknowledge that he or she is in a privileged position, awarded an authority under which he or she can influence the lives and minds of his or her pupils. Should the teacher ever abuse his or her authority, or should he or she ever become domineering or tyrannical as a result of this authority, that teacher is to be stripped of it by the community from which he or she comes. If the teacher's authority masks the message that he or she seeks to pass on to pupils, that teacher is to be removed from his or her position as a representative of his or her practice. If the teacher oppresses originality or rejects new ideas, particularly from his or her own pupils, that teacher is to consider himself or herself a failure in his or her duty. The teacher has a responsibility to keep up to date with the changes within his or her discipline, so that the message that he or she conveys to the pupils is the most up-to-date version available. The teacher is to self-scrutinize, to ensure that his or her message is pure.

The teacher must also always remember the community and practice to whom he or she is answerable. The teacher is not a renegade; he or she is a representative, and his or her behaviours should reflect this.

The community and practice from which the teacher comes themselves have similar responsibilities to the learners under their charge. First, the practice must act as a guide for the actions of the teachers who represent it. In the same way, the accepted ways of working adopted by the community are to serve as the teacher's guidance in the mannerisms that he or she conveys to pupils. Thus the pupil can have direct access to the practices of the teacher and to his or her ways of working. The community must consistently scrutinize its own adopted practices and the actions that it is suggesting as appropriate via its representatives. If the message becomes stale and outdated, or if the message is faltering in its correctness, it must be overthrown and replaced with a message and a practice that are justifiable and pure. In adhering to a form of self-regulation, the community – whose responsibility it is to cultivate and disseminate its adopted practices – can ensure that its message is clear, concise and beyond reproval.

8 WITTGENSTEIN ON AUTHORITY

A foundationalist approach

The final section of this book is dedicated to perhaps the most unlikely of educational contributors; in equal measure, however, he is the philosopher who contributes the most to the debate for authority in knowledge, teaching and learning, and education in general, in his typically deflationary approach. The author in question is Ludwig Wittgenstein. He has made several contributions to the discourse regarding the significant role that authority – and particularly training – plays in a successful education. The purpose of this section, therefore, is to examine the nature of these contributions, in an effort to finalize this discussion on authoritative approaches to teaching, learning, knowledge development and, generally speaking, education.

Rather strangely, the contribution that Wittgenstein makes to the educational 'authority debate' is lesser in terms of content than those of others, but arguably more pertinent in terms of its profound connection with why authority is at the core of a successful education and all that this encompasses. Perhaps this is typical of Wittgenstein the scholar: to say less and yet to achieve more than most of his academic counterparts in any debate with which he considered it worth engaging. This discussion of Wittgenstein's writings must begin with developing the ideas of distinguishing *categorially* between certainty and knowledge. This inadvertently (and rather conveniently, for the purposes of this discussion) solves the 'Aristotelian problem'[1] of knowledge founded in knowledge, outlined in Chapter 4. However, the distinction serves a more salient cause – namely, to demonstrate that learning is founded in the development of bedrock certainties that emanate from an initial trust in one's teacher and the training that one receives on the back of such a trust. Learning can therefore be successful only when one trusts one's teacher and the training that he or she provides. I will elaborate on these points in more detail in the next few sections.

The categorial distinction between certainty and knowledge

I must begin this section with some preliminary definitions, in order to ensure that what follows can be more readily understood. First, in the subheading to this section, I have used three words that need explicit definition if they are to be clear: 'category', 'certainty' and 'knowledge'. I have already discussed the notion of knowledge at length in previous chapters, and so the interest in this case is the *distinction* between knowledge and certainty as concepts from a purely philosophical stance.

First, however, the notion of a category in this sense can be described as a collection of objects that are governed by a set of accompanying rules. Knowledge, for example, is a category the objects of which are the 'set' of propositions, and these propositions are governed by the rules of logic and propositional calculus. Therefore the propositions of knowledge can, generally speaking, be established as true or false, reasonable or unreasonable, on the basis of an adherence to the rules that govern them. In this way, knowledge propositions can be doubted, and the doubt in a knowledge proposition is removed or reduced only when there is some evidence for its removal. However, even in the case in which the doubt is removed, it is not unintelligible – that is, doubt can be removed or reduced only once it is permitted as possible (that is, conceivable) in the first place. To understand why the notion of a category is important in this debate, the reader needs only to understand the importance of being able to distinguish between *different* categories, on the basis of the objects that belong to them. Therefore, if there is an object that does not adhere to the parameters and construction of the 'knowledge category' outlined, then one cannot place the object into that knowledge category. Categories are therefore useful in determining which objects are similar to each other in terms of their construction and the rules that they obey; as such, these objects can be grouped together, along with a set of rules to govern them, into a category of their own.

What, then, might this definition of a category have to do with the notions of certainty and knowledge? Indeed, perhaps a more sensible question would be to ask what gave Wittgenstein (1969: 39e) grounds for claiming that: "'Knowledge" and "certainty" belong to different *categories*. They are not two "mental states" like, say "surmising" and "being sure". The answer provides one of the most profound contributions to modern philosophy, and also highlights Wittgenstein as a most profound and notable thinker in terms of how certainty and knowledge are distinct, and yet connected, concepts. In claiming that knowledge and certainty belong to different categories, Wittgenstein is saying (according to my definition of categories) that certainty and knowledge – as two concepts – are of different constructions and are governed by different rules. The greatest distinguishing feature between these two concepts is, according to Wittgenstein, the role that *doubt* plays in each of their respective constructions and subsequently the rules by which they are governed.

Knowledge, for Wittgenstein, is a concept that results when a proposition has been subjected to doubt and has required some form of justification – that is, a consideration and subsequent rejection of doubt in the concept involved. Certainty, on the other hand, is at the bedrock of knowledge and requires no such justification or doubt – that is, if one is 'certain' of something, one is making a claim that there was *not* an absence of doubt, but a logical *impossibility* of doubt. In essence, certainties emanate from concepts in relation to which doubt is incoherent, as opposed to rejected as false or improbable. In contrast, knowledge emanates from concepts that have been subjected to doubt and which doubt has been dispelled on the basis of some form of logical justification. Knowledge therefore is propositional in nature, whereas certainty is non-propositional to the extent that it is not to be derived from logic or propositional calculus.

This distinction is a profound contribution to the philosophical doctrine, which still permeates the mainstream understandings of knowledge and certainty (even though many scholars continue to be careless with these terms and continue to exchange them freely as though they were mere different *kinds* of the same 'thing'). Never, before Wittgenstein, had philosophers articulated so profoundly and elegantly a situation in which the foundations of knowledge could be *categorially* distinct from the knowledge itself, which was henceforth to rest upon these certainties. Wittgenstein (1969: 59e) outlines his own acknowledgement of the lack of distinguishability between certainty and knowledge: 'There are cases where doubt is unreasonable, but others where it seems logically impossible. And there seems to be no clear boundary between them.'

In this acknowledgement, Wittgenstein is outlining that knowledge results from considerations of which doubt has been discarded as 'unreasonable', whereas certainty results from rendering the notion of doubt as 'logically impossible'. However, notice also that, at his time of writing, Wittgenstein was elucidating a clear misconception (perhaps within the philosophical literature at the time) in where the 'boundary' between knowledge and certainty lies. Wittgenstein therefore seeks to establish such a boundary by outlining that the key concept that distinguishes knowledge and certainty is doubt (and its natural counterpart, 'justification', which is the tool required for dispensing of doubt in the cases in which doubt is logically permitted). This boundary is established in the acknowledgement of the fact that, as one passes from the notion of knowledge to the notion of certainty, 'doubt gradually loses its sense' (Wittgenstein, 1969: 9e).

Therefore certainty belongs to a different category from knowledge in as much as the construct of knowledge permits doubt and has rules either to which to submit or with which to dispense with doubt in any knowledge propositions, whereas certainty is a construct that renders the notion of doubt logically incoherent – that is, doubt is not only absent from certainty, but is, in fact, also logically prohibited. In this way, Moyal-Sharrock (2007: 80) asserts: 'For Wittgenstein, it is *not* true that a mistake gets more and more improbable as we go from a hypothesis to a rule. At some point a mistake has "ceased to be conceivable".[2] A change of category, not of degree, has occurred.' Therefore, since knowledge and certainty have different constructs and are governed by different rules, they belong to different categories. This categorial distinction will become ever more relevant in the next section, when I will display the importance of such a distinction as a prerequisite to the claim that knowledge is founded in a concept that is categorially different from it, hence sidestepping the Aristotelian problem of knowledge founded in knowledge.[3]

Bedrock certainty: Trust and training

In considering the distinction between certainty and knowledge, Wittgenstein made a significant contribution to the understanding of the philosophical epistemic doctrine known as 'foundationalism', perhaps unintentionally. Foundationalism encompasses a range of philosophical ideas that, until Wittgenstein's unique contribution, purported knowledge to be constructed within a 'knowledge foundation' that is *different in kind* from the knowledge that rests on it. *The Oxford Dictionary of Philosophy* (Blackburn, 2008: 139, emphasis added) defines 'foundationalism' as '[t]he view in epistemology that knowledge must be regarded as a structure raised upon secure, *certain* foundations. These are found in some combination of experience and reason, with different schools (empiricism, rationalism) emphasizing the role of one over that of the other.'

It is interesting to note that the distinction is made in this definition of foundationalism that the foundations of knowledge are to be *certain*, as opposed to them being another *kind* of knowledge. Until Wittgenstein, such a distinction *in category* was never achieved or recognized. Wittgenstein pioneered the construction of indubitable bedrock certainties, from which doubt was logically excluded as opposed to merely rejected, to give the first coherent account of a foundationalist approach to knowledge – that is, Wittgenstein seems to have made a pioneering contribution to the notion of foundationalism, to the extent that he put forth an argument that knowledge is constructed within a foundation of bedrock certainties. He succeeds other (what I believe to be) failed attempts at solving the potential problem of foundationless knowledge, or knowledge founded within knowledge. For Wittgenstein, doubt was not a default position, as it was with Descartes, for example; rather, doubt was induced only when justification or verification was required. In this way, doubt was housed inside 'not-doubting'.

Indeed, the notion of foundationalism was given significance when Aristotle put forth the argument that there simply had to be a foundation to knowledge, lest we result in circular reasoning, proof of self-evident statements or an infinite knowledge regress (all ideas of which I have spoken elsewhere in this text). Aristotle therefore argued that knowledge was to be founded in indubitable precepts that depended on the faculties of perception and memory. Such faculties, however, are clearly not indubitable, since one can doubt one's own perception of things and one can have a hazy memory.

Descartes, another prominent foundationalist (rationalist), put forward the alternative argument that knowledge was to be founded within the indubitable notion of one's own existence and all of the ideas encapsulated under one's own existence. Such a belief came as the result of Descartes' famous claim *cogito ergo sum*, or 'I think, therefore I am', which was Descartes' attempt at connecting knowledge – and its construction – to the supposedly indubitable beginnings of his own existence. Descartes' foundationalism was predicated on the notion that the foundations of knowledge were to be discovered in the 'clear and distinct' ideas of reason. But this is equally as unappealing as Aristotle's attempted solution, since by invoking the faculty of 'reasoning' at the foundation, one naturally invokes the corollary of reason: doubt. And if one can doubt at the foundational level (since one must reason to get there), one does not have indubitable foundations, purely on the basis of the fact that one may have reasoned incorrectly. However 'clear' or 'distinct' Descartes' ideas of reason were posited to be, they could never *logically exclude* doubt. Similarly, as outlined in Chapter 4, Descartes brings himself to the foundations of knowledge, rejecting everything that can be open to doubt, and leaves himself there, unable to rebuild the edifice of knowledge without the very tools that he has cast aside to get to the foundations in the first place. By attempting to find a 'demon-proof' method, Descartes 'has a basis, but no way of building on it without invoking principles that will not be demon-proof, and so will not meet the standards he has apparently set himself' (Blackburn, 2008: 232).

I, like Wittgenstein, find both of these notions unsatisfying in their quest to solve the knowledge foundational problem, or the 'Aristotelian problem' as I have already called it. Without a foundation, one must either find that knowledge is circular in its construction or that it induces an infinite regress. Therefore both Aristotle and Descartes (and indeed many other philosophers) chose to place perception and memory, and one's own existence, respectively, at the foundation of knowledge to avoid such foundational issues.

However, the difference between both of these foundations and knowledge itself is a *difference in kind* – that is, the foundations of knowledge were to be considered as a *different kind* of knowledge that depended on no further justification: it was 'indubitable knowledge' (two words that, for Wittgenstein, could never have been juxtaposed coherently, on the basis of his certainty–knowledge distinctions) at the bedrock and all other knowledge was to be reasoned from within on the basis of this bedrock.

Wittgenstein, however, pioneers a more satisfying solution to the problem of foundationless knowledge by distinguishing between 'certainties' and 'knowledge', and thus founding knowledge *inside* bedrock certainties. That is, at the basis of knowledge, for Wittgenstein, are certainties: truly indubitable concepts that are irrefutably constructed in their very nature. Moreover, certainties are regarded as indubitable to the extent that we act on the basis of a certainty in such a way that we *demonstrate* our lack of – that is, the inconceivability of – doubt. Certainties, therefore, are not of a different *kind*, but are of a different *nature* – or a different *category*, as it were.

By distinguishing between the categories, Wittgenstein has developed a foundationalist system of knowledge that prevents knowledge from being foundationless, but also has succeeded where his predecessors had failed – that is, in founding knowledge in truly indubitable beginnings, of a different *nature*, rather than of a different *kind*. Therefore knowledge is founded in indubitable, non-knowledge foundations. Indeed, as Stroll (1994: 145) argues: 'Wittgenstein's genius consisted in constructing an account of human knowledge whose foundations, whose supporting presuppositions, were in no ways like knowledge. Knowledge belongs to the language game, and certitude does not. The base and the mansion resting on it are completely different. That is what Wittgenstein means when he says that knowledge and certainty belong to different *categories.*'

Wittgenstein, perhaps a 'closet foundationalist' as opposed to being an overt foundationalist, has therefore succeeded in foundationalizing knowledge where Aristotle and Descartes failed (along with others, such as Moore – to whom Wittgenstein directs much of his writings – and Quine). Aristotle's supposedly indubitable foundations of knowledge – perceptions and memory – are called into question when one realizes that the faculties of perception and memory are *not* beyond doubting. Indeed, perceptions can be mistaken and memory can be faulty or misleading. Descartes, in attempting to take his own existence as the indubitable beginnings of his own knowledge, failed to the extent that he demanded that one must be knowledgeable of one's own certainties. Malcolm (1986: 211) distinguishes between Wittgenstein and Descartes, while highlighting the inherent similarities that exist in both of their respective understandings of knowledge:

There are two points of agreements between Descartes' conception of 'metaphysical' certainty and Wittgenstein's conception of 'objective' certainty. Both conceptions have these two features: first, being certain of something, in either sense, entails the impossibility of being able to seriously entertain any doubt about it; second, this certainty entails the impossibility of one's being mistaken. Descartes' conception has the third feature that this certainty entails that one *knows* what one is certain of. But in Wittgenstein's conception this is rejected.

Other authors have made a similar note on Wittgenstein's work and on how it stands in contrast with other scholars who write on the same concepts:

> But one principle that all foundationalists, including Wittgenstein, accept is that if p is foundational, p is certain. If follows that if p is not certain, then p is not foundational, and this entails that being certain is a necessary condition for p's being foundational. Moore also accepts this principle. So at least Moore and Wittgenstein agree in this respect. Where they differ is over the question of whether the foundations are *knowable*.
>
> (Stroll, 1994: 155, emphasis added)

Indeed, this feature of Wittgenstein's work even serves to separate him from one of the other authors on which this text has focused, Michael Polanyi. Where Polanyi argued that explicit knowledge was to be founded within tacit knowledge – a construction of knowledge that he developed – Wittgenstein's understanding of knowledge and how it is constructed was to deny any notion of knowledge being founded in another form of knowledge, the only distinction of which was to be a distinction in *kind*. Wittgenstein, perhaps typically, demanded more – and, rather paradoxically, provided a more deflationary understanding of knowledge to fulfil this demand. Wittgenstein's foundationalism therefore circumvents the inherent difficulties with which both Aristotle's and Descartes' foundationalist approaches were fraught. It even serves to separate Wittgenstein's thinking from Polanyi's, in that the former circumvents the problems that potentially infest the latter's 'theory of knowledge'. Indeed, as Moyal-Sharrock (2007: 10) outlines: '[T]he message of *On Certainty* is precisely that knowledge does not have to be at the basis of knowledge. Underpinning knowledge are not default justified propositions that must be susceptible of justification on demand, but pragmatic certainties that can only be verbally rendered for heuristic purposes, and whose conceptual analysis uncovers their function as unjustifiable rules of grammar.' In this way, we can also see how 'philosophers have lost touch with the *spontaneity* of our beginnings' (Moyal-Sharrock, 2007: 10, emphasis added).

This particular author continues:

> In an excessive subservience to reason, they have rationalized our every act and thought, seeking to trace reasoning that often never was. In *On Certainty*, Wittgenstein attempts to reverse the process, to release us from the hegemony of the intellect and remind us that where we look for a thought or a reason, it is often a 'direct taking-hold'[4] that has occurred. Here, at the origin of our knowledge, there are no such preliminaries as proposition, judgement and inference, but spontaneity, automatism, reflex and instinct.
>
> (Moyal-Sharrock, 2007: 10)

By demanding less, Wittgenstein achieves more. Indeed, he makes no claims to have a 'theory' of knowledge. Moreover, he demonstrates by way of example that 'certitude' is a category that rejects the notion of doubt as incoherent – an achievement that had previously been overlooked (and perhaps has since been overlooked, in Polanyi's case) by other scholars who were determined to solve the Aristotelian problem and yet failed in the very fact that they ignored this most profound achievement, attributable to Wittgenstein for championing its cause. For, in acknowledging that the basis of knowledge is certainty, which is of a different construction (or different category) to the extent that it is not to be subjected to doubt in the way that knowledge can be, Wittgenstein has created a model of knowledge construction that is foundationalist in nature and which, as such, circumvents all of the problems inherent in the Aristotelian problem, while remaining non-contradictory by virtue of the fact that he insists on a distinction between the foundations and the building that rests upon them.

On the basis of this coveted solution to the knowledge problem, Wittgenstein set on foot the solution for how learning was to be considered possible. Taking certainty as the foundational bedrock to knowledge – a foundation that differs entirely from the knowledge itself – was only the beginning of the story. It has, perhaps rather pre-emptively, shed light on the notion of learning as being possible only when the pupil trusts his or her teacher and his or her reliable resources, and the 'training' that the pupil receives in the process.

The notion of trust and the idea of training are at the core of Wittgenstein's description of how knowledge is constructed, and indeed this description demonstrates the true value of learning and the subsequent value of the teacher in these processes. In *On Certainty*, Wittgenstein gives the connective between this notion of 'certainty' that I have described in the above paragraphs and knowledge by means of a process that encompasses the notions of learning, training, belief, trust and authority. The attraction of Wittgenstein as a scholar on this topic is the ease with which he forms his propositions and, in doing so, seems to make extremely intuitive, yet irrefutable, claims about the concepts and processes of interest to us – namely, authority, trust, belief, doubt, training and so on. The process, for Wittgenstein, begins in trust. Indeed, Wittgenstein (1969: 22e) poses the following question of trust, attempting to outline how absurd life would be without a foundational trust: 'Must I not begin to trust somewhere? That is to say: somewhere I must begin with not-doubting.' In posing such a question, he is attempting to highlight the ridiculousness of a life in which *all things* are subjected to some level of doubt. He addresses this issue by suggesting that, 'in the beginning', there simply has to be 'a trust' – that is, an absolute rejection of doubt as impossible at some foundational level. It is important to note that such a claim is *not* attempting to say that one must reason about one's foundational beliefs and *reject* doubt as improbable; rather, Wittgenstein is demanding more. He is suggesting that, 'in the beginning', doubt is to be forbidden and neglected, in place of trust:

> To say that something *stands fast for me* is to say that I rely on it;[5] that I regard it as solid,[6] that I have an attitude of *trust* towards it. Wittgenstein calls objective certainty a trust[7] in an effort to distance it from reasoned belief. Indeed, we might say that objective certainty is a kind of trust or belief *in*, without that belief being reducible to a proposition. It is nonratiocinated and nonconscious trust, or *un-trust*, which we share with neonates and animals. This trust is not *experienced as trust*, but rather shows itself in the absence of mistrust – that is, in our *taking-hold* of something, *directly*, without any doubts.
> (Moyal-Sharrock, 2007: 62, emphasis original)

It is for this reason that Moyal-Sharrock (2007: 62) refers to such a trust as a 'blind trust', to the extent that it appears to have no grounds and can be understood and manifested only in our actions, which display a total absence of doubt. It is, rather counter-intuitively, *instinctive*, making no appeal to reason or consideration and making no effort to pause for a moment's reflection. Wittgenstein (1969: 23e) goes on to outline how such a trust plays a part in how we learn:

> As children we learn facts; e.g., that every human being has a brain, and we take them on trust. I believe that there is an island, Australia, of such-and-such a shape, and so on and so on; I believe that I had great-grandparents, that the people who gave themselves out as my parents really were my parents, etc. This belief may never have been expressed; even the thought that it was so, never thought.

Wittgenstein uses these examples to demonstrate how bizarre life would be if we were to question – that is, to doubt – what we are taught as children. He suggests that our actions are to be taken as demonstrable evidence of the fact that there is a complete rejection of doubt in these cases of learning. In essence, our trust is in our teachers and the facts that they convey to us through their teaching.

This trust, therefore, is demonstrated in our actions, which display that we have taken these facts that our teachers have given us and adopted them as our own. We go in no further search of justification, for such a justification would be a mere manifestation of doubt. The message is taken *on the grounds of trust*, and our certainty of the message is demonstrable in the fact that we act on the grounds of this trust to accept the truth of such a message. It is in this way that, according to Wittgenstein (1969: 23e): 'The child learns by believing the adult. Doubt comes *after* belief.' In this simple proposition, Wittgenstein pre-emptively strikes down any potential counter-arguments to his claims that trust is an indispensable aspect of learning. Indeed, this proposition outlines the dynamic nature of learning as a process, but acknowledges the need for a conservative approach *in the beginnings* of learning.

Wittgenstein also serves to distinguish further between certainty and knowledge in such a claim, and demonstrates that learning is a process that encompasses the grasping of both concepts, beginning in a trust and ending in the development of an ability to reason for oneself. But Wittgenstein's message is a warning that the cart must never be put before the horse.

Learning is to begin with trust – an absolute absence of doubt – and is to end with – on the basis of the certainties that will emanate from this trust – an ability to doubt and to reason for oneself. Such a proposition has all of the hallmarks of Polanyi's claim that faith was to precede reason – that is, that at our basis is an innate requirement to trust our intellectual superiors (those whom Wittgenstein calls 'the adult'), in a quest to establish a foundation of certitudes upon which knowledge can be built and about which we can reason. A rejection of such a trust is therefore to result in a rejection of one's access to certitude. Our actions, in such an instance, are guided by an infinite regress of reasoning: essentially, a knowledge without foundation.

The dynamic element of Wittgenstein's model is highlighted further, in his proposition that 'I learned an enormous amount and accepted it on human authority, and then I found some things confirmed or disconfirmed by my own experience' (Wittgenstein, 1969: 23e). Learning is not to be so restrictive that it is to reject an ability to reason; rather, learning is to be a process, the *genesis* of which is to be founded in trust and the *quest* of which is to grant the pupil an ability to confirm or reject a proposition on the basis of the certainties that he or she has attained through his or her initial submission to a trust. This is perhaps what Wittgenstein (1969: 46e) meant in *On Certainty* when he said: 'Doubting and non-doubting behaviour. There is the first only if there is the second.' Thus the precept for doubting is 'not-doubting', and the prerequisite for reason is 'not-reasoning'. Faith and trust come first, a foundation is constructed, and then reasoning can eventually follow. The cart remains forever behind the horse.

Such a requirement of trust at the foundations is also found in how one reads reliable resources and textbooks. Wittgenstein (1969: 23e) claims:

In general I take as true what is found in text-books, of geography for example. Why? I say: All these facts have been confirmed a hundred times over. But how do I know that? What is my evidence for it? I have a world-picture. Is it true or false? Above all it is substratum of all my enquiring and asserting.

Therefore, even in the instances of reading a reliable resource such as a textbook, Wittgenstein remains steadfast in the claim that such resources are to be trusted on the basis of the belief that the facts that are conveyed therein have been subjected to a continued process of scrutiny and, as such, can be considered *trustworthy*.

The interesting word in this proposition is 'substratum', which gives a particular foundational importance to the notion of trust. Indeed, if the notion of trust in one's teacher and one's resources is to be considered the substratum to all of one's 'enquiring and asserting', this demonstrates that 'trusting' is the basis upon which one structures one's future learning endeavours.

This also highlights how to circumvent the notion of learning through inquiry, in that if one has a foundation of certitudes that have been established through a trust in one's teacher and reliable resources, one can *go in search* of solutions to future problems on the basis of these certitudes developed through one's trust. Wittgenstein (1969: 24e) does, however, also acknowledge the inherent difficulties with understanding such a model of learning based on trust: 'The difficulty is to realize the groundlessness of our believing.' This difficulty, however, is not to overwhelm the fact that learning is possible only when it is founded in a trust, or a belief in one's teacher and reliable resources. This is why Wittgenstein (1969: 24e–25e) asserts: 'I believe what people transmit to me in a certain manner. In this way I believe geographical, chemical, historical facts etc. That is how I *learn* the sciences. Of course learning is based on believing.' However difficult it is to grasp the groundlessness of our believing, Wittgenstein suggests that we are to persevere. Indeed, it is clear in our actions and our behaviours that we do not feel compelled to challenge the trust and belief that a teacher naturally commands in his or her position as such. The fact, for example, that we do not feel compelled to check *for ourselves* the facts conveyed to us by our teachers and reliable resources is evidence that learning begins with trust. Our actions become instinctive on the basis of this trust. We do not subject the beginnings of learning to doubt in the same way as we might do had we formed our foundations on certainties. Trust is required to permit reason, but only when it is sensible.

Any scheme that advocates reasoning *all the way down* to the foundations is a scheme that is built on no foundations at all. The permission of doubt arrives, perhaps paradoxically, only after it has been initially rejected. The basis of doubt is – paradoxically – to *exclude doubt logically*. But it was initially excluded with good cause: a rejection of doubt took place at the foundations, where a trust was required to begin the process. The trust was in the teacher and the training with which he or she was intent on supplying us. Such a trust was well placed, regardless of how difficult it may seem to grasp the groundlessness of the belief that emanates from the trust.

The next important concept that seems to appear in most, if not all, of Wittgenstein's writings is the notion of training, with particular reference to how training impacts on the construction and development of our instinctive behaviours and our foundational certainties. Avrum Stroll (1994: 155) suggests how Wittgenstein is to be interpreted in his efforts to connect the ideas of trust, training and certainties, claiming:

> Instead [Wittgenstein] began to conceive of certainty as a mode of acting. The idea that acting lies at the bottom of the language-game[8] (instead of any system of propositions) is a new and radical conception of certainty. Certainty stems from one's immersion in a human community in which rote training and the inculcation of habits create the substratum upon which the language game rests.

In outlining that certainties were a mode of acting, founded in an 'immersion' into a form of habitual practice displayed in training, Wittgenstein succeeds in connecting the notions of training and certainty into a web of intellectual pursuit.

The 'habits' and 'rote training' to which Stroll refers are at the basis of our certainties; our actions therefore are guided by such habits and such training, since certainty itself is manifested in our actions. Training, in this sense, is indispensable in the effort to formulate certainties. It is a process that encourages instinctive reactions, which are themselves manifestations of the certainties that were to be constructed as a product of training. It is for this reason that Wittgenstein (1967: 33e) claims that our understanding of things is 'effected by explanation; but also by training' – that is, that every understanding must have, as part of it, an element of training. To be introduced into the 'way of the world' is a process that is achieved only through training. Indeed, '[b]asic initiation into our form of life is a *training*, not a reasoning' (Moyal-Sharrock, 2007: 109). Our foundations begin in bedrock certainties, which are themselves brought about by a trust in our teachers and the training that they display.

Wittgenstein (2009: 7e) also refers to the paradigmatic example of speech, at which we looked earlier in the text, in reference to the role that training plays in this most primitive form of learning: 'A child uses such primitive forms of language when it learns to talk. Here the teaching of a language is not explanation, but training.' Moyal-Sharrock (2007: 109) goes on to cite David Bloor (1997: 47), who claims: 'At the basic level ... teaching does not proceed by explanation, and hence escapes the sequential and linear requirements of definition. It is concrete and holistic, exploiting a form of trust that does not require each step to be justified in turn, and where the learner is prepared to understand the earlier in terms of the later.' Bloor (1997: 13) goes on to claim (without using these terms) that, in viewing teaching as a form of 'Wittgensteinian training', the learner can view the process of learning as a process of 'instinctive generalization', which equips him or her to go beyond the rules and examples provided in teaching. These instinctive generalizations constitute our bedrock certainties, formulated within our training, and give rise to actions that are the manifestations of the certainties themselves. Teaching is therefore to be by example, since 'we do not reason or infer' (Moyal-Sharrock, 2007: 110); rather, we have 'instinctive responses to the examples used in teaching' (Bloor, 1997: 13).

The recognition of 'sameness' is a skill developed in one's training, and it is this skill that ensures that future problems can be solved in a similar way to previous examples that we will have encountered in the training process. Training therefore equips us with an ability to 'spot' a similar problem and to solve it in the same way as we were shown. Our action, however, is instinctive and is not founded in justification or reasoning; rather, it is founded in certainty. That is not to say that we cannot be mistaken; rather, we learn to react in 'such and such' a manner when presented with an example that we believe to be of a similar nature to a previously encountered problem – a problem that would have been demonstrated to us among the examples that constituted our training. This training does *not* encourage reasoning; instead, it encourages action – instinctive action under certain prompts. In this way, Bloor (1997: 14) argues that 'we go on from our training in the way that we do because we have a set of dispositions or tendencies that happen to be activated in this way by the examples used in training'. These 'dispositions' and 'tendencies' could be thought of as the instinctive reactions to our foundational certainties. They have been constructed and developed in training, and they encourage us – when required – to go on in the same way as was demonstrated to us in training.

Such an explanation develops the ideas put forward by Oakeshott in the previous chapter, in grasping that training seems to equip us with information (inert facts) and judgement (an ability to act). This is perhaps why Moyal-Sharrock (2007: 110) – in keeping with Wittgenstein – describes training as having an 'interplay' with instinct and learning:

Particularly in the learning of rules, 'rules are mastered via a process of inculcation which involves our deepest drives and instincts and blind learning.'[9] Teaching a child that 'This is a chair' is analogous to teaching it to walk or eat with a spoon. Analogous also to taming an animal, '[c]hildren do not learn that books exist, that armchairs exist, etc. etc., – they learn to fetch books, sit in armchairs etc. etc.'[10] When we learn rules, we do not learn a content but a technique, a skill, a method: *how to proceed*. A rule is transmitted to a child as something it can *go* on: an enabler.

Moyal-Sharrock continues this discussion by way of reference to several analogies that seem to make the point rather more succinctly. She claims that learning by example in the knowledge sense can be thought of in the 'same way the child is physically propped up and taught to walk' (Moyal-Sharrock, 2007: 110), to the extent that, in learning how to walk, the child depends on and trusts in the training that it receives from the adult superiors who guide the process of teaching.

Similarly, '[l]ike rules or instructions that a coach gives to a novice in the teaching of a game, these are handed down as the only acceptable *moves* in a game, not open to discussion or stemming from it' (Moyal-Sharrock, 2007: 110). What, then, are the lessons for learning in an educational sense? Training is to be a process that requires a teacher in whom the pupil is expected – nay, *required* – to display a trust. The 'rules' are transmitted through training, by way of example, in such a way that the pupil is not invited to challenge; rather, he or she is invited only to attain an instinctive insight into the way in which he or she is expected to behave and act in similar future situations. Such an insight becomes a part of the pupil's bedrock certainties, which guide his or her future endeavours. This pupil will accept such an insight in acknowledgement of the fact that the rules of the 'game' enable 'us to play the game' (Moyal-Sharrock, 2007: 110). Indeed:

[U]pon being told that 'This is a chair' or that 'The ace has such-and-such a value in blackjack', we do not ponder but register. Considering these basic *givens* as requiring justification would only hinder us from playing. The certainty with which parents or teachers show us, teach us or make us alert to anything merely fortifies what is already a basic or innate or instinctive trust.

(Moyal-Sharrock, 2007: 110)

Who better to take up the mantle of a leader than the teacher or the parent, who continue (in their respective natures) to have the best interests of the children under their charge at heart? In an educational sense, the teacher seems to be the *only* candidate for such a leader, in that he or she has the experience and the expertise, and the backing of the subject from which he or she comes, to substantiate a claim to an authoritative educational position.

In an effort to connect these ideas to teaching and learning, Moyal-Sharrock (2007: 110) appeals to Wittgenstein once more, quoting: 'For how can a child immediately doubt what it is taught? That could mean only that he was incapable of learning certain language games.'[11] Moyal-Sharrock (2007: 110) goes on to expand on Wittgenstein's claims, asserting: 'Unconditional absorption is possible because the child's natural attitude to the rules that are handed down to it is the same as its attitude to the milk it is fed: it swallows them whole – or with hardly a hiccup. Here, learning is blind; our eyes are shut.'[12] The fact that the child does not generally challenge the training that it receives from its teacher displays, in action, the child's certitude that the message that is portrayed to it through training is a message that is of value to it. There is an instinctive, innate understanding that its training is required and it is not open to scrutiny, since the child does not yet possess the requisite skills to offer a serious and sensible challenge to it. And even in the instances in which 'inquisitive or recalcitrant children demand explanation for the rules, ... the questioning invariably finds its natural halt in the teacher's pronouncement of such words as: "That's just how it is"' (Moyal-Sharrock, 2007: 110–11).

In this section, therefore, in an appeal to Wittgenstein's writings on trust and training, along with the views found in the secondary literature around the same author, it has been shown that knowledge and what knowledge rests upon – certainty – are not only different in *kind*, but are also different in *category*. That is, where knowledge is to be developed through a process of reasoning and the rebuttal of doubt in light of such reasoning, certitude is to be at the bedrock of such knowledge and is to be found not only in situations in which doubt is rejected as improbable or unreasonable, but also in instances in which doubt is to be logically incoherent. The foundations upon which the knowledge house is built are to be constructed in such a way that doubt is prohibited.

In ensuring that the foundations differ from the building, Wittgenstein ensures that the 'knowledge problem' can be avoided. I have shown that certainties are to be constructed on the basis of a trust in one's teacher, or in reliable resources such as textbooks and the training that the teacher conveys. Trust is to be the cornerstone of the certainties that form the bedrock for our ability to know.

Training, also, is to be the font from which such instinctive certainties emanate. In this way, as Wittgenstein so succinctly demonstrates, training is seen as a mechanism that is instigated by the intellectual superiors in the learning process (adults, parents and teachers); moreover, training is the tool that is used to curb our reactions and instincts to enable us to go on in the same way as we were originally shown within our own training. Training, in this way, takes the indeterminate human being to the cusp of determinacy.

Conversely, in the absence of both a trust in our intellectual superiors and the training with which they provide us, we are condemned to remain in the realm of indeterminacy. A trust in one's teacher and a belief that naturally protrudes from our training are therefore indispensable facets of the learning process that has, as its aim, the development and construction of knowledge. Indeed, training and trust are required for the very bedrock certainties in which knowledge is to be founded.

Thus a world without trust in one's teacher and the training that the teacher provides is a world in which certainties are unattainable, and consequently a world (and, in particular, an education) in which knowledge is foundationless and inaccessible. The difficulty, Wittgenstein warned, was in grasping the groundlessness of our believing. It seems that we have no choice but to grasp it, lest we endorse a world bereft of knowledge. Perhaps by way of addressing his target explicitly, Wittgenstein (1967: 74e) claims: 'Any explanation has its foundations in training. (Educators ought to remember this.)' Indeed, they ought to – for the entire collection of knowledge, and its accessibility, depends on it.

How 'training' and 'trust' depend on authority: Beyond the Wittgensteinian vision

In concluding on the contribution made by Wittgenstein and his associated authors to the debate for authoritative teaching and education, it seems that there is a requirement for a brief discussion dedicated to tying together the notions of 'trust' and 'training' – to which I alluded in the previous section – with the notion of authority. Wittgenstein (1969: 23e) acknowledges that authority is involved in the processes of teaching and learning, claiming: 'I learned an enormous amount and accepted it on human authority.' It is this claim that I want to examine in more detail now, with respect to establishing that authority is the essential genesis of teaching, learning and, consequently, knowledge development.

The notion of 'human authority' is what seems to be of interest in this instance. Wittgenstein claims that our trust in our teacher is 'blind', to the extent that the grounds for our trust or our believing are difficult to grasp. Our foundational certainties – which are instinctive reactions to our training and the trust that we placed in our teachers – are essentially groundless. That is, they are supported by no further foundation: literally, 'without ground'. Thus, when we have reached certainty, we have reached the axioms – the entire basis upon which everything else is to be built. As much as I agree that certainty is at the foundations, I disagree with Wittgenstein on the notion of our belief being *completely* groundless. I am not suggesting that our certainties require explanation – indeed, that would be to defeat the entire essence of certainties; rather, I am suggesting that a trust in one's teacher and in one's training is not a 'groundless' belief. It seems to me that authority commands that a trust in one's teacher and one's training are, in fact, entirely *grounded*.

To what or whose authority might I be referring? The answer: the authority of the teacher himself or herself, and that of the practice from which he or she comes. Our belief is not groundless, in that the natural authority of the teacher and training that he or she provides ensure that we have *good cause* to believe. This is not a justification of certainties, as opposed to an assurance that trusting one's teacher is not a fruitless pursuit. In each of us, as learners, there is an innate understanding that there is knowledge to be acquired and that we require help to acquire it; it is a feature of our makings as human beings. Few possess the insight required to make pioneering contributions to any subject or discipline. Most of us require guidance – a beacon – to lead us on our way through the darkness. The instinctive, innate understanding that one requires guidance in one's knowledge pursuits is *a certainty in its own right* – that is, our actions point towards the fact that we are inquisitive beasts who require answers and who require assistance in attaining these answers. We inherit a picture of the world and set about our business of establishing more detail about our 'world picture' inheritance. We cannot enquire by means of some mystical 'stab in the dark' to find out more about what makes the world the way it is, no matter how much the fire of inquiry burns inside us. Our submission to our teachers in the process of learning to speak, for example, demonstrates that our nature is to submit to authority in a quest to satisfy our innate appetite for knowledge and skill.

The authority of the teacher and the practice from which he or she comes, in itself, commands that a trust in one's teacher and one's training are not groundless. We believe because it is in our very nature to do so. That is, as human beings, we are creatures who have an innate understanding of the fact that an intellectual authority – a teacher or a practice, such as mathematics or language – is an authority to which we *must* submit if we are to inherit and gain understanding of our 'world picture'. Authority therefore *commands* certainty and belief. Thus Wittgenstein (1969: 65e) could exclaim: 'So this is it: I must recognize certain authorities in order to make judgements at all?' As Meredith Williams (2010: 20–1) notes:

> The fundamental feature of our human life is that it is so fully immersed in normative structure that even our natural reactions and ways of seeing are normatively shaped in ways that are shared: 'the common behaviour of mankind is a system of reference by which we interpret an unknown language'.[13] The medium of entry is initiate learning. . . . The initiate learner is one who does not have the basic skills or competence to participate in language. Such an initiate learner requires a master of the practice or technique to shape the learner's environment and behavior so that he can acquire mastery of the practice as well. The initiate learner is the novice, the one who is first acquiring a skill, technique or competence. The novice is the very young child just acquiring a natural language or the pupil just learning mathematics or history. It is important that the novice does not have the linguistic ability to engage in these practices autonomously. The importance of this central fact about all human beings, that we learn a language, leads Wittgenstein to distinguish (though not in these terms) *the domain of the novice* and *the domain of the master*. The domain of the master concerns those who are linguistically competent; they are the skillful participants of language games. The domain of the novice is that of the initiate learner.

The novice therefore requires the master and depends on that master for guidance in his or her learning. In this sense, the master possesses the authority that commands and thus yields a trust in his or her teachings. Such authority is established in his or her very nature as a 'master' – as one who is an intellectual superior to the novice learner under his or her charge. The importance of the teacher, the master, is found in the acknowledgement of Stroll (1994: 158), quoting Wittgenstein, that: 'All animals, including humans, inherit their picture of the world, and like other animals much of our inheritance derives from early training – "something must be taught us as a foundation".'[14] This 'foundation' to which Wittgenstein is referring is an instinct, a certainty, the reaction to our early training. Such training requires a trust in one's teacher, the master of the practice of which we hope to become more aware, and in recognizing the use and application of which we hope to become more skilled. And such training has as an indispensable facet: an acknowledgement of the authority that the teacher's position naturally commands.

Given, therefore, that knowledge depends on the bedrock of certainties being well formed and that such certainties depend on an acknowledgement of the teacher's authority, it follows that one who hopes to be knowledgeable must first acknowledge the natural authority that the *domain of the master* commands. The process is therefore simple: it all begins with an initial acknowledgement and then a subsequent submission to the authority of the teacher who represents the practice. On the basis of this instinctive acknowledgement (it need not be a conscious choice, but may be an innate part of our tendency as human beings to submit to the authority of our intellectual superiors), we have grounds for trusting our teachers and the messages that they convey through their teaching. Through listening to the teacher's message, we can be trained in the ways that will develop our instinctive reactions to future problems of a similar nature. These instincts constitute our certainties, our ways of acting without any notion of doubt. And, finally, the journey ends, rather satisfyingly, with knowledge founded in these certainties, which have been reasoned and developed on the solid, unshakable bedrock of what has come before them. This is a journey that begins with authority and ends with knowledge: a journey on which it is well worth embarking.

CONCLUSION

There is one fact that unites every educational philosopher's thinking since time began: education matters. Education, regardless of your philosophical, sociological or political dispositions and beliefs, is a matter of grave importance. And because of this importance, the significance of *how* education is delivered becomes ever more pertinent.

In this book, I have offered an argument for authoritative teaching and learning, knowledge development, and consequently education, by invoking the writings of three major philosophers, Michael Polanyi, Michael Oakeshott and Ludwig Wittgenstein. These philosophers were not chosen by chance; they are, for me, philosophical titans of authoritative thinking, each of whom is required to bring something to the table in this debate. The notion of authoritative education and all that it encompasses is a notion that is losing its appeal in favour of the modern-day, child-centred approaches to education. For me, this signals the demise of what makes education so special; it destroys the entire essence of education and what makes it possible – and it gives rise to worrying times ahead. In the absence of authority – the authority of the teacher – teaching becomes less about guidance and more about facilitation: a worrying prospect. In the absence of authority – the authority of the community and the practice – the notion of 'correctness' loses its meaning: an unforgivable consequence. And in the absence of authority – the combined authority of the teacher and the practice from which he or she comes – knowledge becomes inaccessible: a saddening result. Teaching and learning *need* authority. Knowledge development *depends* on authority. And, as a consequence, education *rests* on authority. Therefore the demise of authority results in the demise of education.

I appealed to the writings of Polanyi, Oakeshott and Wittgenstein individually because, when taken together, they offer insight into the importance of authority in teaching and learning, knowledge, and education in general. The reader will notice that I have talked extensively of the importance of knowledge in an educational context. Such a view, rather unusually, has come under a severe degree of scrutiny. Indeed, many educational theorists and philosophers suggest that an education system founded in knowledge accumulation, acquisition and development is an education system that is narrow-minded and shallow. Such theorists and philosophers suggest that a more holistic approach to education is required. Rather than discuss this any further than it has been already, it seems intuitive to note that it is entirely inconceivable to propose an education system that is bereft of knowledge and its accumulation, acquisition and development – that is, that any education system in which knowledge plays no part is not an education at all. This is why I give knowledge such a pride of place in the educational context: by anyone's reckoning, knowledge forms an indispensable part of education. I have also talked about the notions of teaching and learning as the essential, immovable cornerstones of education. Once again, I noted that an education system that does not require the teacher as a specialist is an education system that has a misconceived view of what the *process* of education involves and *should* involve. Indeed, the very thing that separates formal education from 'worldly experience' is the exposure to an expert from which one benefits within formal education. The only sensible and responsible candidate for such an expert is the teacher, and so the teacher is of particular significance in *any* understanding of education. I have made the case too that to view the teacher as *an* authority and *in* authority in his or her classroom need not give rise to the view that education is a 'top-down', coercive and restrictive process; rather, the teacher is viewed as the master expert who guides the pupils with whom he or she has been charged towards intellectual emancipation. This process of guidance is not a facilitation, as opposed to being an initiation into a custom – a disciplined manner of working towards which the teacher is able to guide the pupil. Guidance, therefore, is viewed as responsible leadership rather than chaotic, *laissez-faire* facilitation. Intellectual freedom comes only after an initial submission to one's intellectual superiors.

In discussing these notions, I drew on all three influential authors. Polanyi was cited for his views on authority, in relation to tradition, communities and a practice. Indeed, Polanyi's writings were used to demonstrate that learning begins in submission to the authority of a master expert, with a view to becoming part of a practice and a way of working. Polanyi invoked the 'community' in his writings as a collection of people who shared the same or similar views about the nature of the practice and how it was to be transmitted. The community therefore ensured that its expert representative – the teacher – was reminded of his or her obligations to protect the practice that his or her message sought to convey to the pupils under his or her charge. And, finally, traditions were at the core of Polanyi's writings, used to strengthen the organic nature of learning, knowledge development and education in general. Indeed, Polanyi argued that traditions were necessary to remind the present generation that a failure to grasp the traditions of the past was to condemn itself to repeat the errors of previous generations in the future. Moreover, in failing to recognize the traditions, the learner could hope for only a blurred view of learning, knowledge and education.

The final contribution made by Polanyi's writing – and perhaps the most insightful – was to inject dynamism into what could otherwise be recognized as an overtly traditional view of education. This contribution was to demonstrate that, although the beginnings of learning, knowledge and education were to be considered as rooted in traditions, practices and submission to an authority (all of which were encompassed in Polanyi's 'fiduciary framework'), there was a need for the *final* goal of education to be the successful initiation of the learner into the very practices and traditions to which he or she initially submitted. In this way, Polanyi described the process of learning as the learner's way of seeking to comprehend something that was, initially, beyond his or her understanding. Indeed, Polanyi argued that to engage with these practices and traditions was to be considered equivalent to the learner *making his or her own* contribution to such traditions and practices. Moreover, Polanyi insisted, where perhaps others had not before him, that the pursuit of a traditional and authoritative education was not permission to oppress originality and moments of true genius on the part of the learner. In this way, I argued that Polanyi had delivered a traditional, authoritative model for education, which resulted in a liberated learner: the supposed end-goal of *progressive education*, not traditional education. In this way, it was clear that, by putting the teacher and the practice at the centre of education, the pupil's eventual emancipation remained unscathed.

Next, Oakeshott was cited to demonstrate the nature of knowledge and the nature of an education in which knowledge was not held to be important. Oakeshott put forward the argument that any education must see, as its primary aim, the inculcation of the learners into a knowledge inheritance: the inheritance of human achievements. In considering the teacher and learner as separate, yet connected, entities, Oakeshott managed to sidestep many of the problems with which other understandings of education are fraught. Furthermore, Oakeshott rather brilliantly pulled apart knowledge into two intertwined components of 'information' and 'judgement'. He demonstrated that neither can be dispensed with and that both require the teacher to 'teach' them. Oakeshott also contested that only the teacher could carry out the process that we know as 'teaching' – that is, that teaching was to be seen to be the *domain of the teacher* – and that the learner who was to learn from such a process was to be viewed as a special type of learner: a pupil, the natural counterpart to the teacher. In understanding teaching and learning as conduct as opposed to behaviour, Oakeshott induced the need for an arbiter of truth and knowledge, the only possible candidate for which could be the teacher. In Oakeshott's writings, therefore, we saw the need for a teacher in the process of acquiring knowledge, which he believed to be an indispensable facet of *any* education. The teacher was to focus on deliberately initiating the pupils into their knowledge inheritance and, as such, was to equip them with the ability to become the best that they could be. The pupil, on the other hand, was to focus only on avoiding the ignorance that would have befallen him or her in the absence of the teacher shedding light on the pupil's knowledge inheritance. In this way, I concluded that Oakeshott portrays the teacher as a beacon of light in the darkness of ignorance. In understanding this pivotal role that the teacher plays, there is no other option but to submit to the authority that such a position commands – that is, if the teacher is to be viewed as the torch-bearer leading the way through the darkness, there is but one option open to the pupil under his or her charge: to follow that lead.

Finally, Wittgenstein was invoked for his remarkable insight into the true nature of how knowledge is formed, and the role that trust and training play in forming the bedrock certainties upon which learning and knowledge development are to be positioned. Wittgenstein – rather typically of his philosophical methods – delivered the final blow: his insight demonstrated that the genesis of thought, inquiry and knowledge begins in trust. Moreover, the training to which we are exposed equips us with an instinctive reaction in solving problems that are similar to those shown to us in training. A trust in one's teacher and the training to which we are exposed, therefore, are indispensable aspects of learning and knowing. The bedrock certainties that are not thrown open to doubt had to be different from the knowledge that rested upon them, if Wittgenstein was to be comfortable that he had sidestepped the 'foundationless knowledge problem' that had troubled Aristotle, Descartes and Moore. Wittgenstein's foundationalism was needed to form a foundation of indubitable certainties from which everything else was to emanate. I then went on to argue that our belief and our trust were perhaps not as 'groundless' as Wittgenstein had suggested. The 'ground' for trusting in our teachers lies in the fact that the authority that they naturally command in their role as such assures us that the message that they seek to portray in our training is a message to be trusted. The position of the teacher was that of an experienced, expert, insightful, reflective and, most importantly, authoritative master, who held the capacity of training his or her pupils in their inherited world picture. On the basis of the teacher's authority, we could be *certain* that his message was both valuable and acceptable. The teacher has the backing of his or her practice, and the expertise with which to support and sustain his or her message. A trust in the teacher is not an *option*, but a *requirement* in the discourse of learning.

These three major philosophers have each brought something unique to this discussion on authority in various aspects of education. Polanyi's 'fiduciary framework' establishes a context into which pupils step when they begin to undertake their education. A framework of trust is necessary if learning is to be possible. Polanyi's fiduciary framework, set in the foundations of customs, practices and traditions, serves as a perfect starting point. Oakeshott, too, demonstrates that knowledge is to be viewed as a collection of intellectual riches, to be inherited by the pupil under his or her teacher's guidance. The institution of the school should provide a platform from which this initiation can take place. The teacher's authority must, as a consequence, be firm and steadfast, in order for these intellectual riches to be passed on successfully.

In this view of education, we come to appreciate why all talk of 'fitting the school to the child' rather than 'fitting the child to the school' reeks of propaganda, fuelled by educational do-gooders intent on selling the product of so-called 'child-centred' education. However, when we get down to the bare bones of the discussion, we come to realize that what is sold to us as 'child-centred' is, in fact, a smoke-screen for an educational 'free for all', in which the child takes precedence over the bedrock customs, practices, traditions and institutions. We are in a modern-day era of doubt, and we are in danger of being unable to repair the damage. The charge of the child-centred liberalists has cast a shadow over education for long enough. The inexcusable theft of the term 'child-centred' is a shameful attempt to give credence to an otherwise unfounded ideology. This type of educational jargon is unforgivable – for who would disagree that education should be centred on giving each and every child the best possible opportunity in life? But Polanyi's arguments demonstrate that such a modern-day obsession with 'child-centred' approaches to education is, rather paradoxically, set within a framework that prohibits the child's freedom *in the first instance*. Trust must be at the foundation. The child must be shown the custom, must be exposed to the prevailing practice and must be initiated into the tradition. A truly child-centred teacher must therefore concur that, to give his or her pupils the best opportunity in life, he or she must instil discipline and habitual practice in them, all the while representing his or her custom, practice and tradition with integrity and sincerity. Protecting the teacher's authority should therefore be of particular significance to us moving forward. The authoritative teacher is the linchpin between knowledge and its dissemination. The teacher possesses the 'information' and can pass on his or her 'judgement'. If knowledge is power, then the teacher reigns supreme.

To embrace an authoritative education, then, is to embrace an understanding of what Allan Bloom claimed when he said: 'Education is the movement from darkness to light.'

Step into the light.

NOTES

Chapter 1

1 See Chapter 5 for a development of these ideas. I will invoke Polanyi to demonstrate the overriding importance of communities, traditions and authority within the transmission of values and ideals to a younger generation.

2 This distinction will be made clearer in Chapter 3, in the definitions of authority.

Chapter 2

1 If this was a 'modern ambition' in 1952, it has most certainly become part of mainstream educational thinking in many countries across the world in the second decade of the twenty-first century, with teachers often described as 'learners' and 'facilitators', and principals calling themselves 'head learners'. It is a frightening prospect that, some sixty years after Bantock warned against the problems inherent to such a move, we have managed to smuggle this outlandish idea into practice in many schools.

2 For a detailed overview of Stenhouse's contribution to the role of knowledge within education, as well as the role of authority in the development of such knowledge, see the bibliography to Hendricks (2002), in which the reader will find a raft of Stenhouse's work for further reading.

Chapter 3

1 See also R. S. Peters (1973: ch. 2) for another discussion about the 'nature' of authority.

Chapter 4

1 There is a hidden component to this argument. This concept of learning through inquiry is founded in a discussion of learning theories, particularly

with reference to varying forms of constructivism and, at the other end of the scale, Platonism. Rather than spend extended amounts of writing space with these arguments, I will assume that the reader can find out more about these theories in relevant texts. Useful references on constructivism can be found in the works of Piaget and Vygotsky, who discuss the concepts of learning as a constructed entity attained through experiencing the world. The demise of all forms of constructivism is found in discussions of the Meno paradox, at which we look shortly. A detailed discussion of this demise can be found in Bereiter (1985). For an understanding of Platonism – the notion that learning is achievable through discovering a Platonic realm that coexists independently of the natural word – key authors include Sir Roger Penrose and, self-evidently, Plato.

2 The basis for the rejection of Platonism can be found in Wittgenstein's rejection of the belief that a mental object or a mental image can guide. If the Platonic realm were to exist, it would be little other than a collection of mental images and objects, stored somewhere within the boundaries of the mind (or brain?), but such a realm could never guide our future behaviour in its own right. Wittgenstein deals with this view of things over the course of *Philosophical Investigations* (2009), as well as in Wittgenstein (1922, 1967, 1969, 1975, 1980, 1982).

3 This argument is perhaps more complex than is suggested here. The foundation of the argument is found in Wittgenstein's account, and subsequently in secondary literature accounts, of learning as 'rule-following'. This seems to be at the basis of everything so far discussed in relation to the concept of correctness. Wittgenstein argues that following rules is a practice that requires an accepted way of following them; otherwise, we cannot claim to have a rule.

I acknowledge the potential counter-argument to correctness requiring authority at its foundations. Indeed, it could be argued rather convincingly that correctness does not require a submission to an authority; rather, the notion of correctness resides in practices and rules, such as the practices of mathematics or the rules of grammar. Such an argument would suggest that rules and formulae guide our actions towards correct answers. Moreover, the notion of correctness in such a system would reside within the practice of the discipline. However, the practice is not a stand-alone entity, which guides us towards correctness; rather, we attain a privileged participation with the practice when we are trained by our teacher. Such training, unsurprisingly, requires an initial submission to authority, and a faith in the teacher who invites us to participate in the practice and its associated rules and formulae. In this way, correctness cannot reside in a practice, since the rules and formulae that emanate from a practice are no more than inert entities, which provide no guidance as to their appropriate application. Such guidance is attained only through a submission to the authority of one's teacher.

Rather than discuss this any further and risk compromising the integrity of this in relation to the relevant arguments for our purposes, I refer the reader to Wittgenstein (1967, 1975, 2009), as well as Malcolm (1986) and Wright (2001), for a more extensive explanation of rule-following and the need for an accompanying training to align a judgement alongside the rules.

4   A more detailed account of Aristotelian foundationalism can be found in various articles and texts. To avoid a major development of these ideas in this text and risk venturing away from the topics of importance to this discussion, the reader should refer to Aristotle (1994).

Chapter 5

1   Which can be translated as: 'Unless you have believed, you will not understand.' In Polanyi's text entitled *Personal Knowledge* (2009), from which this quote is taken, Polanyi himself provides a reference to a quote from St Augustine from *De libero arbitrio*, Book I, para. 4, which reads: 'The steps are laid down by the prophet who says, "Unless ye believe, ye shall not understand".' In this sense, we can see even more profoundly how Polanyi is seeking a return to this Augustinian foundation of faith. Such is the importance of this quote to Polanyi that he also cites in another one of his books, *The Tacit Dimension* (1983: 61).

2   The teacher is taken as the candidate for the expert master in the classroom environment. However, Polanyi himself talks of having faith in reliable sources such as textbooks. In this way, the learner must still submit to a wider authority: the authority of the practice and the traditions that the teacher or the reliable sources represent.

3   These comments were made by Polanyi with specific reference to how a student becomes part of the scientific culture. However, they apply generally in any discipline to a development of knowledge through a submission to authority.

4   I refer to this as 'quasi-independence' in a deliberate attempt to avoid appealing to the concept of *total* independence from one's master. I will discuss later, in keeping with Wittgenstein, that the learner never truly escapes the influences of the master; rather, students carry the hallmark of the masters – the students' training – throughout their lives, and into their own contributions and discoveries.

5   This 'inner guidance' is an internal barometer that the student has developed through imitating the master. I will describe it in the next section as an 'indwelling'.

6   This notion of 'inheritance' will be considered further when we look at Oakeshott's discussion of what learning is in Chapters 6 and 7.

7   Indeed, this paradigmatic example is used in many other authors' works. I will talk briefly of how Oakeshott discusses the example of language

development in his works on authority and knowledge, as well as considering the most prominent proponent of these arguments, Wittgenstein.

8   Nor can reason or doubt be purely private things: cf. Wittgenstein's 'Private language argument', in *Philosophical Investigations* (2009: §§243–315).

9   For another example of how authority and traditions are needed within knowledge development, see Polanyi's *The Tacit Dimension* (1983: 63–70), in which Polanyi discusses the example of how one pursues knowledge in the natural sciences: 'Let me display the inescapable need for a traditional framework in one example of great modern endeavour, which may then serve as a paradigm for other intellectual and moral progress in a free, dynamic society' (Polanyi, 1983: 63).

    In this example, Polanyi outlines that a revolt against tradition and authority has become commonplace within modern science, but goes on to make the case that a return to authoritative approaches to scientific endeavours is an inescapable necessity if scientific advancements are to be enhanced.

10 Oakeshott also talks of how important 'judgement' is in the development of knowledge. I will outline this in the next chapter.

11 Compare Aristotle and Descartes, for example.

12 The details of precisely why Polanyi's 'theory' of tacit–explicit knowledge is insufficient will become clearer in light of the chapters based on Oakeshott (Chapter 6) and Wittgenstein (Chapter 8). What Polanyi has missed is pertinent when examining each of these two philosophers. For the meantime, we will accept that Polanyi's most significant contribution to the debate on authority is the so-called 'fiduciary framework', as well as his discussions of traditions, practices and communities.

13 We build towards such analysis in working towards Wittgenstein via Oakeshott. Oakeshott talks of knowledge as information and judgement, and in doing so encompasses Polanyi's tacit–explicit model with more careful language. Indeed, what Polanyi might call 'tacit knowledge', Oakeshott would call 'judgement': a *component* of the totality of knowledge that cannot be articulated in terms of rules and propositions, but which is a feature of our knowledge edifice. Wittgenstein, however, as it is argued in Chapter 8, makes clear that knowledge does not rest on knowledge, but on certainty, which is conceptually distinct from knowledge in that it is logically exempt from doubt.

14 Consider reading Saul A. Kripke's *Wittgenstein on Rules and Private Language* (1982: esp. 7–15), for his famous 'plus-quus argument' as well as David G. Stern's detailed commentary of Wittgenstein's writings in *Wittgenstein's Philosophical Investigations: An Introduction* (2004: 139–70) and Norman Malcolm's *Nothing is Hidden* (1986: 154–82). The most detailed account of rule-following, however, is Crispin Wright's *Rails to Infinity* (2001).

15 For a detailed description of knowledge construction and the nature of knowledge, see Mitchell (2006: 70–9). In the section of that chapter entitled

'Tacit knowing', Mitchell outlines how Polanyi talks of the way in which knowledge is constructed through subsidiary awareness and focal awareness. There are also references to how Polanyi appeals to Gestalt psychology in his effort to find a theory of knowledge construction.

Other references to Polanyi's tacit knowledge can be found in any of Polanyi (1969, 1983, 2009).

Chapter 6

1   This independence is the same as the 'quasi-independence' to which I referred in the last chapter (see Chapter 5, n. 4).

2   It seems, therefore, that information forms only the factual part of knowledge. The notion of 'knowing', however, seems to require a more dynamic approach, other than simply being aware of items of inert information or stand-alone facts. However, being aware of the facts is an indispensable facet of knowing, even though there appears to be another component required to complete the picture. See Oakeshott (2001: 47–9) for more detail of this discussion, where Oakeshott discusses the two different ways in which information can be related to knowledge.

3   The argument put forward here – that a formula or a 'mental object' *in itself* cannot guide – is discussed extensively by Wittgenstein (2009) and in other texts. The argument is a combination of what has become known as the 'rule-following argument' (see Chapter 5) and the 'private language argument'. Other authors to which I refer readers include Wright (2001), Malcolm (1986) and Kripke (1982).

4   This analogy has the potential to be misleading. I want to be clear that this does not mean that I am suggesting that, when things are learned, they are stored somewhere (usually assumed to be the mind or brain) and recalled when required. The details of my contestation to the 'storage' problem are for another time and I hope to develop them later in my career. The pertinent point of this analogy is that information without the judgement on how to access and apply it is useless. No other parallels should be drawn from this analogy.

5   I say 'quasi-passive' because I believe that no teaching is an entirely passive process. Even in the forms of learning that seem to require little pupil input, the pupil must still engage with the material to understand its essence fully. Even by simply listening to the teacher to avoid their own ignorance, pupils are playing an active role in their own learning.

6   In this case, the pupil is never truly 'on his or her own' in any future solutions – that is, the teacher is always present when the student solves a problem, manifest in the judgement that the teacher imparted through his or her teaching.

7 An extension of Oakeshott's ideas can be found in *Rationalism in Politics and other Essays*, in the essay entitled 'Rational conduct' (Oakeshott, 1991: 99–131). In this essay, Oakeshott outlines that the notions of a human mind bereft of predispositions and of a human being who is capable of reasoning from 'within' such a mind to produce the coveted 'rational' conduct are nothing more than empty idiom. He goes on to outline that we are guided by our engagements with the activities that we pursue, which endow us with the ability to reason. Reasoning, therefore, is not done from 'within' the human mind, but from the *outside in*. This acknowledgement by Oakeshott gives my arguments a renewed justification for demanding acceptance of the authority of the teacher, and the traditions and practices from which he or she comes. Indeed, Oakeshott makes a compelling argument for the notion that a so-called 'virgin mind', free from authoritative inputs, is a romantic notion at best, but a notion that surprisingly has many philosophical supporters. Rather than go into this argument further and offer little more to the argument than that which Oakeshott has already provided, I refer the reader to the essay itself.

Chapter 7

1 I place the word 'discovery' inside quotation marks because such learning is described as discovery as a result of an unfortunate language deficiency. Learning as discovery, in the literal sense, results in radical determinism (Platonism) or radical indeterminism (constructivism), to the extent that unless there is an accompanying guidance – that is, a teacher or a practice – the learner is in a world in which 'correctness' loses its meaning and is replaced by the notion of viability. Indeed, to discover something and to attach a meaning to it without the guidance of another (the teacher), one either has to have all of the possible solutions already 'in mind' or in the ether (Platonism) or one has to be free to choose the solution that 'works best' (constructivism). Therefore, in rejecting these notions in favour of the guidance of a teacher or a practice (and the training received in accordance with both of these), I am referring to learning as discovery in the experiential sense. The need for authority in such a form of learning will still be made clear.

2 'Correctness' is the key term. The notion of correctness finds its roots in an acceptance of authority: the authority of the practices and the community, which decided on the notions of 'right' and 'wrong' by acting in the way that it does. That is, 'correctness' in the public sense is intrinsically linked to an understanding of an 'agreed' way of working. If such an agreement is not in place, then *any* way of working can be considered viable. As such, correctness is replaced with viability. Imitation of the ways of one's teacher gives an insight into correctness as a concept. The teacher is therefore the authoritative representative of the community and practice.

3 This 'authority' could be either the authority of a teacher who guides towards a correct interpretation or the authority of a practice – that is, an accepted way of working.

Chapter 8

1 I will show how these notions solve the Aristotelian problem in the next section.

2 Citing Wittgenstein (1969: Proposition 54).

3 For an extension of the distinction between 'certainty' and 'knowledge', see Moyal-Sharrock (2007: 13–32), Malcolm (1986: 201–35) and Stroll (1994: 141–5). In these sections, the three authors elaborate upon these ideas to extend them into the full versions of the arguments that Wittgenstein constructed – arguments that, if I were to develop them here, would digress from the relevant topics relevant for this book. Moreover, the arguments that these authors outline are extensive and I could add little to what is already found in the three texts.

4 Citing Wittgenstein (1969: Proposition 511).

5 Citing Wittgenstein (1969: Proposition 603).

6 Citing Wittgenstein (1969: Proposition 151).

7 Citing Wittgenstein (1969: Proposition 603).

8 The term 'language-game' is defined in Wittgenstein's writings. The explicit definition can be found in Wittgenstein (1969: Proposition 7).

9 Cited as '(Typescript, 125)' in Moyal-Sharrock's references.

10 Citing Wittgenstein (1969: Proposition 476).

11 Citing Wittgenstein (1969: 37e).

12 Citing Wittgenstein (2009: Proposition 224).

13 Citing Wittgenstein (2009: Proposition 206).

14 Citing Wittgenstein (1969: Proposition 449).

BIBLIOGRAPHY

Anscombe, G., 1985. Wittgenstein on rules and private language. *Ethics*, 95: 342–52.

Aristotle, 1994. *Aristotle: Posterior Analytics*. 2nd edn. Oxford: Clarendon Press.

Bantock, G., 1970. *Freedom and Authority in Education*. Whitstable: Latimer Trend & Co. Ltd.

—— 1971. Discovery methods. In C. Cox and A. Dyson (eds) *The Black Papers of Education*. 2nd edn. London: Davis-Poynter Ltd, pp. 101–20.

Bereiter, C., 1985. Towards a solution of the learning paradox. *Review of Educational Research*, 55(2): 201–26.

Black, M., 1970. Rules and routines. In R. Peters (ed.) *The Concept of Education*. 5th edn. London: Routledge & Kegan Paul, pp. 92–105.

Blackburn, S., 2008. *The Oxford Dictionary of Philosophy*. Oxford: Oxford University Press.

Bloor, D., 1997. *Wittgenstein: Rules and Institutions*. London: Routledge.

Chaitin, G., 2007. *Thinking about Gödel and Turing*. Hackensack, NJ: World Scientific.

Curtis, S., 1965. *Introduction to the Philosophy of Education*. 2nd edn. Cambridge: University Tutorial Press Ltd.

Dearden, R., 1970. Instruction and learning by discovery. In R. Peters (ed.) *The Concept of Education*. 5th edn. London: Routledge & Kegan Paul, pp. 135–56.

Dempster, W. C., 2008. The foundations of knowledge in Aristotle and Epicurus: A comparative analysis. *Stance*, 1: 20–5.

Descartes, R., 1986. *Meditations on First Philosophy*. J. Cottingham (ed.). Cambridge: Cambridge University Press.

Dyson, A., 1971. The sleep of reason. In C. Cox and A. Dyson (eds) *The Black Papers of Education*. 2nd edn. London: Davis-Poynter Ltd, pp. 84–9.

Furedi, F., 2009. *Wasted: Why Education Isn't Educating*. London: Continuum.

Grice, A., and Judd, J., 1999. Labour Party Conference: Education – Parents of truant pupils face arrest and £5,000 fine. *The Independent*, 13 February. Available online at http://www.independent.co.uk/news/labour-party-conference-education--parents-of-truant-pupils-face-arrest-and-pounds-5000-fine-1123188.html [Accessed November 2012].

Hamlyn, D., 1970. The logical and psychological aspects of learning. In R. Peters (ed.) *The Concept of Education*. 5th edn. London: Routledge & Kegan Paul, pp. 24–44.

Hendricks, C. C., 2002. A review of the work of Lawrence Stenhouse: Questions, ambiguities, and possibilities. *Journal of Research in Education*, 12(1): 117–22.

Hersh, R., 1997. *What is Mathematics Really?* Oxford: Oxford University Press.

Kripke, S., 1982. *Wittgenstein on Rules and Private Language.* Oxford: Blackwell.

Lynn, R., 1971. Streaming: standards or equality? In C. Cox and A. Dyson (eds) *The Black Papers on Education.* 2nd edn. London: Davis-Poynter Ltd, pp. 77–84.

Malcolm, N., 1986. *Nothing is Hidden.* Oxford: Basil Blackwell.

Mitchell, M. T., 2006. *Michael Polanyi: The Art of Knowing.* Wilmington, DE: T. Kenneth Cribb Jr.

Monk, R., 2005. *How to Read Wittgenstein.* London: Granta Books.

Moyal-Sharrock, D., 2007. *Understanding Wittgenstein's On Certainty.* Basingstoke: Palgrave Macmillan.

Oakeshott, M., 1970. Learning and teaching. In R. Peters (ed.) *The Concept of Education.* 5th edn. London: Routledge & Kegan Paul, pp. 156–77.

—— 1975. *On Human Conduct.* Oxford: Oxford University Press.

—— 1991. *Rationalism in Politics and other Essays.* Indianapolis, IN: Liberty Fund, Inc.

—— 2001. *The Voice of Liberal Learning.* Indianapolis, IN: Liberty Fund.

Panjvani, C., 2008. Rule-following, explanation-transcendence, and private language. *Mind*, 117(466): 303–28.

Peters, R., 1970. What is an educational process? In R. Peters (ed.) *The Concept of Education.* 5th edn. London: Routledge & Kegan Paul, pp. 1–24.

—— 1973. *Authority, Responsibility and Education.* 3rd edn. London: George Allen & Unwin Ltd.

Polanyi, M., 1946. *Science, Faith and Society.* Oxford: Oxford University Press.

—— 1958. *Personal Knowledge: Towards a Post-Critical Philosophy.* Chicago, IL: University of Chicago Press.

—— 1969. *Knowing and Being.* London: Routledge and Keegan Paul.

—— 1983. *The Tacit Dimension.* Gloucester, MA: Doubleday & Co.

Rogers, C. R., 1983. *Freedom to Learn for the 80s.* Columbus, OH: Charles E. Merrill Publishing Co.

Rousseau, J. J., 2013. *Emile, or On Education.* New York: Dover Publications Inc.

Ryle, G., 1970. Teaching and training. In R. Peters (ed.) *The Concept of Education.* 5th edn. London: Routledge & Kegan Paul, pp. 105–20.

Steiner, G., 2003. *Lessons of the Masters.* Cambridge, MA: Harvard University Press.

Stenhouse, L., 1983a. The relevance of practice to theory. *Theory into Practice*, 22(3): 211–15.

—— 1983b. *Authority, Education, and Emancipation.* London: Heinemann Educational Books.

Stern, D., 2004. *Wittgenstein's Philosophical Investigations: An Introduction.* Cambridge: Cambridge University Press.

Stroll, A., 1994. *Moore and Wittgenstein on Certainty.* Oxford: Oxford University Press.

Vygotsky, L., 1987. *The Collected Works of L. S. Vygotsky.* New York: Plenum Press.

Waterfield, R., 2005. *Plato: Meno and other Dialogues.* Oxford: Oxford University

Press.

White, J., 1970. Indoctrination. In R. Peters (ed.) *The Concept of Education*. 5th edn. London: Routledge & Kegan Paul, pp. 177–92.

Wick, D., 1995. *The Infamous Boundary*. New York: Copernicus.

Williams, M., 2010. *Blind Obedience: Paradox and Learning in the Later Wittgenstein*. London: Routledge.

Winch, C., 2008. *Learning How to Learn: A Critique*. Keynote lecture at the Philosophy of Education Society of Great Britain Annual Conference, Oxford, 28–30 March.

Wittgenstein, L., 1922. *Tractatus Logico-Philosophicus*. Oxford: Routledge & Kegan Paul.

—— 1967. *Zettel*. G. E. M. Oxford: Basil Blackwell.

—— 1969. *On Certainty*. Oxford: Basil Blackwell.

—— 1975. *Wittgenstein's Lectures on the Foundations of Mathematics: Cambridge 1939*. Chicago, IL: University of Chicago Press.

—— 1980. *Remarks on the Philosophy of Psychology, Vols I and II*. Oxford: Blackwell.

—— 1982. *Last Writings on the Philosophy of Psychology, Vols I and II*. Oxford: Blackwell.

—— 2009. *Philosophical Investigations*. 4th revised edn. Oxford: Wiley-Blackwell.

Wright, C., 2001. *Rails to Infinity*. Cambridge, MA: Harvard University Press.

—— 2007. Rule-following without reasons: Wittgenstein's quietism and constitutive question. *RATIO*, 20(4): 481–502.

INDEX

rules
    acting in accordance with/following
        105
    and correctness 184n.4.3
    and information 126
    and knowledge 97–100, 104–5,
        131
    and learning 184n.4.3
    learning of 170
    simplest rule 103
Ryle, G. 40

safeguards, to authority 57, 58,
        152–3
Sages, teachers as 117
sameness, recognition of 169
schooling, formal 13
self-evident truth 68
self-regulation 152
self-teaching 148–9
simplest rule 103
skills-based education 17, 18
socialization of children, and adult
        authority 15
societal problems, and education 12
society, educated 16–17
sociological perspective, education
        11–17, 21
Socrates 65
Socratic method 65
speech, acquisition of 45, 91–5, 132,
        168
Spinoza, B. 79
Stenhouse, L. 34–5
Stroll, A. 69, 162, 168, 175
subject knowledge, undermining of 13
subsidiary awareness 106

Tacit Dimension, The 186n.5.9
tacit knowledge 96, 97–100, 104, 105,
        128, 162, 186n.5.13, 187n.5.15
teacher-led learning 60–1
teachers
    authority of 14, 15, 31, 46–7, 114,
        142, 144, 145–6, 173, 174–5, 181,
        182

as facilitators 44, 48
faith in 123, 184n.4.3
importance of 114, 116, 117
as instructors 136
judgement of 123–4
responsibility of 46, 48, 152–3
role of 14, 31, 46–7, 48, 118, 122,
        123, 124, 135–6, 180
role of authoritative 25
as Sages 117
status of 14, 15
submission to 174
trust in 156, 167, 172, 173, 174, 175,
        180, 181
teaching
    and authority 113, 146–52, 173,
        177
    defined 112–13, 120
    and education 178
    by example 141, 169
    of a judgement 138–9, 187n.6.6
    and learning 112–13, 114, 119,
        148
    as a process 118, 120–1, 122, 124,
        133, 146, 147
    remit of 121
tendencies 169
textbooks
    faith in 185n.5.2
    learning from 149
    and trust 166
traditional education 40, 41
traditionalism 87, 88
tradition(s) 84
    and art of knowing 86
    and authority 77, 78, 80, 81, 82, 84,
        89
    and community(ies) 84–91
    education as 21
    and freedom 88
    importance of 87, 179
    and knowledge 80, 84, 85, 86,
        186n.5.9
    plasticity of 85, 87
    and progressivism 30, 87
    submission to 111